BOY SOLDIERS
OF THE GREAT WAR

Richard van Emden

B L O O M S B U R Y

LONDON · NEW DELHI · NEW YORK · SYDNEY

First published in Great Britain 2009 by Headline Book Publishing

This paperback edition published 2012

Copyright © 2012 by Richard van Emden

The moral right of the author has been asserted

Bloomsbury Publishing Plc
50 Bedford Square
London WC1B 3DP

www.bloomsbury.com

Bloomsbury Publishing, London, New Delhi, New York and Sydney

A CIP catalogue record for this book is available from the British Library

ISBN 978 1 4088 2472 6

10 9 8 7

Typeset by Hewer Text UK Ltd, Edinburgh
Printed and bound by CPI Group (UK) Ltd, Croydon, CR0 4YY

MIX
Paper from
responsible sources
FSC
www.fsc.org   FSC® C020471

This book is dedicated to the memory of my father,
Wolfgang van Emden, 1931–2002

CONTENTS

New Introduction to the 2012 Edition

In August 1914 a young private named John Parr was shot and killed near the Belgian town of Mons. Officially recorded by the Commonwealth War Graves Commission as aged twenty, he had in fact just celebrated his seventeenth birthday when he died. That he lied about his age on enlistment and had fallen in the service of his country was hardly a revelation. It was who he was that was so significant. This former golf caddie from London was the very first of three-quarters of a million British servicemen to die in the Great War and the truth about his real age came as a shock. I had never investigated the British Army's first casualty because I thought I knew his age.

It is seven years since *Boy Soldiers of the Great War* was first published, time enough to collect much additional material for a revision. All authors know to their irritation that a book is never truly finished, no story fully told: it is always a work in progress. The story of how Britain passed a generation of young boys as fit to fight on the Western Front is one that continues to grip my imagination, and since 2005 I have kept a keen look out for new facts and details.

There are many new and poignant stories. There is the thirteen-year-old boy who impersonates his elder brother and reaches the Western Front with no knowledge of even how to hold a gun; there is the sad case of an apparently healthy sixteen-year-old who, after serving for months on the Western Front, dies within hours of finally gaining his release from the army, and there is the boy who deserts after breaking down under fire. Such additional stories have helped to broaden the scope of the book, adding new original source material to what was already published.

It is not just the stories of boys' own experience that have been developed but also those of families at home, the nervous, sometimes panic-stricken, parents who fought to get sons released from the forces. Their correspondence with the military authorities is analysed in greater detail, throwing new light on the official attitude to under-age soldiering, as well as the plight of parents, many of whom had already lost one or more sons in the war. In particular, as voluntary recruitment slumped in the summer of 1915, the degree to which recruitment sergeants harried and chased boys into the forces has been further explored, with remarkable hitherto unpublished stories.

During the course of my research, I studied in depth the service records held at the National Archives, in particular the pension records (WO364), from which I extracted the histories of 2,046 lads discharged as having made a 'mis-statement' about their age. Within this number, I also identified details of 251 boys who served in a theatre of war while under age. From the size of the sample and from the wealth of information collected, it has been possible to make the first-ever assessment of their service as a group or class, not just as individuals. Fascinating patterns emerge. What was the difference between stated and true age? What proportion of all under-age soldiers was discharged quickly or managed to serve overseas? When did they enlist and did the numbers ebb and flow depending on external factors, such as news of enemy atrocities? What was their average height and weight, where did they come from, and what were their jobs? How long did they serve overseas and does the evidence point to boys who were unable to cope? These and many other questions will be examined for the first time.

In the original book, I suggested that around 250,000 under-age boys served in the forces during the Great War and I based this on good but also circumstantial evidence described in detail in the book's final chapter. This evidence has been revisited and a more mathematical approach taken. The new evidence supports my original core assertion but has also provided some important and interesting qualifications.

In all, I have added approximately 10,000 words to the original text. The result is a more rounded picture of this enthralling story of how under-age boys, some as young as thirteen, served the British Army and the nation during the Great War.

Richard van Emden
December 2011

Introduction

In May 2004, I visited Cecil Withers, then nearly 106 years old and one of the very last veterans of the Great War. It was my third visit to his home on the outskirts of London, where he lived with his eighty-one-year-old son Raymond, and he welcomed me warmly. We talked for a while, and then at an appropriate moment I reached for a cardboard tube, unrolling and handing to Cecil an original copy of *The Times* newspaper, dated Friday, 10 March 1916. I asked him to read an advertisement in the personal column on the front page. Slipping on a pair of black-rimmed spectacles and using a magnifying glass, he slowly began to read the following:

> Cecil C. W. – All's well, will not apply for discharge if you send full address; past forgiven – Father.

Cecil Clarence Withers was reading about himself, eighty-eight years after his father had paid five shillings to place the advertisement in the national newspaper. Cecil, born in June 1898, had enlisted under age in the British Army in 1915, and his father was forgiving his son's action and indeed accepting it, by guaranteeing not to ask for a discharge. Cecil then gave his true identity to the military authorities and sent his whereabouts to his worried family. He was by that time anxious to own up. He had not only enlisted under age but had given false details on the attestation form, changing both his name and address. Now that he was due to go overseas, it had dawned on him that, in the event of his death, no one would ever know who he was or where he had come from.

At seventeen, Cecil had done nothing that thousands of other boys had not already done, by enlisting under age in order to serve their country, but he is almost the last who is able to tell the story. When I spoke to him in January 2005, he was one of only sixteen known veterans of the First World War alive in the United Kingdom: six served in the infantry, one in the Army Service Corps, two in the artillery, one in the cavalry, two in the air services and four in the Navy; a further two British veterans lived in Australia. No doubt there were a few elsewhere but, in all, the number of those who could bear witness to the war was surely fewer than twenty-five: twenty-five out of six million servicemen.

In 2004, the year before I spoke to Cecil, ten British veterans died, including the last man who saw action in the naval engagement at Jutland, and the last man who won a decoration for bravery. The former, Henry St John Fancourt, enlisted as a twelve-year-old and fought at Jutland at sixteen; the latter, James Lovell, enlisted at sixteen and went abroad at nineteen, the age at which he won the Military Medal.

Britain has a long tradition of taking young soldiers overseas; what was different in the First World War was their sheer number. Among all those serving in France by the end of 1915 were more under-age soldiers than the entire force that Wellington took to Waterloo exactly one hundred years earlier.

The connection to that event is stronger than one might imagine. A veteran who died at the end of 2002 remembered that in 1905 he had met a former boy soldier who had served at Waterloo. His mother had impressed on him how remarkable the meeting was, and the memory had stayed with him all his life – a twenty-first-century link to the great battle of 1815.

My own interest in the First World War began while I was still at school, and on my first visit to the battlefields I was the same age as many of the young soldiers whose graves I saw. On my second, to the Somme in late June 1986, I met my first veteran. He was Norman Skelton, then eighty-seven years old. He had enlisted at sixteen and had been sent abroad a year later. He told me that as a seventeen-year-old wireless operator on the Somme, he had had his eardrums burst by a shell explosion, steel fragments of which had killed several of his mates. At the time, I saw no great significance in Norman's age; he made no issue of it himself. He was one of a group of veterans making a trip to France, and over the next two days I met a further twenty old soldiers, a third of whom, I discovered, had enlisted under age. They included Donald Price, aged eighty-eight, formerly of the Royal Fusiliers, who had joined up in December 1914 aged sixteen, and Frank Lindley, aged eighty-six, who had enlisted in 1914 and gone over the top on 1 July 1916, when he was sixteen. There were Alec Stringer and Harry Goodby, aged eighty-eight and eighty-seven respectively, both of the London Scottish, who had enlisted, independently of each other, when they were both also sixteen. There was Horace Calvert, then eighty-six, formerly of the 4th Grenadier Guards, who had been recruited shortly after his fifteenth birthday and had served in France from March 1916.

Meeting them and seeing so many graves of under-age soldiers strengthened my interest in the whole subject, and the question of how many such young men there had been. Amazingly, this had never been researched. These lads had undergone some of the fiercest and most costly fighting in the history of the British Army. Why had they, and other youngsters, joined up?

There were many reasons for enlisting in the army in 1914 and 1915: boredom with work, a longing for adventure, a desire to escape family pressures or responsibilities, as well as a belief in King and Country. Most Britons still believed in the innate superiority and righteousness of their country, and had little interest in, let alone knowledge of, other cultures. Within society, there was a broad acceptance that the rich man had a God-given right to his castle while the poor man stood eternally by his gate. These are, of course, oversimplifications, but few would have questioned a man's abiding duty to his country.

Whatever the motive, one characteristic was particularly pronounced among boys aged eighteen or less – described most clearly to me by a South African telephone engineer working at my house. He had been called up at eighteen for a period of compulsory military service under the old apartheid regime. During training, he had asked his sergeant why boys were called up at eighteen when they would have been fitter, stronger and generally more competent at twenty or twenty-one. The answer was simple: not only were eighteen-year-olds very susceptible to propaganda and more willing than older men to accept orders, but they were also great believers in their own indestructibility, with a general incomprehension of risk or danger. Today, we can see this on every ski slope or skateboard park. In 1914, boys climbed high trees or ice-skated on frozen lakes. They had also survived childhood illnesses that frequently took siblings or friends, and seen men injured at work. They were aware of death and injury but inured to their ramifications. If they had thought for one moment that they might actually die in France, I wonder if as many would have enlisted so willingly.

Anecdotes about boys enlisting under age are commonplace. In researching this book, I had only to bring the subject up in conversation and there would be recollections, if sometimes vague, that someone, perhaps a great-uncle, had been sixteen on the Somme. Inevitably, there would be some incidence of false memory: it is easy to see how a lad of nineteen who served on the Somme in 1916 becomes a lad of sixteen who served on the Somme. But, mistakes apart, there is no doubt that, when the 'myths' about the First World War have been unpicked, the belief that thousands of boys as young as fourteen and fifteen served at the front has never been challenged. What has perhaps not been previously considered is the *total* number of lads who enlisted under age and fought and in many cases died for their country. Given the enormous volume of literature on the Great War, it is surprising that the story of the under-age soldier has not been researched. Campaigns are studied in depth and the life of the individual soldier explored, and in many of the books and articles a comment has been made about a lad of fifteen killed in action or about the grave of a sixteen-year-old, but nothing has brought all these stories together.

On the Western Front, the younger the boy soldier was at the time of his death, the more 'popular' his grave has become, often with several poppy crosses in front of the headstone. The graves of the very youngest victims are well known. Two of the most visited are those of Private 6322 John Condon, 2nd Battalion, Royal Irish Regiment, who was killed in May 1915; and Private 5750 Valentine Strudwick of the 8th Rifle Brigade, killed in January 1916. Condon was reputedly fourteen years old (although there is currently some dispute about this) and, according to the Commonwealth War Graves Commission (CWGC), the 'youngest known battle casualty of the war'. The CWGC notes that Private Strudwick was 'one of the youngest battle casualties of the war' when he was killed at fifteen. Strudwick's grave is famous, in large part, because of the cemetery he lies in. Known as Essex Farm, it was where Lieutenant Colonel John McCrae wrote his famous poem 'In Flanders Fields'.

The extreme youth of these two boys is by no means unique. Strudwick, in particular, is just one of a number across the battle-fields who were aged fifteen when they were killed; most of them lie uncelebrated – indeed, unidentified as being so young. Nor does the death of Condon at fourteen make him the youngest soldier to have served at the front. There are cases of boys as young as thirteen, or even twelve, serving in France. I met one veteran, George Maher, who served briefly in France when he was thirteen years and nine months. He was sent back to England, along with five other under-age boys. As George recalled with a smile:

One of them, as I discovered, was even younger than myself. A little nuggety bloke he was, too! We joked that he could never have seen over the trenches, that they would have to have lifted him up.

The story of the boy soldiers is one that may yet raise passionate debate. It is too easy to see it as one of innocent lads being sent as cannon fodder to the front by uncaring generals and politicians – lion cubs led by donkeys. The truth is far more complex. Whatever the failings of Great War politicians, their sons were not absent from the forces or, more importantly, from the front line. The Members of Parliament who voted on war issues were doing so in the full knowledge that their sons were likely to be the beneficiaries or victims of the decisions. By the time the war ended, those votes, however indirectly, had cost many leading politicians the lives of their children. They included the Conservative leader Andrew Bonar Law, who lost two sons, James and Charles; the Prime Minister, Herbert Asquith, who lost his eldest son, Raymond; and the Undersecretary of State for War, Harold Tennant, who lost his son, Henry, and three nephews including the poet Edward Wyndham Tennant. Nor, given the extent of intermarriage between families of the political and social elite, did the death of one MP's son leave other Members unaffected: Herbert Asquith was, for example, married to Harold Tennant's sister.

When considering the story of the boy soldiers, it is important to remember that such politicians were men of their time. They had to make hard decisions and carried huge responsibilities, but they were not heartless; they could not afford to be.

However passionately I feel about the boy soldiers in the First World War, this book has no hidden agenda. Such an emotive story does not necessitate an attack either on the political elite of the time, who might have turned a blind eye to under-age enlistment, or on the military or civil officers who frequently overlooked a boy's palpable youth so that he could fight. The connivance needed to enlist the number of under-age soldiers who fought in the war was required at all levels, including the boys' own parents and, not least, the lads themselves, who were willing to go in their thousands and who in many cases rejected an escape even when it was offered. This book will look at the political and social pressures that brought about their enlistment in the first place, and at the subsequent campaign to secure their discharge. It will, for the first time, make an assessment of how many fought and died between 1914 and 1918. But most of all, it is the boys' own stories, told in their own words, about what inspired them to enlist and what made them continue to serve when the full horror of warfare became apparent.

Back in 2005, there was some speculation, largely among devotees of the First World War, about the origin and accuracy of the figures available. While any such assessment must rely on extrapolation, hypothesis and crude mathematics, there is, I believe, genuine historical value in the numbers given, and an extended note on how they were arrived at is set out in the last chapter of this book. A definition of what constitutes a 'boy soldier' is crucial. In August 1914, the age at which boys could enlist as full-time soldiers was eighteen; to serve overseas, they had to be nineteen. This rule lasted until 1918, and underpins what this book describes as under-age soldiering. Even so, problems of definition abound. Is a boy who enlists at fifteen, serves overseas at sixteen, and is killed the day after his nineteenth birthday counted as an under-age soldier or not? Is a boy who is killed at seventeen, but who, under military exception, was allowed to go to war, under age? It is not possible to reconcile all such conflicting issues, for much will depend on the attitude of the reader and the strict interpretation of the law as it then stood. Exceptions that enabled boys to go to France legitimately will be highlighted, but the basic premise is maintained that a boy had to be nineteen to see overseas action.

'A bullet,' wrote one veteran, 'is no respecter of age', and it is true that many incidents were not age-related and would have been the same if they had happened to an older person. Nevertheless, the reaction might be that of a boy rather than a man, as, for instance, in the case of a sixteen-year-old lad consuming alcohol and so breaking his word to his mother:

> Well, Mum, I am sorry to tell you that I have not kept my promise to you not to touch intoxicating drinks. You see, we got rum when we were in the trenches and I used to drink the rum but I give you my word it was only to keep the cold out that I drank it. I haven't touched anything else.

There were innumerable incidents during the course of the war when such under-age soldiers willingly took part in a general attack. Once again, the experience is not in itself age-related, but I felt that there were times, particularly in direct combat with the enemy, when the boy's story must be told to show the extraordinary ability of young lads to focus their thoughts and actions and to act like much older men. The actions of the Battles of Loos and the Somme, related by Dick Trafford and Frank Lindley respectively, took place when they were both just sixteen, and their descriptions are astonishingly mature and for that reason especially shocking.

There are many sources that refer to an individual as 'a boy' without any clarification of his precise age. I have, however, tried to quote only from young soldiers whom I know to have been under age when they enlisted and served on the Western Front. As time passed, there was an inevitable crossover. Almost all the boys who enlisted in 1914 and 1915 eventually came of age, if they survived, during their military service. In such circumstances, I have sometimes continued their stories rather than stopping the narrative on the day they became officially old enough to serve.

The incidents recalled in this book are in approximate chronological order, but at times the need to group related experiences in order to highlight a common theme has meant that the time sequence is not seamless. My aim has been to describe the experience of under-age soldiering rather than primarily to maintain the strict order of the events of the war.

In preparing this book, I met the last surviving veterans who fought under age on the Western Front. I am immensely grateful to centenarians such as Cecil Withers, Tommy Thomson, Alfred Anderson, Albert 'Smiler' Marshall and Harold Lawton for sharing their experiences with me. Dick Trafford, who died in 1999, put their point of view:

> The only thing I am pleased about is I can help; I can help the likes of you and my comrades, the First World War veterans. I feel I'm helping in some way, I can't do any more. I put them on the same level as me. It's nice to think that they've been through what I've been through. I also know what they've suffered.

This book is based essentially on oral history, but the story would be too complex to tell without the input of diaries, letters, newspaper columns and journals, all of which added new perspectives to an aspect of the war that has been widely acknowledged but consistently under-researched.

The boy soldier's story in the Great War is an enormous subject, which encapsulates every theatre of conflict and medium of fighting, on the ground, by sea and in the air. It covers military ranks from private to captain, and includes everyone with an interest in the ages of those who served, from parents to politicians. For this reason, it has been necessary to concentrate almost entirely on the primary crucible of the conflict, the Western Front, including the Royal Flying Corps, which became the Royal Air Force in 1918. Other important theatres of war and one arm of the services, the Royal Navy, have had to be excluded.

While wandering around the Great War cemeteries that dot the battlefields of France and Flanders, I, like many people, have been fascinated by the inscriptions that appear at the foot of many gravestones. These were written and paid for by the families of those who died and, while all are heart-felt, a few are deeply poignant. At the start of each chapter I have reproduced one of the dedications that appear on the graves of under-age soldiers, choosing especially those that stress their youth.

I

Youthful Dreams

ONLY A BOY BUT A HERO

4214 Private Frank Grainger,
16th Battalion Australian Infantry

Killed in Action 30 August 1916, aged 17

Patriotism was not universal in early twentieth-century Britain, but most people did not question their life-long allegiance to their native land. Communities demonstrated this through popular activities such as pageants and processions, celebrating the continuing prosperity of the nation and its empire.

On a more personal level, newborn children were often given names that reflected the nationalism of their parents – George Baden White, for example, was born in August 1900, the son of a gunner serving with the Royal Garrison Artillery in Malta. Thomas White, his father, was a patriotic man and, in choosing names for his son, he turned to military leaders made famous in the Boer War. Sir George White, holder of the Victoria Cross, had successfully defended the South African township of Ladysmith until its relief in February 1900; Colonel Robert Baden-Powell, better known now for founding the Scout movement, had similarly defended Mafeking until relieved in May that year. Across Britain there had been wild public celebrations at the news and both became national heroes. So the choice of names for the newborn baby sleeping soundly on the island of Malta was obvious: George and Baden.

Between 5 and 10 per cent of all children born in 1900 were given names associated, in one way or another, with the Boer War. After May, and for the next year, over 6,100 British children, mostly boys, were christened Baden and another 1,000 Powell. A few parents went further, christening their children Mafeking Baden or Baden Mafeking. In England alone, over 700 children, both boys and girls, were christened Mafeking, and over 800 girls were called Ladysmith or, after the other besieged town of 1900, Kimberley. Even General Sir Redvers Buller VC, who, as commanding officer in South Africa, had overseen many of the war's military failures, had nearly 7,300 British children named after him, either Redvers or Buller; while in 1900 another 3,000 children were named Roberts after Field Marshal Lord Roberts VC, the man sent to replace him. Indeed, almost any name in South Africa mentioned in the press that year found its way into baptismal records, from Modder River Lampard to James Spion Kop Skinner. Thirty-five equally unfortunate children had Bloemfontein inserted in their names, thirty-four had Majuba; fifty-four had Transvaal; and six had the name of Stromberg.

No one came more highly respected than the Queen herself. The names Victoria and Victor became fashionable; 'Victoria' was fourteen times more common in 1897, the year of the Queen's Jubilee, than in the previous year. The word 'jubilee' itself was sometimes given too, if not as a first then as a second or third name. Bertram William Jubilee Rogers was born during the fiftieth anniversary of the monarch's accession to the throne in 1887; James Jubilee McDonald was born during the Diamond Jubilee celebrations ten years later. Both were to be killed during the Great War.

Adult patriotism had always permeated down to children. At school, headmasters had noted famous days in the military calendar, such as the Battle of Waterloo or the defence of Rorke's Drift, and children dutifully stood in respect. The portraits of great military commanders adorned school walls, along with explorers and adventurers, men to be admired, respected and emulated. Such tangible expressions of patriotism may seem extreme today but, for a great number of boys, young life was steeped in military glory and the great campaigns of the past.

A few of the children who would serve under age in the Great War could just about recall the joyous, Union-Jack-waving behaviour of adults during the Boer War, when Mafeking was relieved and a school holiday granted. They remembered, too, the national sorrow at the Queen's death in 1901, when children wore black as a mark of respect. Her birthday, 24 May, was celebrated as a public holiday during her lifetime and from 1902 as Empire Day, a manifestation of pride in the nation's achievements. In schools up and down the country, the day was rigorously observed: children turned out to parade banners on promenades and in parks, as brass bands played and local dignitaries made rousing speeches. George Baden White, who arrived in England in 1901, saw it all:

> Each year we had a pageant. That was Empire Day, and most of us really revelled in it. The pageant consisted of somebody appearing as Britannia as the centrepiece, and the boys representing the major colonies, like Australia, Canada, New Zealand and South Africa, paying homage to her. As part of the proceedings, we all wore either a red, white or blue cap, lined up to form the Union Jack, and, of course, finished up singing the National Anthem. I loved every minute of it.

This was a world in which monarchy, Church and army were fused together in impressionable minds as the bulwarks upon which the nation state's security, peace and prosperity rested, each integral to the others' survival. The Boy Scout's three-fingered salute expressed this ideal, representing service to God, King and Country.

The Scouts were one of a number of uniformed youth organizations formed in the late nineteenth and early twentieth centuries, helping to promulgate, perhaps to engineer, future social cohesion; others included the Boys' Brigade and the Church Lads' Brigade. These all offered boys a taste of outdoor adventure within a framework of healthy Christian discipline and obedience.

Thousands of young boys joined the Scout movement when it was formed in 1907, benefiting from activities that encouraged cooperation as well as self-reliance, personal discipline and fun. The organization professed not to encourage militarism and to an extent this was true. The elementary drill that the boys practised was said to be similar in character and purpose to that undertaken by children in a school playground so that they could move in numbers without misunderstanding or delay. The long list of badges, of which there were about a hundred, was held up as another example, for few could be associated with military training. Yet the essence of Scout training was self-government, self-discipline, loyalty and good citizenship, and all these had military applications. Boys were taught to march, wave banners, and win medals. They were taught camping, signalling, tracking; they learnt first aid, Morse code and semaphore. In camp, they frequently slept in bell tents and deployed sentries; they built fires and cooked, and in the evening they sang songs:

> Scouts will be Scouts
> Scouts can be heroes too
> By striving to aid
> A man or a maid
> And seeing the scout law through.

The Scouts' motto 'Be Prepared' was very pertinent, as war with Germany had long been expected. Since the 1880s, Germany's industrial rise had been meteoric. As a nation, it had been founded in 1870 and led since 1888 by Kaiser Wilhelm II, a grandson of Queen Victoria. The Kaiser, envious of Britain's Empire, had been an enthusiast for rapid industrial and military expansion, soon leading his country into a naval arms race with Britain that only helped foster mutual suspicion. Britain was well aware of the threat of an increasingly strong German nation, and the expectation that war might one day break out between the two slowly seeped into the public consciousness through books and newspapers.

Britain relied on the Navy to impose her will and defend the home country. The conflict in South Africa had thrown into sharp relief the difficulties of fighting a war ranging over thousands of miles, and it had been fought at a time when Britain's pre-eminence was just beginning to ebb. Security through alliances would have to be the way forward: Britain entered into agreements, first with Japan in 1902 and most notably with France in 1904. These ententes were significant because they were, in effect, an acknowledgement that in a changing world Britain would have to cooperate with other nations if she were to maintain her Empire intact.

No country wants to join an unnecessary war, but understandings with other nations such as France ensured that if a major conflagration broke out, Britain would probably side with her nearest neighbour. This likelihood was increased when Britain concluded an Anglo-Russian convention in 1907, as France and Russia were already in alliance. Through these agreements, the Empire was safeguarded but Britain had been drawn into European affairs to an extent that would have seemed impossible a generation before. The only country in Europe with whom Britain might come to blows was Germany, and in this case no pact of any sort had been attempted. If Germany became an aggressor in a European war, the chances of Britain siding with France and/or Russia were high. When Germany invaded Belgium in August 1914, Britain had reason to go to war, not first and foremost because she treasured that country's neutrality, but because it was in her national interest to side with France and Russia with whom she had concluded pacts and who were already at war with Germany.

The imminence of the conflict in no way hindered the recruitment of youngsters who, if anything, could now see the possibility of military glory won fighting for their country. If the Scouts or other boys' organizations did not deliberately act as a fertile recruiting ground for the army, their culture of 'good citizenship' certainly encouraged such ideas, and prepared their members for active work when war did break out.

For boys interested in a more direct route to an army career, there was Boy Service, catering for those who wished to join up in their early teenage years. They signed on from school as young as thirteen, or, if they were the sons of serving soldiers, from the age of twelve. Over 2,500 such boys were in fact serving at home or in the colonies by 1914. They were predominantly trained as drummer boys, and were also taught trades such as tailoring. They were paid a shilling a week until the age of eighteen, when they became soldiers proper. Still far from being the finished article, they required many months of further preparation before they were full participants in the regiment.

Britain's Regular Army was small by European standards. Reliance, perhaps over-reliance, on the Royal Navy to defend the nation's sovereignty had allowed the army to remain purely professional, with, in all, about 250,000 men, half of whom were stationed overseas, and a reserve of a further 225,000 former soldiers who had returned to civilian life but were available to be called up at short notice. Nevertheless, it provided an ever-present backdrop to daily life in large swathes of the country. In 'army' towns such as Winchester and Richmond in Yorkshire, there was a high concentration of military personnel frequently witnessed on manoeuvres. Country boys who were keen on the army were offered opportunities to watch the soldiers at summer camp, to walk alongside as the men tramped country lanes or help look after horses in the transport lines. One boy from Hartlepool recalled:

These bronzed infantry soldiers marched through the village with packs and rifles on long route marches. They went down into the Dene and up the other side of the valley to Nesbit Hall and disappeared into the distance, while we awaited their return. When they came back, their shirts were open at the neck and they looked really exhausted and we offered to carry their rifles. Then, if we were allowed to do so, we made our way up to the camp where the soldiers were making full use of the Ship Inn and there was a lot of singing going on. It looked very romantic with the field kitchens going, preparing the meals, and the smell of the food, the smell of the horses in the lines, the jingle of the harnesses and the bits. It made a fourteen-year-old boy long to be a soldier.

There were always boys who were destined to join up, like Benjamin Clouting, the son of a groom working on a large estate in Sussex, who volunteered in 1913 at the age of fifteen:

As a child I brandished a wooden sword, with red ink splattered along the edges, and strutted around the estate like a regular recruit. I daydreamed about the heroic actions of former campaigns, and avidly read highly charged stories of action in South Africa.

Like many children, Ben had close family links to the army. He had two uncles, one of whom served in the 11th Hussars and taught his young nephew how to ride 'military style' while the other, Uncle Toby, served in the Scots Guards.

He was a great character and a sergeant major. Even though he had been too young to fight in South Africa and later somehow avoided the First World War, he nevertheless nurtured my interest in the army.

When it came to war and death, the experience of childhood in the early twentieth century was very different from that experienced a hundred years later in one way in particular: today's children are graphically exposed to images of war but protected from the effects of death; Edwardian children were all too well aware of death but largely naive about the effects of war.

The Victorian 'culture of death' was well developed and continued up to the First World War, with children being encouraged to take an active part in death rituals such as wearing black and kissing the hand of the departed. The sight of a body was not unusual, the dead often resting in an open coffin at home before the funeral. Illness was rife and contagious diseases hard to control when so many families lived in cramped, back-to-back houses, in frequently insanitary conditions. With infant mortality high – 20 per cent of children failed to reach their fifth birthday – it was common to lose a sibling, especially in large families. Overall life expectancy was around fifty for men and slightly higher, fifty-five, for women, and so the loss of a parent or other near relation in childhood was also unremarkable. George White had lost his father by the age of five, but that was far from his only contact with death. During his childhood, George lost a cousin, Ernie, killed playing on a railway line, and a school friend named Sutton, who was drowned in a creek, while a Scoutmaster was accidentally killed during camp. In addition:

A pal of mine, Theobald, lost his mother, who died from consumption, and a neighbour in our road, named Stevens, was killed in an explosion in one of the powder mills.

Death was commonplace but the effects of war less so. Britain's colonial conflicts had been described but not seen, drawn but hardly photographed. The medium of film, still in its infancy, was capable of taking anodyne images of soldiers fording a stream, or baggage trains crossing the South African veldt, but nothing of the actuality of fighting. A combination of unwieldy cameras and the restrictions of public taste ensured that explicit war cinematography would wait another generation. Instead, war artists drew the conflict, presenting stirring scenes of battle that were never ignoble. The effect was to create a generation of war romantics. Thomas Hope, who was to serve in France aged just sixteen, wrote of this effect:

> War, glorious war, with its bands and marching feet, its uniforms and air of recklessness, its heroes and glittering decorations, the war of our history books ... From the cradle up we have been fed on battles and heroic deeds, nurtured on bloody episodes in our country's history; war was always glorious, something manly, never sordid, uncivilized, foolish or base.

When the war broke out, 'the height of my ambition', he wrote, 'was to fight for King and Country'.

Stuart Cloete was just as intoxicated. He was not much more than three years old when he saw a black and white drawing in his father's copy of the *Daily Telegraph*. It was the time of the Boer War, and the image, as Stuart recalled, was:

> of a boy trumpeter with a bandaged head, galloping madly through bursting shells for reinforcements. My father coloured the picture for me. The horse brown, the boy in khaki with a red blob of blood on the white bandage round his head. The picture was hung in my nursery.

Stuart was raised on the stories of ancestors who had served, including his great-great-uncle who, at the age of fifteen, had fought at the Battle of Waterloo. As a child, he played with hundreds of lead soldiers and guns and forts, and read books with titles such as *Boy Heroes* and *Heroes and Hero Worship* as well as magazines such as the *Boy's Own Paper*.

> Without knowing it, I was being formed, compressed as it were into a semi-hereditary mould. It resembled in a way the old

apprenticeship to a trade which was often carried on from father to son. Perhaps being a soldier and a gentleman was in those days a kind of trade.

George White also had designs on the army although, with hindsight, August 1900 was an unfortunate date of birth for a boy with warlike ambitions. In theory at least, George's participation in the Great War should have been utterly frustrated, the boy consigned to dreaming of military heroics and unable to realize his dreams. Only in August 1918 would he have become eligible for compulsory service. Called up, he would have undergone at least fourteen weeks' basic training, the end of which would have coincided with the signing of the Armistice. At best, George would have been dispatched to the Army of Occupation in Germany, the war over, no medals won. In practice, George, like tens of thousands of other young boys, would be driven by a deep-seated patriotism and a desire for adventure. In his case, this inclination was intensified after his father died and his mother took in a lodger, a former cavalryman, whom she later married.

It was nice to have a man living with us, especially one like Mr Burton, who we could look up to like a hero, especially as he was so good to us. We thought him our hero because he had served as a regular with the 9th Lancers and, in the Boer War, was wounded and still had a bullet in the leg. We boys were fascinated with his medal which was displayed in a glass case with a few accessories such as regimental cap badges and buttons.

Mr Burton's connections with his old regiment gave George access to cavalrymen and he was taken frequently to see them.

In the afternoon we watched some of the troops practising combat in the form of sword vs lance while on horseback. I had never seen anything like it before, but later I was to see something really spectacular. That was watching the Lancers rehearsing the musical ride which they were evidently to perform publicly later. Being able to watch the men on their horses and listening to the band was really thrilling. I had always thought I wanted to be a soldier when I grew up but after that wonderful day, realized it would have to be the cavalry for me.

The army may have had a romantic attraction for the young, but the wider public view of the forces was not positive. The army's stature had suffered during the Boer War after repeated debacles. It had learnt hard lessons, but, despite reforms, the public image of the services remained poor. The reaction of one mother to her eighteen-year-old son's enlistment was typical of many. 'Oh,' she said, 'you little fool, don't you understand there's only thieves and vagabonds join the army, you go back and tell them that you've changed your mind.' Her natural concern for his safety had merged with her long-standing derogatory view of the military.

Nevertheless the army was for some a refuge from ordinary life, and so it attracted recruits running away from personal problems, domestic disputes or small-time acts of criminality. The army also drew in those who lived on society's margins, men who had no family and few friends. Ben Clouting recalled:

A good proportion came from orphanages, joining for the comradeship and the sense of belonging more than anything else. One man in my barracks at Seaforth had come from a Dr Barnardo's home; he had no relatives and to him, as to all these men, the army was their new family, most, not surprisingly, never receiving any mail from the outside world at all.

Social misfits, criminals, tramps, tearaways and orphans: it was a hotch-potch army and hardly a profession that recommended itself to families with even modest ambitions for their sons.

Although the army offered a bolt-hole for a few, peacetime soldiering was no easy option. Men initially signed on for twelve years, undertaking a minimum of three years' full-time service followed by nine on the reserve. The training was hard and it was thorough, forging those who enlisted into some of the best fighting soldiers in the world. For those who found they could not take to army life, there was the possibility of being bought out by a kind relation or friend, but this was prohibitively expensive for most working-class people.

The desperation that had brought many to the sanctuary of the army sometimes drove the same unhappy men to desert when they had had enough, with a midnight flit over the camp wall the usual tried and tested method.

This form of 'personal demobilization' was a major problem for the pre-war army, which found that nearly 5 per cent of its annual recruitment did a bunk with little fear of being caught. Once a soldier was reported missing, a twenty-one-day 'search' would be made, after which his uniform and kit would be sold off and the man officially designated a deserter. For those who left the army in this way, there was always the possibility of a return. Re-enlisting under a fictitious name was easy in a world in which there were no computers to cross-reference names, no National Insurance numbers to check identities, and no requirement to show a birth certificate on enlistment. A name, any old name, was taken on trust.

The army had to weigh up conflicting interests, capturing those who abused the enlistment process while not putting off genuine recruits. Pre-war recruitment was already insufficient to meet requirements and for this reason practical proposals to curb the problem of fraudulent enlistment had been rejected. Checking birth certificates was abandoned on the basis that too many 'good' men did not possess one and would be unable to recall where their birth had been recorded. While registering births had been compulsory since 1837, in practice it became widespread only in 1874 when a

£2 fine was imposed on any parent caught failing to register a baby. However, many never bothered to purchase a copy of the certificate for future reference, and therefore their sons would be incapable of presenting one on enlistment. Using fingerprints was another option, as was the idea of introducing compulsory smallpox vaccination on the forearm. Both were rejected, as the former appeared to criminalize the innocent, while the latter would have left a scar – proof of previous service but also an act tantamount to branding. In the end the only tentative reform introduced to curb fraudulent enlistment was the character reference.

In October 1910, one case was forwarded to the military authorities as a prime and particularly bad example of fraudulent enlistment. On reading the file, one senior officer wrote:

> I hardly know what to advise, and perhaps you will prefer to leave the matter alone; but everyone who reads the adventures of Private Stacey will realize the extent to which we are victimized by men of his type.

Private Stacey's case was exceptional but not unique. He had first enlisted in 1902, aged fifteen, after the death of his parents. He was left, as he acknowledged, with only two options: either to present himself at one of Dr Barnardo's homes or to join the army. He chose the latter. His story of the next eight years, in and out of the forces, underlined how difficult it was for the military authorities to keep track of a young man utterly bent on enlisting, deserting, and re-enlisting. Finally, in 1910, Stacey revealed and revelled in his military exploits in a brazen statement entitled 'One of the King's Bad Bargains by Himself'.

Stacey enlisted in the Essex Regiment and for a while enjoyed army life, until his first leave.

> At Christmas time I was given a ten-day furlough. On returning to barracks, however, I found that not one particle of my kit

was left and no doubt it had been sold by someone who wanted
a drink. I was put down for practically a new kit and given 1/- a
week as pay. That I could not stomach, and one night I sold everything I had and deserted. I had three or four days' holiday on the
strength of the sold kit, and then walked to Reading. I stopped in
the town one night, and the following morning presented myself
at the Barracks as a promising young recruit.

Stacey gave himself the new name of Charles Cousins.

I liked the Berkshires very much, and no doubt would have got
on well, but after being at Reading two or three weeks, one day
I was surprised to see two men come up to enlist who were in
my company in the Essex Regt at Warley. I told them how to go
about enlisting but one of them was very slack and apparently
gave himself away, and of course the other fellow was caught too.
Not only did they give themselves away but me also. However, I
got wind that they were going to cross-question me in the morning about the Essex Regt, so the night previous I sold up and
'bunked over the wall'.

From Reading, Stacey went to Aldershot where he enlisted
in the King's Royal Rifle Corps under the name Fred Bailey;
after five months he deserted and joined the Royal West Kent
Regiment at Gravesend using the name Cotton. When Stacey
presented himself yet again, this time at Woolwich, he was
asked by the recruiting sergeant if he could supply a 'character', references having just been introduced. Stacey's answer was
typically brash.

'Oh yes,' I said, 'I have only just left a five years' job so I suppose
he will give me a Character' . . . I then gave him my real name
as my employer, and the following morning called at the house
which I told him to write to, and filled in the Character form as

having worked 5 years as a painter, honest, sober, and everything puffed up to make a spotless Character.

Over the next six years, he deserted and re-enlisted a further seven times, serving for a short time in India – 'too hot for a white man' – before feigning illness to get home.

How much longer Stacey could have cocked a snook at the military authorities will never be known, for when he heard of a special army order pardoning deserters and those who had fraudulently enlisted, he decided to come clean.

I made a full confession of having fraudulently enlisted into twelve corps . . . I have finished with the army now. Not that I disrespect it for I would fight for old England tomorrow if there was a war. But the army does at present not require my services. Let us hope they never may.

Part of the problem with fraudulent enlistment, as identified by the army, lay with the rewards paid to recruiting sergeants for each new man attested. 'The present system of rewards does not tend to make the recruiter too particular or careful as the more men, good or bad, he recruits, the greater his reward,' acknowledged the Army Council. It was a quandary that would remain largely unresolved, for the desire to halt the abuse of the system ran counter to the requirement for more peacetime volunteers. The difficulties met in cases such as Stacey's were exasperating but ultimately manageable in peacetime. Yet if it was hard to clamp down on fraudulent enlistment in the pre-war Regular Army, how much more difficult would it be if the army expanded fivefold in the first few months of an international war? The same none-too-particular sergeants would still be signing men up, only this time, instead of arriving in ones and twos, they would be queuing round the block, beating a path to recruiting desks to enlist. Many would be boys, as keen as anyone else to serve.

Some of these eager recruits would have served their time in the Territorials. This force had been formed in 1908, as an attempt to build a national force of the disparate arms of part-time service, namely the Yeomanry and the Volunteers, but it already had a mixed history. Bringing these units into one unified force did not meet with universal approval, and many older soldiers resented what they saw as an unnecessary change to a hitherto unbroken system.

Nevertheless, for boys who did not want to make the army a career, the Territorials offered an attractive and alternative way of serving. They had been established for home defence only and for this reason seventeen had been designated as the minimum age to enlist. Thousands of boys had enthusiastically responded and continued to do so. By 1914 as many as 40,000 were aged eighteen or less and almost as many again were under twenty. In all roughly a third of the entire force was made up of teenagers.

One such was Alfred Anderson, who, at sixteen, joined the Territorials of the 5th Black Watch regiment in 1912. These were the so-called 'Saturday afternoon soldiers', who worked during the week on farms or landed estates, and in the small towns of Perth and Newtyle. In truth, part-timers were looked down upon by regular soldiers, but that did not worry lads like Alfred. He worked in the family business, a joinery that his father had set up in 1902, and he worked hard. His father was strict: holidays were taken by other people and, as was frequently the case among family members at work, pay was indifferent. Joining the Territorials gave Alfred an escape. He could link up with good friends such as Jock Mackenzie, Jim Ballantyne and Lyon Jeffrey, and look forward to fun at weekends. Just as important to Alfred – and one of the allures of the Territorial Force – was that he was entitled to fifteen days off to attend annual summer camp, a release from work that his father could not veto.

The summer camp of 1914, his third, began in the last full week of July, in glorious weather. One day, Alfred, just turned eighteen, was on a route march with his regiment when the order came to fall out by the side of the road. It being a warm day, the men were in shirtsleeves. They had just passed through the town of Crieff where they picked up a few local boys who ran alongside them and now sat among them as they halted for a statutory ten minutes' rest. As the lads from the Black Watch sat soaking up the summer sun, a photographer strolled up. This was an opportunity for him to make some money, taking pictures of the soldiers and selling copies to them later that week in the town.

'We didn't have any idea the war was about to break out, not the slightest. It was a beautiful day, that was all, and we were having a rest,' recalled Alfred, who died in November 2005 aged 109. Alfred was the last of the 268,777 pre-war Territorials.

The coming of war brought a change in their role. For several years, soldiers had been given the opportunity to sign a legal document, the Imperial Service Obligation, to signify their willingness to 'accept liability for service outside the United Kingdom in time of national Emergency'. There were, however, vast discrepancies among battalions in the numbers of men signifying their agreement. In 1912 the 6th Notts and Derby Regiment (raised predominantly in Chesterfield) had the agreement of twenty-six officers and 730 other ranks; the 7th Notts and Derby Regiment (Nottingham), the agreement of two officers and eighteen other ranks. The 7th and 8th Middlesex had almost their entire complement signed up, the 7th having secured the signatures of twenty officers and 841 other ranks, the 8th twenty-three officers and 837 other ranks. However, the 4th Royal West Kent Regiment had the signatures of two officers and twelve other ranks, and the 5th Battalion no officers at all and just two other ranks. The 5th Black Watch, with whom Alfred Anderson was serving, had no officer and only one other rank in agreement. There had been one simple reason for this, according to Alfred Anderson: 'no one ever asked us until the war broke out'.

Whatever the reason, the fact remained that by the start of August 1914, only 18,683 currently serving soldiers had agreed to serve overseas and, with time-served men leaving the service, that was almost 2,000 fewer than two years before. In other words, only about one in fourteen of the men currently serving with the Territorials could legally be sent to fight. With the continuation of voluntary enlistment, the country could hardly force abroad men who had signed to serve on home shores only. Nevertheless, it was soon to become clear that these men were needed in France once the Regular Army found itself confronted by an enemy vastly superior in numbers.

Germany's huge armies advanced into Luxembourg on 2 August and into Belgium the following day, part of the opening gambit of the meticulously honed blueprint for an attack on France. This plan would use pre-emptive speed and devastating force. Belgium was a convenient backdoor by which to invade from the north, and in due course to seize Paris and knock France out of the war before German attention would turn to Russia.

In the event, Germany failed to respond to a British ultimatum to withdraw, and when that expired at 11 p.m. on 4 August, Britain entered the war. Immediately, general mobilization of the nation's professional army was ordered and within hours it had swung into action. The following day, thousands of reservists began to stream into their regimental depots across the United Kingdom, bringing the first battalions of the British Expeditionary Force (BEF) up to strength – in the end, reservists made up 60 per cent of the BEF. Soon they were sailing to the Continent, to take up a position on the left flank of the French, to help counter the German thrust from the north. They were the advance guard of six divisions, a total of 80,000 troops.

The plans for sending an Expeditionary Force to the Continent had been carefully drawn up and its departure met with few hitches. It came as a welcome relief to Members of Parliament, many of whom had doubted that Britain was capable of dispatching any such force. In March 1914, there had been angry debates in the House of Commons about the size of the army and the average age of volunteers. The Army (Annual) Report had been grim reading for MPs. Recruits were overwhelmingly young, around half being under nineteen. The fear was expressed that in a European conflagration, 14 per cent of the Regular Army, according to its own estimates, would be legally ineligible to serve abroad, while many of the rest would be physically disadvantaged in a fight with other nations who generally took their soldiers at the age of twenty-one.

War brought a change to the qualification for enlistment. Before the war, it was recommended that lads under nineteen should not be able to join the Regular forces while those under twenty should be ineligible for service overseas as their stamina was not yet considered sufficient for the job. With war, enlistment into the army was altered to a minimum of eighteen years, while there was a broad rule that overseas service should be permitted for those aged nineteen or above. There were certain dispensations. Those in Boy Service, boy drummers, buglers, trumpeters or pipers, could proceed overseas if specifically authorized by the commanding officer, as well as those with specific technical abilities among units such as the Royal Engineers.

Boys who had enlisted at eighteen or younger and who had not completed the recruits' course of training became panic-stricken at the prospect of being left behind when the regiment proceeded overseas. Across the country, confrontations between boys and officers occurred in almost every regiment. They asked for audiences with their commanding officers, appealing to be allowed to go, but they were frequently refused.

Sixteen-year-old Ben Clouting, by now a trooper in the 4th (Royal Irish) Dragoon Guards, was one of those who intended to go. He had completed all his drills in July and had just finished annual manoeuvres to qualify as a regular trooper in the regiment. The conflict came at just the right moment.

With the news that hostilities had broken out, Tidworth [Barracks, in Wiltshire] went crackers. Everyone was very excited at the prospect of a fight. We were going to war; we were going to do something. No one stopped to think about what that actually meant. We were about to wipe the floor with the Germans and anything else was inconceivable.

Within days, the troop lists had been pinned on the notice boards but Ben was in for a shock. 'My eyes scanned the notice. I was dumbfounded; my name had been omitted.'

Stubbornness overrode bitter disappointment. Twice, Ben scrubbed the bottom name off the list and added his own; twice, Ben's troop sergeant amended it as before, until, in exasperation, he took the young trooper before Captain Charles Hornby, second in command of the squadron.

'You know your age. You are not entitled to come out with the regiment.'

'According to my enlistment papers, sir, my age is officially nineteen, and, with all due respect, I am coming out.'

Hornby was well aware of Clouting's real age, having connived to let the boy join the regiment a year before, and in the end he relented. 'Fair enough, it's against my wishes, but you shall come.'

Just ten days later, the regiment was on its way to France with its young trooper – one of the first of thousands of under-age soldiers.

2

For King and Country . . .
and Your Mates

FAREWELL BELOVED
SO YOUNG AND BRAVE
FOR KING AND COUNTRY
HIS LIFE HE GAVE

10675 Private Alfred Clark
1st Royal West Kent Regiment

Killed in Action 9 October 1915, aged 18

BACK HOME, THE BRITISH public heard of the declaration of war in their newspapers, on placards and, for the most part, by word of mouth. It came almost as a release from the anxious years of expectation. Although there were small demonstrations against the war, these were swamped by jubilant expressions of support indicative of pent-up excitement and nervous energy. Horace Calvert, a lad from Bradford, was fourteen years old.

I was going home from work at about seven o'clock in the evening and as I got up the top of Richmond Road, there was a newsagent's shop and outside there was a big placard: 'War declared on Germany'. Mobilization had taken place. I went to Bellevue Barracks, home of the 6th West Yorks, a Territorial battalion, and found there were crowds round there. Everybody was excited and

every time they saw a soldier he was cheered. It was very patriotic and people were singing 'Rule Britannia', 'Land of Hope and
Glory', all the favourites. A challenge had been laid down over
Belgium and they were eager to take it up. I should have been
home at nine but I stayed there until late at night. Everybody
stood in groups saying 'We've got to beat the Germans' and quite
a number were already setting off to enlist.

Two hundred miles to the south, in London, seventeen-year-old
Vic Cole was swept along in an eruption of public fervour.

In the afternoon, I went up to town and wandered about in front of
Buckingham Palace and down the Mall. There was a great crowd
of people outside the palace and other crowds were congregating
in Whitehall and towards Westminster. Later on that night, just
before midnight, the word went round that the ultimatum had
expired and we were now at war with Germany. I don't remember
getting home but I was terribly excited. The thing that people
had been talking about for years had at last come about.

The expressions of wild enthusiasm in the two cities belied the
fact that there was no great urgency on the part of the British
public to gear up for conflict. Some uniformed organizations,
however, being readily available, were able to react to the declaration of war. The Scouts, for example – like the Territorials, on
their summer camps – were prepared and keen to act. These boys,
25,000 in all, were used straight away to safeguard railways,
telegraphs and reservoirs, or to run messages or act as dispatch
riders. Down in Exmouth, Devon, fourteen-year-old Christopher
Paget-Clark had just broken up for his school holidays and, being
a Boy Scout, volunteered to help patrol the coastline to look out
for anything suspicious. This he did for several nights a week
on an isolated stretch of land midway between Exmouth and
Budleigh Salterton, before being withdrawn. He then enlisted

into the Devonshire Regiment, being made a lance corporal, one of 10,000 ex-Scouts and Scoutmasters who enlisted in the first four months of the war.

George White was also sent on duty as soon as war was declared.

We senior Scouts were released from school to do a cycle patrol along four miles of the London Road to guard the telegraph wires, apparently to prevent any sabotage. This duty lasted for a couple of weeks, then some of us were dispatched to Harty Ferry [in Kent] for service with the coastguards. Each night, one coastguard and two of us boys rowed across the Swale carrying rocket equipment with us. The object of the exercise was to watch for any attempted landing by the enemy in darkness.

In marked contrast to this activity, 'business as usual' became a common phrase in civilian life. Even so, the decision for war created a degree of economic uncertainty, which over the following month resulted in the loss of around 500,000 jobs; nervous employers temporarily shut factory gates, in part to encourage workers to enlist but in the main because of anxiety about the future and the implications for their work of a widespread conflict. There was still no general conception of what war would mean. Newspapers – practically the only source of information on national matters – were often content to run patriotic stories in the face of a dearth of hard news, until it arrived at the end of August with the retreat from Mons.

Popular belief today is that there was an immediate and overwhelming rush to the colours. In reality, peak enlistment – of almost half a million men in two weeks – was a month away. The majority of people were prepared to wait and see, while the machinery of government cranked into action and the first appeals for men were printed and issued.

Calls for recruits were not long in coming. Sixty-four-year-old Lord Kitchener – Britain's most successful soldier and military governor of Egypt from 1911 – was in London at the outbreak of hostilities and was immediately appointed Secretary of State for War, taking office on 5 August. Within two days he had issued an appeal for 100,000 volunteers. The age group first specified, nineteen to thirty, was soon adjusted upwards to include all men up to the age of thirty-five, and raised again intermittently throughout the war.

Young boys who desperately wanted to enlist had to resort to lying, and that did not always come easily to lads brought up to eschew deceit. Officially, of course, the age for recruitment into the Regular Army was eighteen, and nineteen the minimum age to go overseas on active service. If a boy was keen to go to France before the fighting was over, nineteen he would have to be, a point clarified by the recruiting sergeant when one lad, George Head, tried to enlist.

'How old are you?' asked the sergeant. I replied, 'Eighteen.'

'Yes, that will do for enlisting but not for Imperial Service Overseas. If you want to join in the war, go over there,' and he pointed to a table on which lay some newspapers. 'Have a read and perhaps when you return you will have grown another year older.'

Burney, who was with me, being over nineteen, explained this riddle and so I returned and when asked the age question again, I replied, 'Nineteen.'

No such deception could help the very youngest volunteers. These boys, whose ages had barely broken into double figures, were patted on the head and escorted from the recruitment halls. Most went home to rue their lot and return to school, but an optimistic group persisted. Their only hope was to make a direct appeal to anyone who might listen, even the Secretary of State himself. Indeed, it was not unheard of for a boy to assail Kitchener on the steps of the War Office or Scotland Yard. One Reginald Smith was reported in the press as having made a sixty-five-mile journey from Ramsgate to speak to the great man himself. 'We will talk about it again when you are older,' Kitchener is reputed to have told him.

If a personal meeting was impossible, then there was always a letter to explain a young boy's plight, certain in the knowledge that the Secretary of State for War knew a good sport when he saw one. Alfie Knight had a touching faith in Lord Kitchener.

21 Park Avenue
Dublin
Dear Lord Kitchner
I am an Irish boy 9 years of age and I want to go to the front. I can ride jolley quick on my bycicle and would go as dispatch ridder. I wouldn't let the germans get it. I am a good shot with a revolver and would kill a good few of the germans. I am very strong and often win a fight with lads twice as big as myself. I want a uneform and a revolver and will give a good account of myself.

Please send an ancncer
Yours affectionately
Alfie Knight

Far from ignoring the letter, Kitchener asked his private secretary to reply.

17 August 1914
Dear Sir
  Lord Kitchener asks me to thank you for your letter, but he is afraid that you are not quite old enough to go to the front as a dispatch rider.

Yours truly
H. J. Creedy
Private Secretary

Quite how many boys were willing to lie is difficult to ascertain. However, in a study undertaken on a surviving Company Roll Book belonging to E Company of the 16th Battalion Royal Welch Fusiliers, a statistical anomaly is evident. The book reveals that 21 per cent of all volunteers claimed to be nineteen, while fewer than 1 per cent were eighteen. This evidence is put into perspective when compared with other age groups: on average, each year broadly 7 or 8 per cent of those who enlisted were older than nineteen.

The frequency with which boys gave their age as exactly nineteen should have alerted recruiting sergeants to the fact that there had either been the most remarkable explosion in the birth rate in 1895, or a number of boys were consistently giving the wrong age. Most boys, if they thought about it, were careful to use their day and month of birth and subtract one, two or three years as required; a very few, aware perhaps that boys were using the age of nineteen, boldly claimed to be twenty for greater authenticity.

Inevitably, among the first to volunteer were those with few family ties, working in dreary dead-end jobs. These would-be recruits were likely to make a snap decision to join up, whereas men with steady jobs and a family to feed were more likely to ensure that their affairs were in order before offering themselves to the country.

Seventeen-year-old John Laister was in just such a dead-end job and was one of the first to join up immediately on the outbreak of war, on 6 August. His motive for lying about his age was less military glory and more that he was bored and keen for a change of scenery – typical of unattached youth.

I worked at Oldbury Carriage Works as a fitter and turner from six in the morning until six at night, with a long walk to and from work. I was on my way home and I'm looking at the evening paper and there was a picture of men queuing up to join the army in James Watt Street in Birmingham. 'I'd like to join the army better than slogging down at the Works for a few shillings a week,' I thought, so without telling Mother I got my bike in the morning and went to enlist. I never bothered telling my employer what I was up to; I didn't feel I owed them anything.

I had great difficulty in finding James Watt Street but I found an alleyway to park my bike and I went to get in the queue which was almost the length of the street. I almost gave up. I'd been going for about two hours to reach the building, one person going up a flight of stairs as another came out, before I was called to go up.

The sergeant major opened the door. 'Come in.' As soon as I got in, he says, 'Take your clothes off.' It wasn't too warm and there were two doctors there in white coats and an officer sitting behind this table and they examined me and measured me. I was five foot one inch tall. I didn't think I was so small. The officer looked up. 'How old are you?' 'Nineteen, sir.' 'Are you sure you're nineteen?' 'Yes, sir.' 'Well, I'll tell you what. You come back here in about two years' time and then perhaps you will have filled out.'

So I'm making for the door with tears in my eyes, and a corporal who was there said, 'Half a minute' and he went to the sergeant major and he whispered something, and he went in front of the officer, saluted and said, 'Do you think he'll fill out, sir?' 'Well, I don't know,' replied the doctor. 'Oh, all right, put him in the army and let them sort him out.'

According to John's surviving enlistment papers, he was just 7 stone 8 pounds, and the doctor's comments are revealing: 'A little underweight but well proportioned and will develop.' Development was the key: what he could be, not what he was.

John was far from alone in being disenchanted with the daily grind of work. The vast majority of children left school at the age of fourteen, and even earlier if they had an excellent record of attendance. In Lancashire a child could begin part-time work at the mill at eleven and full-time work at thirteen. Leaving school on the Friday meant adult work on the Monday. Invariably, pay was poor and hours long in frequently dangerous conditions. At the end of the working week, parents expected the child to hand over wages in their entirety for lodgings and keep. If the child was lucky, he might be handed back what was known as 'odd' money, perhaps a shilling or two in return, but rarely any more. It hardly eased the treadmill of work. Horace Calvert remembered:

> Civilian life was a dull life when you looked at it, just work. Mine was a dirty job at an engineering firm, always lots of grease and the smell of metal being turned. I didn't like the machinery, either. I was always frightened I might get caught up in it.

It was ironic that Horace should naively think that machinery in the factory was a greater threat than that of war.

> I looked upon war as a big adventure, having read all those adventure stories in the *Wide World* magazines in the library. It made me feel what a nice life it would be.

If the war happened to be morally just, then all well and good, but boys like Horace did not need such a reason to enlist. They were just happy to escape hard, humdrum lives.

Dick Trafford enlisted not so much to escape his job as to keep up with the other men. He had been a miner for the best part of two years, although only fifteen, and was fit and strong.

> I was working down a coal mine at a place called Rainford from the age of fourteen. About six men from Ormskirk and me used to be on night work, and this particular night we'd all turned up for work but one chap was late turning up. When he arrived, he said, 'There's no work tonight, chaps'; the war was going to break out tomorrow and, he said, we had better go and report to the drill hall. They were Territorials and had to report there and

I followed them to enlist. It wasn't that I actually wanted to go, it was because the other men were going and I thought, 'Well, I might as well be with them.'

It was always possible during enlistment for a boy to give a false name in the hope of escaping detection. Cecil Withers enlisted under the name Sydney Harrison, George Maher under his mother's maiden name of Ashton. Morris Kroffsoff served as Jack Phillips. 'It is customary for these boys to adopt their father's first name,' wrote his father, Phillip Kroffsoff, by way of explanation to the army. Other under-age boys made slight but clever adjustments. Richard Kerr served in the artillery as Richard Farr; Michael Cohen enlisted in August 1914 giving the name Michael Cowan. Harold Lautenberg, from Hackney in London, became Harold Lawton, although in his case jettisoning his ancestry was probably as much a motive as concealing his identity.

Stuart Cloete, an eighteen-year-old officer in the King's Own Yorkshire Light Infantry (KOYLIs), recalled one fourteen-year-old in his company who had made it all the way to France.

He was big for his age, had lied about it when he enlisted under a false name, and then had sufficient self-restraint to write to no one. I had noticed that he received no mail and wrote no letters, but had never spoken to him about it.

In this particular case the boy was traced by his family and sent home, but the graveyards of France are littered with those who enlisted under assumed names and will for ever be lost to posterity.

There was another possible route to France for a keen young boy. The Territorials would take him at seventeen, and, although he was not officially eligible to go abroad until he was nineteen, they were desperate for men. Any assumption at the onset of war that all their existing part-time soldiers would patriotically sign up for overseas service had proved wide of the mark. Many older men resented what they saw as the government's attempted change to their conditions of service, and refused or were slow to sign.

This caused a problem, for there was no proper reserve for the Territorials, no pool of men upon whom the force could call to fill the gaps. Official sanction, allowing these soldiers to jump ship to the Regular Army, only exacerbated the problem. As a result, anyone, boys included, who was sufficiently well trained could expect to go overseas and youngsters were aware of this possible short-cut. They grasped the fact that the Territorials might take lads who had attempted and failed to get into the Regular Army. What was more, the Territorial Force's pre-war attestation form, E.501, did not ask for a statement of age, and although in time new forms were brought out requiring such a declaration, many recruitment offices were still using the old examples well into the following year.

Seventeen-year-old Leslie Walkinton wanted to join a Territorial battalion of the London Regiment, the Queen's Westminster Rifles (QWR). He was anxious on two counts: that he looked too young to be accepted and that the war would take place without him. He need not have worried. Boys as young as fifteen were enlisted into the battalion and Leslie was readily admitted. He was delighted with his choice, finding himself 'amongst a congenial lot of men whose one idea was to train us as quickly as possible in the hope that we might all be lucky enough to see just the end of the fighting'.

Leslie's vision of war was little short of quixotic.

We were a normal lot of healthy young men afflicted with romantic minds and large reserves of pent-up energy. Our real need was to rescue beautiful maidens from terrible dragons, but the beautiful maidens were so capable and standoffish and all the dragons had been slain long ago, so that when the *Daily Mail* told us that beautiful Belgium had been violated and France was in distress, we all rushed to the rescue. But I think we did it for our own sakes very largely. The uniforms, the bands, the open air life, and most of all the feeling that one was a devil of a fellow, attracted us irresistibly . . . this wave of patriotic emotion which carried us into the army received its impetus from the publicity and the glamour of it all.

John Auguste Pouchot, born in April 1899, was one of the fifteen-year-olds who joined the regiment. His father worked as an auctioneer's manager and lived in Belgravia, but, for reasons that are not recorded, Jack – as he was known – was fostered. When he left school, he took a job at the Army and Navy Store in London, but in August 1914 he joined the QWR. He was probably attracted to a Territorial battalion because of his age, but even so had to add a couple of years in order to enlist. His medical must have been perfunctory in the extreme, as he appears to have grown two inches in height and two inches in chest measurement between signing his attestation papers and being passed by a doctor.

Ernest Steele, aged seventeen, from Leytonstone in east London, was another who joined the QWR. A quiet, reserved boy, Ernest was fond of reading and noted for his studiousness. He had not been averse to outdoor activities, however, and while a member of the Island Rangers, a local military and scientific corps, he won several silver spoons for shooting. He had been working in the family business as a box maker when war broke out and enlisted, signing the Imperial Service Obligation as he did so. Leslie Walkinton also signed but in his case he was told to get parental consent as well.

My platoon commander wouldn't take me abroad unless I got written permission from my father. This was a bit awkward, but by dint of assurances that we should probably be sent to India or

Egypt on garrison duty, or merely to the lines of communication in France, I managed to get the required signature.

Although the Obligation should have been signed individually, consent from serving Territorial soldiers was often obtained collectively, and in a manner that was more than a little underhand. In one case an entire battalion on parade had been asked to step forward to signal its group assent, sergeants being ordered to look down the line to check that every man had obliged.

This was not an isolated case. In Parliament, Liberal MP George Esslemont cited a similar example. He had been to see a battalion billeted nearby and had been struck by the number of obviously young boys in the unit.

> I took the opportunity of having an interview with the commanding officer. I referred to the case of these lads and expressed the view that they should not have been mobilized at all but allowed to continue their education ... The commanding officer said that those boys would not be sent away [overseas]. The next thing I heard, only a few days afterwards, was that he had paraded the whole battalion, delivered a speech and invited all the men and boys in the battalion to volunteer for foreign service. I would have no cause for complaint if in making that appeal he had clearly and distinctly said that it must be understood that he did not expect any lad under nineteen years of age to make application for foreign service. He did nothing of the sort. He asked those willing to volunteer to slope arms and of course the majority of the boys sloped arms along with the older men. I thought this was rather an extraordinary thing after the representations I had made and the assurances he had given me. I wrote respectfully calling attention to the matter and asked him how it had come about. He said he had acted on instructions from Headquarters.

Alfred Anderson's company of the 5th Black Watch was paraded and asked one by one whether they would agree to go overseas.

The quartermaster sergeant called the roll out. He was sat at a table in the middle of the hall and he just took us as we were in the roll book. I was about the first to volunteer because my name is A. Anderson. I didn't sign anything. You had to declare your willingness to go abroad in front of the others. That was enough. Only one or two said they couldn't volunteer for home reasons, parents to support and things like that, but very few refused to go. We did have talks amongst ourselves about it and the main thing I remember was that we would stick together. We had drilled together, been at camps with the same fellows, what else could you do, you couldn't say 'I'm not staying with the battalion'.

If Territorial battalions had been forced to eject all aged under nineteen, then most units would never have set sail at all. It seems inconceivable that the authorities had any alternative but to turn a blind eye and send these units overseas, boys and all, as they did from the second half of September.

Meanwhile, the first troops had arrived in France only a week after the rapid mobilization of the BEF. From the coastal ports the first British divisions advanced only cautiously. The French had been optimistic that the Allies might make a stand near Charleroi in Belgium, but such hopes soon evaporated; instead, the first meaningful contact took place on 23 August near the town of Mons, much closer to the French border than anticipated.

One of the first battalions to arrive on 14 August was the 4th Middlesex Regiment. They had wasted little time in leaving Boulogne where they had disembarked, moving off in an easterly direction. A week later they were near the Belgian town of Mons, pushing forward, searching for the enemy who were as yet to be located, although they were known to be close and in great numbers. As no contact had been made, pairs of scouts were sent forward on bicycles to see what they could discover and report back. One of those chosen was Private John Parr, a golf caddie in civilian life, born in North Finchley, London. He had enlisted in August 1912, stating his age as eighteen and one month; he was in fact fifteen and one month. Despite his age he was a fully trained regular soldier by the time he went overseas.

No one was certain precisely what happened to Private Parr once out on reconnaissance but he and another man named Beard were engaged by small arms fire. Private Beard returned to the battalion, Parr did not, and he was noted as missing. In the weeks following, Parr's mother, Alice, first contacted the War Office, then wrote to the Infantry Record office in Hounslow asking for news, but no one could confirm his whereabouts; the War Office did not even know he was missing. Then Alice Parr received a letter from a British prisoner in Germany who informed her that John had 'been shot down at Mons', partly confirmed by Parr's Company Commander, Captain Hanley, who wrote that her son had not been heard of since. The date was recorded as 21 August 1914 making No 14196 Private John Parr the first British soldier killed in the war. He was seventeen years and thirty-three days old.

Among the units slogging their way forward were an unknown number of under-age soldiers who, despite the vigilance of commanding officers, had somehow contrived to go overseas, some as young as fifteen or sixteen. At Mons the units formed up and took part in the first set-piece engagement of the war. It was there that a young private by the name of James Price, of the 2nd South Lancashire Regiment, was killed. He was sixteen and, quite possibly, the second under-age soldier to die on the Western Front.

The regulars who fought at Mons were able to give the Germans a bloody rebuff. Nevertheless, the small British contingent was faced by a force nearly two and a half times as big and with twice as many guns; it had little option but to fight and retire, and then retreat. It came as something of a national shock when, just three weeks after the declaration of war, news filtered through that the regular British Army was in danger of annihilation. The nation hardly expected such a rapid reversal of fortunes.

In this international conflict, Britain would increasingly turn to her Empire and Dominions for vital help; they were not found wanting. Yet if Britain had only a small Regular Army, the forces of countries such as Canada and Australia were by comparison practically non-existent. Both nations were still technically dominions but Australia had been self-governing since an Act of 1901, while Canada was to all intents and purposes autonomous, though a Governor General still had the right of an imperial veto. Both nations had immigrant populations, large swathes of whom were still intensely patriotic to Britain. In August 1914, Canada automatically entered the war on the Allied side, making no independent declaration of war. Within weeks, 30,000 Canadians had enlisted, while in Australia news of the conflict was greeted with raucous approval. Recruitment was begun straightaway to send an initial force of 20,000 men to help the Allied cause. These men would form the newly established Australian Imperial Force (AIF), the first contingent setting sail on 7 November 1914.

The vast majority of European inhabitants in Australia were of British descent, while in Canada a great wave of emigration over the previous century ensured that large numbers of immigrants had ties to Britain, including many Scots families made landless during the Clearances – though, surprisingly, still willing to help a nation that had treated them so badly. More recently, thousands of young men, both singly and with families, had left for Canada to seek work and a better living, while simultaneously there had been a regular flow of children sent from British orphanages to begin new lives across the water. Alfred Anderson's two elder brothers, Dave and Jack, had both emigrated to Canada before the war. Dave, the eldest son, enlisted in the Canadian Infantry and Jack in the Canadian Royal Engineers. At one point all three brothers were serving in France at the same time; all survived.

It was often the toss of a coin, literally in some cases, that determined whether men set sail for Australia, Canada or perhaps New Zealand. They might have been seeking a new challenge but the emotional link with the past remained.

One of those prepared to help Britain in her hour of need was Wesley Wade from Sydney, New South Wales, a lad with family ties to Britain. He eventually found his way to France, serving with the 17th Battalion AIF, and saw action during the Somme. In August 1916 he was killed. His grave carries an interesting inscription chosen by his English mother, Agnes. It reads: 'A Young Life gone to rest fighting for his King and Country'. It is an inscription that is by no means unique. Roderick Budsworth, a native of West Tamworth, New South Wales, was killed in fighting in November 1916. The inscription on his grave reads: 'He died for King and the Empire'. Similarly, the grave of Sergeant Henry Flynn of the 38th Battalion of the Canadian Infantry carries the inscription: 'Died for King and Country'. These give an indication of the ethos of the time, and, just as in Britain, it encouraged thousands of men and boys to enlist.

Those who were actually born in Britain had by far the greatest affinity with the mother country. While 6.5 per cent of Canadian boys of British parentage enlisted in the forces, a staggering 37.5 per cent of eligible British-born Canadian men joined up by the end of October 1916. Typical of the lads who enlisted were Thomas Tombs and Percy Layzell. Thomas was born in Worcester in 1900. He had emigrated with his parents to Vancouver, enlisting in the Alberta Regiment. Percy was a few months younger than Thomas. A lad from Brighton, he had emigrated with his parents, Charles and Bessie Layzell, to Kingston, Ontario, before he enlisted into the Canadian Field Artillery. Both Percy and Thomas later served on the Somme, where they were killed within a week of each other in November 1916. Both boys were then aged just sixteen.

Although most chose to enlist in Canada, a few boys preferred to return to Britain. James Hodding was born in Portsmouth in 1899, the son of Major James Hodding, a former Royal Fusilier and an ex-Indian Army officer. Soon after war broke out, fifteen-year-old James travelled from Vancouver back to Britain where, at sixteen, he was commissioned into the 10th Royal Fusiliers. He was killed the following year. His forty-nine-year-old father also reported for duty, and served with the 2nd Royal Fusiliers; he survived the war.

Bill Taylor was one of the British orphans sent to Canada – he had left London in 1908. He was never sure where he had been born and did not know precisely how old he was, although he was aware he was under age when he enlisted. In November 1914, Bill had been working as a farm labourer and, during some time off, had been watching the 20th Battalion training in Toronto. Mistaken for a new recruit, he was directed to take a medical and, before he knew what he was doing, was a member of the battalion. By September 1915 he was out in France where he continued to serve until he was seriously wounded in 1917.

Back in the mother country, just short of 300,000 men had volunteered for enlistment in August 1914, and the queues were thinning when press reports of the military crisis, the retreat from Mons, caused a second surge in recruitment. In September the enlistment figures rose dramatically to 460,000, most in the first two weeks of the month. It was a never-to-be repeated rush to the colours.

In spite of his initial excitement, Vic Cole had been one of those who opted to wait. He was studying wireless telegraphy at a school in Clapham and returned to work the following week, but his mind was elsewhere.

My work suffered greatly during the next few weeks. I wanted to be in the army with a gun in my hand, like the boys I had so often read about in books and magazines.

Vic was keen to go but he was unsure whether to take the irreversible step of enlisting. He attended a recruitment rally in early September 1914, listened to the rabble-rousing speeches, and then with his sixteen-year-old friend George Pulley decided to make the leap of faith. 'George and I considered the matter, made our decision and approached the Sergeant who already had his eagle eye upon us.'

Once both boys had made their intentions clear, they were whisked away to sign up at once. As volunteers, they were offered the chance to pick their regiment, the last act of free will, as Vic saw it, for four years.

Lolling back on the nice cushioned seats of a fast car, we were rushed to a nearby hostel called The Crooked Billet. This was the Recruiting Office. In an upstairs room we stood before the Recruiting Officer who demanded particulars. Age? Nineteen years nine months! Occupation? Student. What regiment do you wish to join? Pulley behind me whispered, 'West Kents' so I said, 'Make it West Kents.'

The R.O. with a smile (looking back on it, I feel inclined to say with a sinister smile) said 'Sign this form.' I did so. He handed me a railway warrant and a slip directing me to report at Bromley Drill Hall at 9 a.m. on the 7th inst.

Early on Monday morning, then, George and I, pockets stuffed with sandwiches, went forth to war. Arriving at the Hall without incident, we found some fifty other fellows wandering about in various stages of undress, undergoing medical inspection. Our turn came. We dutifully walked on our toes, exhaled and coughed when ordered, read jumbled letters on a card and passed as fit.

Vic and George were part of the surge of recruitment that followed the epic retreat from Mons. This had finally come to a juddering halt on 6 September, with exhausted British troops now southeast of Paris. Around this time the first lurid stories of atrocities perpetrated by German soldiers began to filter home, the details of which were not forgotten at recruitment rallies. The civilian population of Belgium and northern France was being raped, robbed and randomly shot and it was up to Britain to save them.

Don Price was sixteen.

We heard about the Germans and the stories of their cruelty and the Uhlans we used to think were terrible people. Stories like that built up in my mind until I decided I wanted to do something for my country.

In Manchester we had the *Daily Dispatch* and what they said about the Germans, as far as I was concerned, was gospel. We believed it instinctively, no question.

Jimmy Rushworth was an apprentice with me, a tall lad, and he influenced me. We were talking one day in the warehouse and he said 'I'm going down to enlist' and I said 'Right, Jimmy, I'll come down with you.' We went down to a hotel in Piccadilly, Manchester, to join, without any second thought about the consequences. We just believed we'd have a damn good time for about six months. Work was so tedious and people wanted a bit of fun and this was a way to get it. This would be a holiday.

I had no idea when I went to work that morning that I was going to enlist that lunchtime. I came home that night and said, 'Mother, I'm in the army,' just like that. When I told her, there was weeping and wailing. She wasn't happy at all, but when I explained it would only be for about six months, she calmed down somewhat.

The Germans needed to be stopped and taught a lesson, Don believed. His was an abstract anger, the sense of a moral affront to decency. There was no personal hatred about it.

In the case of Frank Lindley, there most certainly was. As the war expanded, more and more boys would find themselves in his position, wanting to avenge the loss of a father or a brother. Frank had left school in March 1914, on the day of his fourteenth birthday, to become a dental technician, a 'posh job', in his words. It was not what he wanted to do. He wanted to go to sea like his brother Harry, but his father had put his foot down and ended that idea, at least for the time being. Frank was immensely close to his brother, who was almost ten years his senior. Harry was an able seaman in the Royal Navy and had travelled widely, bringing his younger brother presents from around the globe.

I had itchy feet, fired by Harry's travels. While he was on leave we used to talk, 'cos we used to sleep in the same bed. He said, 'Now, Frank, I've got it all planned. We're refitting for the Far East and when I get to Australia I shall jump ship and go and take a tract of land. Then I'll send for thee.' That was the very last thing he said to me.

And then war broke out and Harry was sent to join an old cruiser, HMS *Hawke*. In a devastating attack in October 1914, not only the *Hawke* but also two other ships were torpedoed and sunk in the North Sea, causing huge loss of life. Harry was drowned.

Me and my dad were getting ready to go to work and a knock came at the door and there was a telegram sudden just like, about 9 a.m., and it said sorry to tell you that your Harry's down at bottom. We read the bugger and we both collapsed. That finished my dad. He died in 1918, of course his grinding job didn't help. But it nearly killed him that morning. It upset the family a great deal. It made me think a bit. Everybody was wanting us, Kitchener was pointing, so I joined up. I wanted to avenge Harry's death. That was the main issue.

I joined up under age. There was a small bunch of us went, but a lot of them were fetched home by their parents. We all gave our ages as a lot older. I gave my age as twenty. I didn't give my parents a thought in this respect, there was me going off and them living in suspense, having already lost one son. I've thought about that since.

There is no argument that many who enlisted looked the right age. Boys who might have worked for three years since leaving school were often strong and broad-shouldered, like young miner Dick Trafford, and even if the recruiting sergeant had an inkling that the lad was under age, he saw little reason to reject someone physically up to the task and, more importantly, keen to go. Dick's 'grilling' was typical of the type of interview most might expect to receive:

'What do you want, sonny?'
   'Well,' I said, 'I'm with these fellows and I want to join up.'
   'You're too young.'
   'No, I'm not, I'm eighteen.'
   He said, 'I don't believe it.'
   So I said, 'If you don't believe me I'll go home and get my birth certificate.'
   'Oh,' he said, 'It's all right, I'll take your word for it.'

Asking for a birth certificate was well within the rights of a suspicious recruitment sergeant and could be used as a crude method of sifting out young boys without bothering to question a recruit further. Even then, what did its production actually show, other than that the boy could come up with a birth certificate? Whether it was his own or not was impossible to prove. Fifteen-year-old Louis Hardy had been given the same name as his deceased elder brother. When he enlisted he took along his brother's birth certificate as proof of age, and was duly accepted into the army. An unusual example, perhaps, but indicative of the fact that simply showing a birth certificate did not prove a lad's eligibility to serve.

The emphasis in sorting out who should or should not enlist

was on physical condition rather than age. Assessments were based on whether a recruit suffered from rotten teeth, poor sight, heart murmurs or rheumatism.

The minimum height requirement in August 1914 was 5 foot 3 inches, and the minimum chest measurement 34 inches, and there were tests too of the senses. Even so, medical examinations might be detailed at one office, almost laughable at the next. Herbert Gutteridge was sixteen when he enlisted with his brother, aged fourteen. Their army ages were put down as twenty and nineteen.

> Our medical examination was a farce: just a few questions asked, with no physical examination. We were then sworn in and declared to be fully fledged soldiers.

Memorizing the letters to pass the eyesight test was a ruse favoured by the short-sighted, such as Don Price.

> When I went in I was wearing glasses and I thought I wasn't going to be accepted if he started testing my right eye. Fortunately the doctor went out of the room and I saw this chart on the wall and learnt the bottom lines. He seemed to know because he said, 'I don't believe you can read that,' but I read them again from memory and he let me through with a smile.

Standing on his toes might explain the discrepancies on James Lock's enlistment papers. James, a labourer from Mile End in London, was reliably measured as being 5 foot 4 inches on his attestation papers, and 5 foot 1 inch by a doctor on his medical form. Either way, the sixteen-year-old did not last long in the army. He enlisted on 18 August 1914 and was discharged a month later when his real age was discovered.

As harassed doctors hurried to push recruits through, a few boys in the general nervousness failed to react in the right way.

George Pollard was sixteen years old when he attempted to join the 11th East Lancashire Regiment, more famously remembered as the Accrington Pals.

> On Tuesday morning, 15th September, I went with my friend Ernie Place for our medical at Willow Street School. The doctor asked me to expand my chest. I didn't quite understand what he meant, so I just stood there. He measured me, then told me I'd failed. Ernie, nineteen on 4th September, passed his medical.

Terribly disappointed, George walked home.

> I told my father what had happened. He said, 'Take your jacket off and expand your chest.' He made me expand my chest a few times, then measured it with a tape. He said, 'What's that doctor talking about? You've got a 35-inch chest. You should have been taken in. Go down and tell him.'

Two days later, George returned, puffed out his chest, and passed.

There was another reason for superficial questioning. Every recruiting sergeant was paid two shillings and sixpence (about £6 in today's money) for each man attested into the infantry, as was the medical officer, frequently a civilian specifically employed for this task. As a result, the standard of probity could vary greatly from one office to another, and those rejected frequently discovered it was merely a question of turning up elsewhere to be accepted.

Considerable sums could be made by less scrupulous recruitment staff, but that would require a quick throughput, passing all but the palpably decrepit. The pre-war fears of the military authorities that the process of recruitment was subject to the (in) discretion of the enlistment sergeant were once again realized. Men were being passed, only to be rejected by the army once they reached their depots for training. By October, the army had reduced the reward to one shilling and there were calls to force those who were paid to return the fee if the recruit should subsequently be discharged as medically unfit. Doctors too required reining in and in December 1914 orders were issued that no doctor should process more than forty men a day, or eight men in one hour. Furthermore, all were ordered to spend no less than seven minutes on a recruit so ensuring each received a proper medical examination.

It would be unfair to point the finger at recruiting sergeants and officers as somehow being more immoral about the enlistment of under-age boys than anyone else. Recruiting sergeants came in all guises, and some of those who colluded in the enlistment of under-age boys did so in order not to deprive them of their chance for adventure.

In the last resort, the onus on telling the truth was placed squarely on the shoulders of the recruit and he signed to that effect. Even so, the flaws in the whole process were evident for all to see. On both sides of the recruitment table there was room to bend the rules and, with no identification being required, abuse was prevalent. The enlistment forms were set up to pursue the question of how fit a boy was to serve, less whether he was old enough. The boy was asked, 'What is your age?' but the form filled in by the doctor asked for a medical opinion as to the *apparent* age, in other words, whether the boy's physical development was such that he would make an efficient soldier. As one MP was later to point out, nowhere was there room for the medical officer to state that he believed the boy to be actually under age.

Although fraudulent enlistment carried the threat of prosecution, there is scant evidence of military law being used against a soldier who made a 'mis-statement as to age'. In a question later raised in the Commons, in April 1916, one MP asked pointedly whether any boy had been court-martialled for the offence; in reply, the Undersecretary of State for War conceded that no such trial had taken place.

The MP may have been referring to a General Court Martial, for during the course of the war around 2,000 other ranks were tried by the lesser District Courts Martial for the crime of fraudulent enlistment and re-enlisting after discharge. However, how many were under-age soldiers is not recorded. One fifteen-year-old boy who was discharged only to be caught again after re-enlisting was punished, the following note being written on to his service record: 'Committed crime – Fraudulent enlistment – trial disposed of but placed under stoppages of pay etc as if he had been convicted by D.C.M.' Loss of pay was hardly a serious rap over the knuckles for a boy who had twice fraudulently enlisted. In December 1915 another under-age soldier, Private John Arnold from London, was awarded a District Court Martial and forty-two days' detention in Wandsworth Detention Barracks for giving 'false answers on attestation'. However, no evidence has been discovered that any recruitment officer or sergeant was prosecuted for knowingly enlisting such boys.

The collusion that enabled boys to enlist in such numbers was endemic, not just in recruitment offices but in family homes up and down the country. It included Members of Parliament, as well as miners and mill workers. It included lord mayors, headmasters of schools and governors of borstals as well as mothers and fathers, and, most of all, the boys themselves.

Any individual who sanctioned the enlistment of an under-age boy was complicit in the act, although the level of involvement varied greatly. Sixteen-year-old Charles Leatherland was working for Birmingham Corporation.

I told my chief I intended to join the army. He said such a thing was impossible. I was too young. I insisted . . . My chief told the alderman how ridiculous the whole idea was. But dear old bearded Alderman Lucas saved me. He said, 'I certainly would have refused to grant permission but tomorrow night I am addressing a recruiting meeting in the Town Hall and I cannot very well do that if I say no to you.' So off I went to the recruiting office. The Medical Officer ran his tape over me, looked rather hesitant, turned to the Medical Sergeant and said, 'He looks rather skinny for nineteen.' But fortune came to my aid again. I recognized the sergeant as the foreman at one of our corporation depots. He rose to the occasion wonderfully. 'That's so, sir,' he said, 'but these ginger-headed lads soon fill out by the time they are twenty.'

The response of parents to the enlistment of their offspring varied widely. Some encouraged their service; indeed, they went out of their way to facilitate it as George Pollard's father had done, while others were furious, and some were bewildered and shocked. Boys could probably guess the reaction of their parents, or simply chose not to tell them that they intended to join up, knowing that permission would probably be refused. A small proportion enlisted without giving their parents a second thought, like Frank Lindley.

And not all parents agreed with each other. The attitude of fathers was generally more robust than that of their wives. In a world in which male and female roles in the family were clearly delineated, the pressure on men and boys to live up to their status was intense. When Dick Trafford returned home after enlisting:

I told my mother what was happening, that I had joined up, and of course my mother played hell because I'd no right joining up at my age and she was going to stop me, but my father said, 'Don't interfere. Let him go if he wants to.'

Horace Calvert had a similar experience, when he joined a territorial battalion of the West Yorkshire Regiment.

I went home and Father said, 'Where have you been?' so I told him I'd joined the army and after a pause he said, 'Well, you've made your bed, that's it.' There were tears from my mother but

I said I think I'd like it. I told them not to try and get me out, because if they did I'd probably go and join up elsewhere.

What happened to those boys whose ambition to enlist outstripped their ability to convince? Not every recruitment sergeant was guilty of turning a blind eye and not every medical officer waved through fit but under-age lads who were willing to serve.

By and large the boys who failed to get in returned to civilian life, perhaps bent on having another go the following year. Yet some adults felt that such a surge of enthusiasm should not be allowed to dissipate and moves were made to harness and organize this collective will, to give the lads a frisson of military standing and a modicum of training. In Newcastle Upon Tyne, for example, several town councillors and moth-balled former soldiers, all well beyond service age themselves, got together to form the Junior Training League, directing lads to attend a meeting at the town hall assembly room.

Basil Peacock was one of the sixteen-year-olds who turned up and had to fight his way into the building. A diminutive figure for his age, he knew he would never be accepted into the army proper, but he felt envious. 'I think it was the sight of schoolfellows in uniform which made me determined to wear one too,' he acknowledged. Basil also had two brothers in the forces and he was not about to sit back and do nothing; the proposed Junior Training League was perfect.

The response was astounding, almost comic, and the elderly founders were engulfed in a seething mob of boys clamouring to join. When I arrived, there were hundreds inside and hundreds more fighting to get in. It was like a modern students' demo, and the councillors had to take refuge on a high platform. The noise in the hall was terrific until an old gentleman in the uniform of a reserve colonel came onto the stage and with lungs of brass shouted, 'Boys, if you want to be soldiers, the first thing you must learn is who is boss . . .'

The Training League soon got under way, and we were given a piece of red, white and blue cord to wear in the shoulder-seam of our jackets to indicate membership. It was the first quasi-military badge that I acquired, and it gave me more pride than real ones did later ... My parents were unenthusiastic about the Junior Training League but relieved to find that I had taken no military obligations; they probably thought that this occupation would take the fidgets out of me ...

There was another organization that had all the trappings of the army even if it was somewhat on its fringes. It was the Forage Department of the Army Service Corps and it employed thousands of boys for home service only. Forage was absolutely vital to the prosecution of the war, with horses and mules providing the power to move guns and supplies around the battlefield, and thousands of thoroughbred horses in the cavalry. More tons of forage were shipped to France than tons of ammunition. Cheap and willing labour in Britain was badly needed: boys who joined were subject to military law and would be employed under older men to cut and bail hay, receiving the basic wage of a labourer plus extra money for every ton of forage bailed. Indeed, wages were higher than for those serving overseas but this discrepancy was not significant for no one working for the Forage Department received any lodging, ration or separation allowances, nor would they be entitled to an army pension and they could be dismissed at short notice. The boys employed would even have to pay for their own army uniform, the cost of which would be taken from their wages in instalments. Nevertheless it was a khaki uniform like any other and that counted for an awful lot.

At the time, boys did not always fully understand their own motives for enlisting, but with hindsight they saw more clearly the pressures both from society and from the attitudes of their contemporaries that had weighed on them. Seventy years after he enlisted at seventeen, Len Thomas wrote a letter in which he looked again at his reasons for joining up.

I have read many accounts of the great rush to join the armed forces in 1914, and my contact with numerous men told me that the great majority, apart from their patriotism, found it a way to escape from the terrible working conditions they were undergoing. To many families this was the way to affluence, with the wife receiving allowances for self and children and no husband to feed and clothe, so far more shillings in the purse. A labourer's average wage was £1 per week. I was a copyholder on the *Daily Dispatch* at 18 shillings a week. A Royal Garrison Artillery gunner's pay was one shilling and tuppence a day, 8/2d a week to squander on myself.

Many modern books contain quite a few inaccuracies on the 1914–1918 war and about the British Expeditionary Force in France. One particular phrase used, also by the media, is that 'These brave men WILLINGLY gave their lives to save their country from German domination and the well-being of future posterities.' What a ridiculous myth. The last thought of those who joined Kitchener's Army was that they had joined to be killed. I'll state that . . . the first priority of all up the line was SURVIVAL. Mine was and I never met anyone who was willing to 'Go West'.

3

The Melting Pot

O SO YOUNG & YET SO BRAVE

24444 Private James Rathband
9th Royal Dublin Fusiliers

Killed in Action 9 September 1916, aged 16

TAKING THE KING'S SHILLING had been the easy part for seventeen-year-old Vic Cole and his sixteen-year-old friend George Pulley. It had been their first and, as it turned out, their last recruitment rally, buoyed up as they were by rousing speeches and praised for their indomitable spirit.

We waited in that drill-hall for some time until all had undergone the formalities of enlistment, then found ourselves sharply ordered outside into the sunlit street and lined up into two ranks by a very smart khaki-clad corporal of the West Kents, whose exceedingly pleasant and friendly manner gave us the optimistic but mistaken impression that life in the army was not so bad after all.

We numbered down, formed fours quite creditably and marched en route for Bromley Station, where, having dispersed about the platform to wait for the train for Maidstone, we listened to a moving speech by His Worship the Mayor, who, addressing us as 'Men of Bromley', wished us all the best of luck and a safe return.

The jovial nature of the recruitment process and the general bonhomie masked the fact that the army simply did not have the capacity to take into its ranks the numbers now joining.

Fifteen-year-old Horace Calvert, who had enlisted in Bradford, was surprised at the lack of organization. He had a boyish ideal about how the army should operate, and the reality was somewhat sobering.

They didn't know what to do with us at the barracks. Parade would be at 9.30 or 10 o'clock. You'd finish after lunch. There were so many men that there was hardly any room for drilling on the square. Form fours, left turn, about turn; there were no rifles at this time.

We used to march round the town with a military band, recruiting, trying to get more, and they used to fall in at the back, wearing civilian clothes, to be marched to the barracks and sworn in. The crowds watched and clapped and cheered. Sometimes twenty or thirty new recruits would be behind and chaps used to call out, 'Come on, Jack or Joe, come on, get in, join up,' and they did, especially if they'd had some drink; that brought them in, in the afternoon, it was laughable.

The class system remained prevalent, and in some regiments middle-class men felt uncomfortable about serving with men of lower status. Battalions were formed to allow like-minded men to serve together in their own units, forming distinctive Tradesmen's, Sportsmen's and Commercial battalions in regiments such as the East Yorkshires and King's Liverpools. In Birmingham, however, things were different. Here men from all backgrounds were thrown together.

Sixteen-year-old Harold Drinkwater had enlisted into the Birmingham Pals, the 15th and 16th Battalions of the Royal Warwickshire Regiment. The Pals were local battalions of men who saw themselves as belonging together because of their loyalty to the area from which they came and the men with whom they worked. Harold's first parade introduced him to: 'an extraordinary collection of fellows', many being the elite of the city, including barristers, solicitors, land clerks, and qualified engineers. Later on I found the fellow next to me had never done a day's work in his life. He had had something in the nature of a valet to do it for him. He was barely seventeen. In the same parade were volunteers from the other end of the social scale, including men and boys who by their looks at least required some good square meals before they would ever be able to stand the conditions which we were beginning to understand existed in France.

One of the well-to-do recruits was seventeen-year-old schoolboy Charles Carrington. He was of discernible officer material but had, in his enthusiasm, enlisted in the Birmingham Pals. He recalled his first impression of army life.

A thousand young men in their holiday clothes (with overcoats and stout boots) appeared in a mob on the parade ground . . . We were subdivided into sixteen platoons, to each of which was allotted a young officer from the OTC [Officer Training Corps] party and a sergeant from the group of old soldiers.

The shortage of non-commissioned officers (NCOs) and officers to train the volunteers was serious. Most were serving in France, and old men were frequently dug out of retirement to take over. Former officers, some in their seventies or eighties, would call out antiquated orders, hastily changing them when they realized their mistake.

It was apparent to Charles Carrington that the officers knew little more about drill than did the men. It was an inauspicious start and Charles looked around to find like-minded spirits.

Since I had no friends yet, I had sidled in among a group of boys of my own age when the line was formed, and presently discovered that two or three, like me, had falsified their attestation forms.

At times it was an eye-opener to see the state of some older men. Vic Cole had not even boarded the train for the West Kents' depot at Maidstone when he had

> a slight altercation with a battered gentleman smelling strongly of hops, who insisted that I bore a resemblance to a sergeant-major of his acquaintance, and was, for that reason, going to punch me on the nose. The train came in at this moment, however, and, in the ensuing rush for seats the Beery One was swept out of my sight.

George Coppard was, like Vic, a south London lad. He described himself as an 'ordinary boy of elementary education and slender prospects' – in truth, an accurate depiction of many of the under-age boys who enlisted. George had joined up at sixteen into the Queen's Royal West Surrey Regiment.

> Looking round at my new companions I could see that several were near-tramps. One wore a faded old morning coat and a well-washed bowler . . . We called him 'Uncle' and he seemed to relish the title.

Just as age had not been the most pressing issue in recruitment, so promotion among such company was not restricted. A young lad, enthusiastic to learn, was often picked out by a sergeant to take precedence over a florid-faced middle-aged man. Harold Drinkwater recalled that one of the boys in need of a 'good square meal' was made lance corporal of his section, though he was only sixteen years old.

Similarly, anyone with even basic knowledge of army life could be made up straight away. Lads from the Scouts or Boys' Brigade were among the favoured, for their perceived self-discipline and previous training. Vic Cole was swiftly parted from his childhood friend, George Pulley, when it was discovered that, as a former

Scout, Vic had a rudimentary knowledge of signalling and some familiarity with telegraphy.

> A few of us were now selected to form a Signal Section and to my consternation I was made lance corporal of same. A special hut was assigned to us, off Battalion Headquarters. There were about twenty of us signallers, including an officer, whom we seldom saw as he probably had another job, and a lovable old-time sergeant, Patsy Sheen, who wore the Indian Frontier Medal and had a seemingly unquenchable thirst. I at first appeared to be the only one with any authority and was well aware that my poor dog's leg stripe was not very popular, as most of the men were older than me and objected to being ordered about by a kid of seventeen.

Vic hardly cut an imposing figure. For the first few weeks, he and other recruits had been allocated out of the quartermaster's stores anything that happened to fit. 'Personally, I did rather well with a set of underwear, khaki tunic and trousers and a pair of boots. Some fellows acquired hats only!' The men looked willing, if peculiar, and there was much leg-pulling and many jokes.

> On parade, some had civilian trousers and coloured socks with khaki tunics, others sported khaki trousers and civilian coats, while one man had a tight-fitting khaki tunic and bowler hat.

The lack of uniforms was a frustration for boys whose apparel was hardly the stuff from which heroes were made. The only time new recruit Ernest Parker saw khaki was during the daily cycle of work, when jobs such as guard duty required for the requisite authority a semblance of uniform.

> On these occasions we rookies were obliged to borrow the khaki uniform of an old soldier and then for twenty-four hours we could imagine that we were real soldiers. This gave us the thrill

of adventure, and after undergoing the ordeal of inspection by the Adjutant, we looked forward to our turn of sentry duty with the feelings of men about to fight their first battle. Apart from the prospect of catching a spy red-handed, which always seemed worth bearing in mind, we knew that inside the Guard Room, and entrusted to our sole care, were several desperadoes whose military crimes might be augmented at any moment by a wild bid for freedom. It was well that inquisitive soldiers did not often test our vigilance, for with such possibilities in our minds, we were ready to shoot on sight.

With so many boys in their teens together, camp life could become a manly extension of school, with attitudes and behaviour to match. Bullying was a problem, with older lads picking on apparently weaker boys. George Coppard was singled out for abuse from one bigger boy, eventually being challenged to fight. The other boys, who had not attempted to intervene before, anticipated a brawl and were keen for George to accept. 'This could only mean a scrape, and before I had time to think it over I was unceremoniously bundled outside the hut.' In the time-honoured school tradition, a ring of boys formed. 'Lord knows, I was not a bit anxious to clash with this bloke, for to tell the truth I was in a state of funk.' Fortune smiled on both George and his assailant. The first blows sent the other boy into an epileptic fit, stopping the fight and so saving George an unwanted tussle and the other lad possible death at the front; he was subsequently discharged as medically unfit.

Most bullying, if it could be called that, was mild boyish behaviour, designed to work out if a lad was game and willing to be one of the gang. Fifteen-year-old George Parker was under canvas at Worksop.

The fellows who had been there some time had evolved a sort of initiation ceremony for newcomers, and I had to go through it.

On the first evening, a bunch of them got me down in the tent, pulled all my clothes off, tied me to the tent pole, and called some of the other hands to come and see. I was very shy then and it was an ordeal. They called me a baby kid, as I was so young, because there were deer with fawns roaming the park. One of the favourite stunts was to put an enamel mug in someone's bed under the blanket, and when a man jumped heavily on it, it was very painful. However, we all played tricks, all meant as fun.

Civilian clothes were gradually being replaced by khaki – and there was nothing more exciting than receiving 'kit'. Weaponry was often the last thing to arrive, the rifle and bayonet being the accoutrements of a real soldier. Cyril José had enlisted at fifteen years and nine months into the 2nd Devonshires. In a series of letters to his family, he could not help but let his excitement spill over.

> Dearest Ivy [his sister]
>
> Stand back! I've got my own rifle, and bayonet, and new ones. Also my equipment i.e. belt, cartridge pouches, trenching tools, haversack, another bag – a valise, a water bottle and oil can for oiling rifle. No live cartridges yet.
>
> Guess the rifle is heavy. The rifle with bayonet fixed reaches up to my ear from the ground. The bayonet is about two feet long from hilt to point. Must feel a bit rummy to run on to one of them in a charge. Not 'arf.
>
> Nearly got it hot today. I had my bayonet fixed in my room with the sheath off and pointed it at another chap. Just then the sergeant walked in. By George, didn't he swear. He told me that it was one of the greatest crimes in the army to point your bayonet at anyone.

All good sergeants inspired some element of fear, but how the boys felt about these men varied immensely. There were those who were hated with a passion, and many a dark, if unlikely, plot was hatched in the barrack block to 'finish off' a certain bastard should he accompany them to France. Other sergeants were hero-worshipped by the lads under them and, although the language they used shocked a few boys, they soon got used to it, as they did the parade-ground patter that was delivered with aplomb. Reginald Kiernan, who enlisted at seventeen, recalled how the lads from the mines thoroughly enjoyed the insults that were thrown.

They think the instructor is a fine fellow, a real soldier. They memorize the lines and repeat them in the hut, and hope some day they will have a stripe on their arms so that they can say them.

Some of the foot drill instructors are really funny, and they are not personal or abusive to any particular recruit. They are all old Regulars. 'Come orn, come orn, leftright-leftright –Yer –broke-yer-mother's-heart-but-you-won't-break-mine ... tike yer eyes orf the grahnd, yer won't find no money there . . .' They run it all off mechanically – they've been doing it for years.

Smiler Marshall joined the Essex Yeomanry at the age of seventeen. A self-confessed rough diamond whose childhood was regularly punctuated by scraps with local lads, he was totally unperturbed by anything he heard. Ninety years later, he could still remember, with a chuckle, the banter thrown at recruits who struggled to stay on their mounts.

When we went to the 20th Hussars at Colchester, you had to ride all different horses, nothing on them, no saddle, no bridle, no nothing. You had to have a stick, a little cane under each arm, and when the riding masters cracked the whip the horses you were on just stopped. The horses were trained for that, they were proper cavalry horses and they'd stop dead from a trot, canter, or gallop.

You had to sit tight, or else. I never came off because I put my arms round the horse's neck – but half of them fell off and the sergeant major used to shout, 'Who the hell told you to dismount?'

Dismounting – permanently – was Frank Lindley's most earnest wish. After his brother was drowned, he had joined the Royal Field Artillery, having been told that his local infantry unit, the Sheffield City Battalion, was full up. He quickly discovered that he had no affinity with horses and was bored.

The NCOs were crap at the Riding School. One of them, Sergeant Major Mullin, he used to take our riding school, and if you didn't suit him, he'd have hands full of horse shit and he'd come up side and say, 'hey, you' and bang, you got a face full. And there was us clinging on bareback horses. It was ridiculous.

Although training was very hard, it was also deeply rewarding for boys who enjoyed army life, such as George Baden White, who had joined the 2nd Dragoon Guards.

We spent days learning marching, physical training, bayonet fighting and, later, rifle drill and firing. There's no doubt it did me good, what with the open air and exercise, I broadened out, gained confidence and went in for boxing.

George loved the challenge, while other boys merely coped. Daily routine typically consisted of a parade, followed perhaps by an hour's intensive drill when men would slope, order, present and port arms ad nauseam. Rifle practice followed, then square bashing, bayonet practice, or a route march with full pack, fifteen or twenty miles. It was exhausting but it hardened everyone, and in what seemed like no time at all.

The only downside to training as far as George and many other boys could see was that robust exercise induced a ravenous hunger. It was never far from the mind of any man, but for growing lads it could be mild torture. Breakfast was typically sugar-laced tea, known as gunfire tea, a bowl of porridge in winter, and bread, butter and jam. Lunch was generally the best meal of the day, when men could expect soup, then vegetables, beef and potatoes or pie. Finally, tea was generally a lump of bread and cheese and a mug or basin of hot tea. It was good food, at least better than many had eaten as civilians, but it was never enough. Ernest Parker recalled:

> Every evening while I was at Longmoor, I paid a visit to the Soldiers' Home where for fourpence, the price of twenty cigarettes, I could obtain a huge basin of porridge floating in milk. The old soldiers would have scorned such food, but for a teenager with a never-satisfied appetite, this was just what was most needed after a hard day's work.

As George Coppard could confirm, growing boys spent much of their meagre wages on extra food from the canteen to keep them going until the next meal.

> The word calories as we know it today never existed at Aldershot. The quartermaster-general never considered the needs of a growing body engaged on hard training, trench digging or route marching. The army clerk at his desk received the same amount of rations.

Eating was George's 'biggest worry' after he had become involved in illicit card games. His luck proved ruinous, and he lost all the money he needed to top up his diet.

> Occasionally word would drift round that there was soup in the cook-house. Only those with no cash took advantage of the offer, and I was generally among the poor and needy.

'We all feel weaker with the little food and the continuous work,' wrote Reginald Kiernan, 'and yet we seem able to stand more of it every day.' The speed at which wheezy, timid and thin boys could metamorphose into tough soldiers surprised no one in camp except the lads themselves. Even so, later in the war, some consideration was given to the requirements of growing boys, with the newest recruits being given double rations at Catterick Camp, in recognition of their youth and their rapid development.

Young lads could broaden out physically, but there was one place that remained a tell-tale problem: the gap between top lip and nose. If there was anything that indicated the age of a boy, it was the 'bum-fluff' as it was known. At times it hardly merited removing, until an NCO noticed the darkening smudge. George White recalled:

One morning, I was asked by the sergeant when I shaved last. This was rather embarrassing as I had to tell him I had not started to shave yet. I only had soft hair on my face but I got the order to 'get a shave'. Hence my first attempt with a cut-throat razor.

Shaving remained an irregular occurrence for most boys. Even after a year's service, George Coppard reckoned that one shave lasted him ten days. Shaving did at least 'even out' a boy's face with those around him. The problem came if the opposite occurred. One disgruntled fifteen-year-old volunteer recalled:

King George V made it known that he liked all his members of the Household Brigade to have a moustache. Of course they all started growing one and I couldn't, all I had was a little mark above my top lip. You can imagine that I was outstanding and the sergeant would come to me and say, 'You've not grown one, then?' 'No, Sergeant.' So I got extra fatigues, peeling potatoes for one hour.

Not all boys were happy with the regime under which they lived, and the thought of doing a 'bunk' to another regiment was never far from their thoughts. Frank Lindley saw no immediate prospect of getting revenge while serving in the artillery, under NCOs he did not like.

> It was too slow, mucking horses out and all that business. Of course we saw a gun or two, but we didn't have much training on them. I used to think 'this is not being a soldier'.

Fed up, he deserted.

> They were a rotten lot, so about half-a-dozen of us decided to clear off and find somewhere a bit more soldier-like. It was a Friday night and we jumped a train at Belper, Sheffield. When the guard came down for the tickets, we said that we'd had to come down in a hurry and they hadn't given us warrants. Fair play to the old boy, he let us through. On the Saturday we were going to meet in the city but only my friend Bert turned up. We changed into what civilian clothes we had and stopped with one of his relatives, sleeping on a rug.

The next day Frank and his friend enlisted once again, this time into the 13th Yorks and Lancs, better known to posterity as the Barnsley Pals.

It was overfamiliarity rather than any unpleasantness that made Horace Calvert desert from the West Yorkshire Regiment. He wanted a battalion that lived up to his childhood impressions of the army, and the friendly camaraderie in his Territorial battalion was just a little too chummy for his liking. 'In our own way, we thought we were a good battalion but the discipline wasn't there from my point of view.' The problem stemmed from the fact that a large number of the men worked in civilian life for those who were their Territorial officers.

They were wool merchants and worked in the warehouses and the boss was on first-name terms with the staff and of course you got it in the regiment, calling one another Bill or Jack, even if he was a corporal or sergeant. I would have preferred orders to have been given in a proper way and then carried out, instead of 'all right, Jack, I'll do it'. To me, that wasn't military discipline, or the sort of discipline that shows up in a tight corner.

In March 1915 the battalion moved to Gainsborough, where Horace and three other men were billeted on a widow.

I was sat in one evening and she produced a lot of photographs of the Coldstream Guards and she told me her husband had been a quartermaster sergeant. I was so taken with these pictures, the smartness, that it set me wondering. One evening I made up my mind, I'd go the following day. When it was dark, I left all my kit, just keeping my uniform, and set off following the road out of town to a country railway station four or five miles away. I had an old pass, which I hadn't handed back in, and I went to the booking office and asked for a single to Bradford. He asked, 'Have you got a pass?' I pulled it out and he just looked to see it was a pass, never checked it, and I got a ticket. At home, I told my parents I was on leave, then, next morning, leaving my uniform in the copper in the kitchen, I went out in civvies and walked into the recruiting office in Bridge Street, Bradford.

Horace was passed straight away for his chosen regiment, the Grenadier Guards. At the beginning of March, he was sent to the training depot at Caterham.

I had to go up a long hill and as we entered the barracks there stood a tremendous figure of a man, Sergeant Major 'Timber' Wood, and he pointed his drill stick at me. 'Hey, you, here. How

old are you? We don't want sixteen-year-olds in this regiment.'
He'd picked me out straight away, but he knew somebody must
have passed me, so he let me go.

At the end of training it was as much as any commanding officer
could do to stop a lad, buoyed up by thoughts of adventure,
from embarking for France. The 1/4th Battalion of the Seaforth
Highlanders had a large number of under-age boys serving in
France, but, as the War History of the 2/4th (Reserve) Battalion
describes, more were willing to go.

> One morning at orderly-room, a young soldier was charged with
> 'breaking into the quartermaster's store, removing a full set of
> uniform and equipment, rifle and ammunition, etc, secreting
> himself in the ranks of a draft and being found under the seat of a
> railway carriage *en route* for France without a ticket'.
>   The young soldier had tears in his eyes while the charge-sheet
> was read over before him – they quickly disappeared when I told
> him he was discharged, with a very big good conduct mark on his
> conduct sheet.

It seemed almost churlish to criticize a boy for wanting to fight.
His actions belonged so much to the ethos of the time and it
was gratifying to commanding officers to see so many patriotic
lads, who wished, in the best traditions of the army, to serve
their regiment and their country. It was also hard to refuse a boy
who had perhaps never failed to finish a route march, had shot
well on the ranges and had, to all intents and purposes, been
a model soldier. When he was fully trained, age remained the
only possible reason for leaving him behind. Leslie Walkinton
was anxious.

> When would we be sent out? Would I be allowed to go with the
> battalion? Even if I was only seventeen, I was as good a man as

the rest of them. I had never fallen out on a route march like some of the older men. I had even carried a man's rifle on one occasion when he was nearly done.

Selection for overseas service, whether as an officer or other rank, was a moment of elation, mixed, if the soldier was honest, with a tinge of nervousness. In most cases, a short period of embarkation leave was granted, a chance to say goodbye. Alfred Anderson remembers:

> We were told in mid-afternoon that we were getting a few hours off to go home and say goodbye to our parents. We went to where the transport was, a lorry and two horses and a driver, Dundee to Newtyle. It took about two hours to get there, it's a nice flat road, you see, and we trotted all the way. I saw some of my relatives and I said my goodbyes and mother gave me a Bible; then it was back on the transport.

Saying goodbye was hard for all concerned. George Parker, who had enlisted at just fifteen, was told after a few months' training that he was on his way.

> I hated goodbyes, and still do. Leaving that weekend was awful. Mum tried to put on a brave show, but the strain for my parents must have been dreadful. I know it was for me. Honestly, I think that saying goodbye to them was worse than thinking of what I might have to face in the near future. Mum and Aunt Annie came to the station with me. Mum kept her pecker up for my sake, but Aunt broke down and I felt terrible.

George was among those being sent out as drafts to reinforce their respective units, already in France. Sometimes a large draft would be lucky enough to receive a proper farewell. In May 1915, William Sims left to join the 4th Rifle Brigade. His draft was not only given a rousing send-off but had the honour of being inspected by Lord Kitchener himself. If that was not enough, as the great man passed by, he stopped and spoke to William.

> He came up and looked at me. 'How old are you, boy?' 'Nineteen,' I replied. 'You don't look it,' he said then moved on. I took it to mean young. I was. I was only sixteen.

In fairness, gauging age could be very difficult, as recruiting sergeants and medical officers had found. To an older man, perhaps one in his fifties, it was far from easy putting an age to a young face. George Louth had enlisted under age late in 1914 but had genuinely turned nineteen when the battalion left for France, yet the commanding officer was decidedly dubious about him.

> We were lined up on Southsea Common when the colonel came to visit us – to size us up, more or less. He came round asking questions, how old we were and such like. I said, 'Nineteen, sir.' He said, 'Nineteen?' 'Yes, sir.' 'Right.' He went to the next man, spoke to him, then came back to me again. 'How old did you say you were?' I said, 'Nineteen, sir,' and he looked at me straight.

It was not the last time George's age was questioned.

> Before we left for France, the sergeant came up to me and said, 'Louth, the captain wants to know how old you are.' I said, 'Why, Sergeant?' He said, ''Cos he doesn't believe you. If you are not nineteen you're not allowed to go over. We're going to France and we don't want you crying when we get over there, saying you are not old enough, because it won't happen, you won't come back, so say it now.'
> 'I'm going with the lads,' I told him.

Within weeks of going to France in August 1914, sixteen-year-old cavalryman Ben Clouting had proved what a boy could do if given the chance, allaying the fears of his troop officer, Captain Hornby. After Hornby was wounded and invalided back to England, he wrote a letter to a fellow officer praising the courage of the youngster: '. . . that boy Clouting, son of the groom, did most awfully well, a real tiger with an exceptional cool head on him . . .'

It had been a risk and officers, such as Hornby, had to take a view that the lad under their command would perform well on active service. The question still lingered nevertheless: should they really flout military law and let them go? It was a tough decision, as the commanding officer of the 2/4th (Reserve) Battalion of the Seaforth Highlanders knew only too well.

A draft which was going to France had been inspected. One youngster, who seemed to me under age but who stoutly contested the fact, was found on reference to the enlistment sheet to be one year under age. I had reluctantly to take him from the draft. On returning to the orderly room, the regimental sergeant major asked if I would see the lad, he was so upset, and I did so. He was physically much fitter than several of the recruits older than himself who were going overseas, and he begged to be allowed to go with his own batch of recruits. I told him to telegraph to his father, and if his father and mother did not object, I would let him go. Their reply was that he might go.

The men of the 1/7th Royal Scots, who had spent the war so far on coastal defence, heard the news that they were finally on their way to the front, and they were jubilant. A and C Companies were to head south by train to Liverpool, to be followed two hours later by B and D Companies. A ship, the *Empress of Britain*, had been earmarked to take them overseas. Among them were a considerable number of under-age boys allowed to go abroad – with, in at least some cases, the connivance of the regiment.

It was the early hours of the morning of 22 May 1915 before they were all on board the train. The wooden carriages were divided into compartments, each holding eight men. As it was dark, the gas lamps had been lit, so the men could see what they were doing before they sat down; most went straight to sleep, while a few dozed. It was routine, once all were aboard, to lock the carriage doors before the train got under way.

The train trundled south, stopping at one point at Carstairs station where a few of those who were too excited to sleep leant out of the carriage windows to exchange some banter with a few local girls who were on their way to work.

It was Saturday morning, and near the village of Gretna Green at Quintinshill station, two signalmen were in the process of handing over just as a late-running London to Glasgow express was given clearance to pass through the station. As two goods wagons occupied the loop lines, a slow local train was temporarily positioned on the down line to let the express through. Almost as he took over, the relieving signalman received a call from a station further up the line to allow the train carrying the Royal Scots to pass. Forgetting that the local train was still at a standstill on the down line, he dropped the signal arm, indicating to the troop train that the track was clear. A catastrophic mix-up had occurred and a collision was unavoidable. Just before 6.50 a.m., there was an almighty crash. Seventeen-year-old Private Thomson recalled the moment of impact.

> The carriage rose up and sank down again, listing dangerously over a steep bank. The cries and screams and the hiss of steam escaping from the engine was deafening! One by one, we climbed out through the window of our compartment and on to the line. What a sight met our eyes! The wreckage was piled thirty feet high and terror-stricken men were staggering about. Worse still, men were trapped in the twisted metal of the wreckage.

The collision with the stationary train was bad enough, but less than a minute later the fast-moving express arrived and ploughed into the derailed carriages, the wreckage of which had spread across the tracks. A fire, which started in the wreckage of the leading carriages, was accelerated as the train splintered and pressurized gas cylinders that fed the carriage lamps ruptured, adding fuel to the flames. It hardly mattered now that the train doors were locked, as all that remained was a tangled wreck, with many men killed, and others wounded and trapped.

Private Thomson recalled:

> I was detailed for stretcher-bearer duties. What a job for a lad not yet eighteen! I wept. I saw many a battlefield after that, but I never saw anything like the things I saw on that terrible day.
>
> It was afternoon before we'd rescued everyone. A lot of the men lay down in the field, they were so exhausted, and some of them thought about the folks at home and how worried they'd be when the news got out and they walked to Gretna Post Office to send telegrams.

After a roll call taken later that day, it was found that in all just fifty-seven men were left to answer to their names. All told, the train crash cost the lives of 216 men of the Royal Scots, and wounded a further 227. The disaster at Quintinshill was, and remains, the worst rail crash in British history.

The casualties included three officers, twenty-nine NCOs and 184 other ranks killed. Of 116 identified ages, 29 of the dead were under age, comprising 17 aged eighteen, and 11 aged seventeen. One sixteen-year-old also died. His name was Private John Malone, a lad from Edinburgh. A drummer boy, he had joined the band with all their instruments in the foremost part of the train. In the aftermath of the crash, Private Malone had been trapped in the wreckage where, despite determined efforts, it proved impossible to release him other than by amputating both his legs. He died that night in hospital.

The stunned few who had helped to rescue their friends were

eventually taken away late that afternoon. Private Thomson remembered:

> About five o'clock they put us on a goods train and took us to Carlisle and then up to the castle for a wash and a meal. A while later they took us back to the station, and there was a special train waiting to take us on to Liverpool.
>
> Early next morning, we were put to work sorting out blood-stained equipment salvaged from the wrecked train. It was a gruesome task and I'm quite sure that there was flesh stuck to some of it. Then we mustered and were allocated our mess decks for the voyage.

It would have been hard to send these men straight to the front and, after some last-minute discussions with the War Office in London, the survivors were sent back north where they received fourteen days' leave.

> We were lined up on the quayside and marched off through the streets to Lime Street Station. Believe it or not, some children playing in the street threw stones at us. We looked so bedraggled and disreputable that they took us for German prisoners!

It would be the best part of a month before Private Thomson was able to rejoin the remnants of his battalion serving at the front.

4

At the Front, at Last

WORTHY OF EVERLASTING LOVE

25793 Private James Walters
9th Sherwood Foresters

Killed in Action 9 August 1916, aged 16

IT WAS A MOMENTOUS occasion for any soldier to cross the English Channel, but for boys it was particularly significant. Embarking, then sailing over twenty-two miles of water, and stepping ashore in France: this was not just a prerequisite of going to war, it conferred on a boy the attributes of a man. Now he was 'on active service', a label of which to be proud, and one that every lad who volunteered prayed would some day apply to him.

During their training, boys wanted to appear like soldiers who had already served abroad, craving the outward signs of such status. They habitually removed the stiffening wire from round their rigid peak caps, following the practice of soldiers at the front who did this to soften the outline and make it harder for snipers to see them. Or trainees would seek out a 1908-pattern web belt rather than the cheaper leather version made for the volunteers of 1914; sporting the older webbing made a boy look like an 'old sweat', a regular soldier who might be home on leave. But such ploys were only playing at war; now this was war itself, and for boys like sixteen-year-old Thomas Hope, who had just set foot in France, the adventure was only just beginning.

Behind me lies the life of ordered things, comfort, security, peace and the hundred and one things that constitute the life I know . . . Ahead is the unknown – danger, hardship, wounds, perhaps death, but these possibilities leave me unmoved. I can only think of heroics, of battles won, of returning heroes, glorious deeds already enacted perhaps on this very ground, the newspaper war I have read so much about. What if I had missed this, if I had been born too late? But why worry? I am here, proud and glad to be here, and that is all that really matters. This is my great adventure.

Thomas Hope was watching from the rear of a transport lorry as it slowly wended its way forward towards the line. He could hardly contain his excitement at the unfolding cavalcade of war.

I am as happy as a new schoolboy at his first picnic, revelling in this new life of guns, limbers, ammunition columns, parties of infantry all going the same way up to the front.

This was a war that demanded a huge collective effort. Private Hope was just a small cog in a gigantic military machine but this was significant neither to him nor to the other young boys keen to adopt the manifestations of manhood that came with being a soldier overseas.

And how long did it take to shatter those illusions? In Thomas's case, it took four days.

Zero day has come and gone and I have lived a hundred years. Four short days ago, I was a youngster with all the ideals of youth, but now I have changed. Everything seems different. I doubt if life can ever be the same. The onetime omnibus sways and jolts over the uneven ground as it carries away from the line what is left of the platoon. Where we are going or what is to happen to us next, I know not and care less. It is sufficient that we are leaving that hell behind.

Drafts from the base camp joined their units wherever they happened to be, and Thomas had been unfortunate enough to find his battalion of the King's Liverpools as it prepared for an attack. He had experienced his baptism of fire: he had been over the top, an unusually quick submersion into total war and about as severe as it could get.

This was not, on the whole, typical, particularly for new battalions out at the front. Emergencies excepted, they might hope to be slowly inducted into trench life, instructed behind the line before being sent to a relatively quiet sector to learn the ropes. This was the experience of the 17th Royal Fusiliers, a battalion that embarked for France in November 1915. They were still in billets when they were given guidance on life at the front by a sergeant of the Highland Light Infantry. His friendly spiel was recorded by one young private in a letter home.

The day before we went into the trenches for the first time, a sergeant from a Scotch regiment came round to our billet to give us a few hints on trench warfare, a lecture in fact. He was a very sensible chap.

'Now see here, you fellows, the war's all right if you take it in the right way and you can have a regular picnic in the trenches if you chum together in threes or fours . . . This war is a war of craft so you've got to be crafty, it's your craft against their craft and the craftiest man wins . . . the more you go into the trenches, the craftier you get.' And so on and so on. I don't know whether I've become any craftier yet but you'd better look out when I come home. Of course I shan't put my head over the parapet again, I always look underneath now! That's craft.

The march up to the front line was always a testing time for both fresh and seasoned troops. Old soldiers knew what to expect, but lads new to France were frightened and curious in equal measure. Stomachs churned at the sound of distant gunfire and nerves frayed at the spectacle of a damaged landscape that became ever more tattered as the front was approached. Finally, there was the eerie illumination of the trenches as Very lights shot up into the night sky, burst, then lingered and slowly faded. The occasional rat-tat-tat of a machine gun might be heard.

Fear was not the only test of their resilience. For any tour in the trenches every man was laden down with equipment not just for his personal use but for the general maintenance of the platoon or company over the following days. Norman Gladden, a young soldier in the Northumberland Fusiliers, noted that his burden had been further increased with personal issues of Mills bombs, Very lights and other portable ammunition.

> As a result, my load, in addition to the normal equipment, ammunition, rifle, overcoat, waterproof, two gas helmets and a steel helmet, included a shovel, two Mills bombs, two Very lights, a ground flare, a smoke bomb, a day's rations, leather jerkin, cap comforter, pair of leather trench gloves joined by a long tape, two sandbags and one hundred extra rounds of ammunition. All these were necessaries in that war but looking back it is incredible that we were able to transport so much under the conditions that prevailed.

If troops were not shelled as they came into the line, then their baptism might begin with the 'morning hate'. This dose of concentrated fire started at dawn and was delivered by both sides, as if to reassure each other of their continued presence and participation in the war. After this brief bombardment, the day was frequently quiet as men slept, wrote letters or undertook menial tasks, before the 'evening hate' at dusk. Only at night-time did the front become alive, as men used the cover of darkness to undertake a multitude of tasks such as bringing up rations, repairing and improving trenches, and patrolling no-man's-land.

Sixteen-year-old Herbert Gutteridge was among a group of twenty men selected to carry water to the troops in the line. He had only recently arrived in France and this was his second night in reserve a couple of miles behind the front, and he had yet to go into the trenches.

> We set out after dark in single file, each man carrying a full petrol can of drinking water. All went well at first, apart from a few stray shells which fell well away from our party, but when we were about 300 yards from our front line, all hell suddenly broke loose. A deluge of shells and trench mortar rifle and machine-gun fire saturated the area. Every man plunged into a shell hole as I grovelled in the bottom of mine, petrified with fear. I expected to be blown into eternity every second, while showers of earth and stone fell upon me from nearby shell bursts and streams of machine-gun bullets tore into the back of my shell hole just above my head. After about ten minutes, the deluge suddenly stopped and our leader ordered us to dash to the front line. This we did, delivered our precious water and got out of this hellish place with all speed. What casualties we had I never knew, as I was very confused and bewildered. I now knew what to expect.

One of the worst tasks was handling the dead, particularly in warm weather when bodies quickly putrefied. The stench could make life intolerable and wherever possible bodies were removed for burial. This was almost the first job on active service that George White had been given and, short of owning up to his real age of fifteen, he simply had to get on with it.

> On the second night, we came across a number of bodies of British soldiers near where we were working. The thing that struck us was that their faces and hands were black as if they had been coloured troops. We soon found that they were not, when we took the identity discs from their necks and went through their pockets

for the paybooks. Each soldier carried two identity discs of different shapes and colours on a cord round the neck: the round one had to be taken from the body and the other one left on. The fact that each one had two discs told us that they had not yet been reported dead but probably missing. We were conscious of the fact that by handing in the discs and paybook of each man, his next-of-kin, who had probably been informed that he was missing and hoped he had been taken prisoner, would now receive the dreaded telegram informing them that he had been killed in action. As we looked through their paybooks, most contained photographs of themselves and their families. We found the whole business very sad and felt sorry that it had fallen on us to disclose it.

Once settled in, a new battalion could expect to be attached to another for tuition and training in trench warfare. In a quiet sector, companies would be sent forward one by one to have the important details pointed out. Men sent out on draft joined their units wherever they happened to be, and for them the procedure was slightly different. It was sensible, if possible, to tag on to someone who had some expertise so as to learn as much as possible. For younger soldiers, this initiation frequently turned to a respect bordering on hero-worship.

Among groups of men with particular unit responsibilities, such as the machine-gunners or stretcher-bearers, teams had to bond quickly. These men implicitly relied on each other and teaching newcomers the ropes was important not just for individual survival but for the life of the group as a whole. George Coppard had no doubt that the example of one man, Lance Corporal William 'Snowy' Hankin, had a great influence on him:

He was very fair with hair almost white, and his cold grey eyes did more than anything else to help me control my fears. When I was with Snowy I always felt confident. He set for me a standard of cool behaviour that I tried to imitate and profit by. He was an expert in his understanding of the idiosyncrasies of the Vickers [machine gun] and in his marksmanship. Wielding an axe in his forester's job had developed a powerful pair of hands and forearms.

Stretcher-bearer Bill Easton was in a four-man team, one of several in a field ambulance unit. Seventeen-year-old Bill's mentor was Tom, a gruff six-foot northerner, while Bill had been bred in the gentle surroundings of King's Lynn.

Tom wasn't my type at all, I don't mind telling you. He would swear and kick up a hell of a fuss at times, but he thought about his companions more than he did about himself . . . he really knew what he was doing, a wonderful fellow.

The first time up the line, of course I was a bit nervous and he said, 'Now when we go in, just hang close behind me. You'll probably be a bit frightened, Bill,' he said, 'but don't show it because some, they like to see you young fellows cut down a bit, so stick your head up and get along,' and he'd talk on the way down about things, anything, I don't know what he was talking about half the time.

Physical power, impressive to young lads on any occasion, was even more important in wartime and could be inspirational. Tom proved capable of repeatedly carrying men out of action when other teams gave up after one or two attempts. He also had a policy of never abandoning anyone once they were collected. Even if the injured man was clearly beyond help, the team would press on.

We never stopped, Tom would have been furious if you had. He kept walking and always took the heavier head end of the stretcher. He'd be as cheerful as anything, talking to the wounded man, and when the other men began to groan or moan he would say, 'Look at young Bill there, he hasn't said a word.'

Absolute faith in these men helped disorientated boys to cope with their surroundings. They set an example, frequently volunteering for dangerous jobs or taking on more than would have seemed to be their fair share of heavy work. In doing so, they made themselves vulnerable and any absence, however temporary, could easily undermine group resolve. When George Coppard's team served for three particularly arduous days, the strain finally told on Lance Corporal Hankin.

> What sleep we got had to be taken in odd snatches in an old German artillery dugout to the rear of the trench. I well remember Snowy fainting in that dugout and it was some while before he recovered. Exhaustion had no doubt caused it but at the time it shook me. I feared that he might lose some of the superb control he always showed, no matter how hard the conditions.

Some lads were lucky enough to have a relatively gentle introduction to war. Sixteen-year-old Cyril José had arrived in France just as the Second Battle of Ypres had drawn to a close in May 1915. A couple of months had passed and just once, well behind the lines, an enemy plane bombed the platoon as it drilled, scattering men into an orchard, but no casualties had been suffered. Since then, Cyril had been in and out of the trenches with desultory shelling and the activities of snipers the principal concern. In August, he volunteered to go out into no-man's-land and by all accounts he enjoyed himself, as he told his sister.

11/8/15

My dearest Ivy

Have been quite adventurous for the past two nights having been out in front with a corporal and another private as covering party while some others fixed up some barbed wire. The first night was quite exciting as the Germans must have spotted something once or twice as they sent over a rapid fire especially when we were

coming in. They continually sent up star-shells so that we had
to keep our nappers [heads] down low . . . To add to the fun our
equipment got entangled in the barbed wire. Naturally this did
not lessen the excitement of the moment. Curiously enough we
did not see the funny point until we had extricated ourselves and
jumped into a shallow trench just in front of our own parapet . . .

This trench had been full of wire entanglements and, in the process of disentangling himself, Cyril had jammed his foot through
an old biscuit tin, compounding his problems.

We weren't out of the fire yet so we began to chuck lumps of earth
into the trench to attract our fellows' attention. Having done this
we asked them to get their bayonets out of the way so that we
might get in. The corporal then hoisted me up out of the trench,
handed up the rifles which I put on the parapet then leaning over
I gave him my hand and the deed was done as it were and we
could smile freely again. I then rejoined my section and on sentry
I didn't half send some ammunition over to our old friend 'Fritzy'.
    Last night was all right but not quite so exciting.

Cyril

'Fritzy', a term of endearment, was an example of the strange love/
hate relationship with the enemy that existed in the trenches.
Abstract sympathy for 'Fritz' or 'Jerry' was typically evident when
the enemy lines were being pounded by artillery, for each side
knew what the other was going through at the hands of a third
party. There was nothing the infantry could do but sit and suffer,
when the shells were obliterating whole sections of the line. On
such occasions veterans recalled feeling that they had more in
common with infantry on the other side of no-man's-land than
with a separate branch of the army such as the artillery or Army
Service Corps, whose men, while frequently exposed to mortal

danger, never saw the inside of a trench and never went over the top in an attack.

Where no-man's-land narrowed, it was even possible to speak to the enemy, a more frequent occurrence than people might suppose. The Christmas Truce of 1914 is the best-known example of fraternization, but there were innumerable occasions when troops shouted to one another, wishing each other good day, or some such cheery comment. 'Morning, Fritz!' answered with 'Bollicks' was par for the course according to one veteran, while another remembered hearing, 'Deutschland, Deutschland, über Alles,' answered with a cheerful reply of 'Deutschland, Deutschland, über Arseholes.'

Conversations were not always so pithy. Bill Taylor, the young Canadian orphan, managed to converse sporadically with one German. To Bill's surprise, he turned out to be a Canadian of German extraction who had returned to the country of his forefathers to enlist, although he himself had never been there before. As they traded shouts, Bill discovered that not only was this lad born and raised in Toronto, close to where Bill had grown up, but he had a brother serving with the Canadian forces while he, simultaneously, fought for the enemy.

Occasionally the two sides were so close that they could exchange not just comments but gifts. Eighteen-year-old Smiler Marshall was barely twenty yards from some Germans who were manning a position forward of their front line. In between was an old communication trench that had been filled with barbed wire. Empty jam tins had been attached to the wire to act as an early-warning system should either side be tempted to encroach on the other.

One day, the Germans sent a stick grenade flying over, to which they had tied a couple of cigarettes. After a bit I went to the bomb, and my mates were saying, 'For God's sake don't touch it.' They thought the bomb would go off and blow me up. But I went and smoked a cigarette and it was all right, so we sent back the same stick bomb with a whole packet attached. I hope they enjoyed them.

In such an extreme environment, fraternal feelings could turn to hatred should either side play a dirty trick. With abstract notions of sport and war so closely aligned in the eyes of many, bad form on the battlefield was akin to cheating on the field of play. Once good faith had been broken, it was almost impossible to restore.

This same sense of fair play and comradeship was an integral part of maintaining morale in the line. Men would take great risks in order to protect or rescue one another, often displaying the highest levels of courage and self-sacrifice – feats that might be recognized by the award of military honours.

Jack Auguste Pouchot had served in and out of the trenches through the harsh winter of 1914/15. By 8 January 1915, the battalion diary records that part of the line had become uninhabitable: 'Parapet falling in – River Lys rising rapidly necessitating evacuation of trenches,' wrote the adjutant. Seventeen-year-old Leslie Walkinton described the events of the morning.

It was just getting light, and there was rifle shooting and excited shouting to our left. We could see two men lying apparently dead about twenty or twenty-five yards behind the barricade. One was a stretcher-bearer, Rifleman Philip Tibbs, who had gallantly crawled out to help Corporal Roche who had been shot by a sniper when running behind the line with some water for his machine gun. As we watched, another soldier crawled out to see what he could do, but when he reached the two men he was fired at and had to turn round and crawl back to safety.

This other soldier was fifteen-year-old Jack Pouchot, and he won the regiment's first Distinguished Conduct Medal for his effort. Both the men he tried to help were killed. Jack remained in France until April 1915 when exhaustion and illness combined to force his evacuation from France. He had just celebrated his sixteenth birthday.

Jack Pouchot was not the only medal-winner who was too young to be serving in the trenches. During the course of the war, several under-age soldiers won the highest accolade, the Victoria Cross. They included John Meikle who enlisted at sixteen, won the Military Medal at eighteen and the VC at nineteen – this last award was granted posthumously; eighteen-year-old George Peachment, like Jack Pouchot, won a medal, in his case the VC, while going to the aid of his wounded captain, stranded in no-man's-land. Like John Meikle, George was killed during his act of bravery.

Contact between soldiers and their families back home was also essential to the maintenance of morale in the front-line trenches. It varied greatly from man to man; in many cases it was initially frequent, war and duty permitting. Descriptions were diverse and often enthusiastic but, as time wore on, a degree of resignation set in. As soldiers felt trapped in an apparently endless war, letters could grow more sporadic, more weary and markedly shorter, the writer less inclined to describe life at the front.

In contrast, Cyril José's letters are full of adventure, like the account of no-man's-land he sent to his sister, and, remarkably, he never turned to the bitterness so evident in the correspondence of others. It is striking to a modern reader that, as new impressions continued to wash over him, he appeared happy to divulge to his family the repeated danger he was in.

Young boys such as Cyril were liable to believe more strongly in their own immortality than men just a few years older, and there is undoubtedly in his letters a tactlessness born of youth. Even so, this naivety does not entirely explain descriptions of battle that were bound to worry any mother, even one who had consented to her son going abroad in the first place.

The answer probably lies in the level of dislocation Cyril felt from his previous civilian life. Faced with death on a daily basis, when casualties were an accepted and normal state of affairs, he had not lost his sense of reality. On the contrary, this was his reality, his everyday, a world incomprehensible to his family. Given the limitations of his environment, it would have been difficult for him to compose anything of note were he not to describe the events taking place around him. Only in time did his words take on an occasional air of healthy cynicism, although he never lost his optimism. Once he had chosen to write about his life, he had adopted, consciously or not, a tone and style that made light of his experiences to avoid unnecessarily worrying his parents. Yet he was not sufficiently mature to know when to rein in his anecdotes. The writing remained jocular and untroubled. Cyril had willingly joined up and he was not about to complain.

When his letter of 11 August reached his sister Ivy, it was his mother who wrote back, clearly concerned at the exploits of her son. His next two replies, while initially reassuring, typically reverted to descriptions of fighting that could only have been alarming.

20/8/15

My dearest Mother

Needn't trouble about the barbed wire biz or any of those little expeditions. I only went out for a bit of excitement, by way of a change. Really it's great fun going out over the top – good for the nerves – espesh when you are back safely and give vent to your exhausted feelings by opening rapid fire on the Germans.

I had a rotten experience though the night before last in the trenches when I went out into a listening post about 75 yards out. There were 4 of us privates and 1 corporal. Some of Kitchener's blessed mob opened fire when the order had been passed down to cease fire as there was a party out on the listening post. The Germans replied and must have had a rifle fixed so as to hit the listening post. One chap 'bobbed up' when it was a bit quiet and got it through the napper. The two other chaps took him in but he died soon after. Guess I didn't 'bob up' so much after that.

Cyril

31/8/15

My dearest Mother

In the trenches this time we have had rather a rough time. We've been working in building the parapet thicker besides doing sentry [duty] so that we can get a little sleep between the reliefs. I hope you've not been worrying.

If I have 3 hours sleep in 24 hours I consider I have done well!! I have only had 1 hour sometimes. Added to work etc we are only 40 or 50 yards away from the Germans – the Prussian Germans too! Hence we've had an exciting time but we go out tomorrow night and we shall all be glad too!

The most exciting day I've ever had was last Saturday. We were just getting our tea ready when a shell came over just behind the trench. 'Hullo, what's up with Johnnie?' I said. Then I saw what I thought was a big piece of shell falling in the next traverse to mine. I ran into my traverse to dodge it, not thinking much about it. Next second, bang went an explosion. Immediately I saw another drop and before I knew where I was I felt myself glide about a foot through the air against the parapet. Didn't know what the joke was for a minute then I saw all the others lying flat against the parapet and sides of dug-outs. I knew what it was then – trench mortars . . . Soon someone spotted one and shouted 'Trench mortar right!' so we all scampered to the left and got behind dug-outs or anything. No sooner had it exploded than we spotted another and so we scampered away again. We soon tumbled to the enemy's wheeze which was to send over a big shell and then follow it up by 2 trench mortar shells. The big shells we can hear shrieking through the air and we looked out for the trench mortars. We had quite an exciting 3/4 of an hour dodging them which isn't exactly as easy as it seems. We had a few casualties naturally but yours truly got through as per usual.

How is father's job progressing? I hope he's getting on alright with it.

God bless you
Cyril

Ernest Steele, the quiet and studious boy from Leytonstone, had also arrived in France in mid-1915. He wrote home too but, against regulations, kept a diary for his own consumption as well. His tone was far less ebullient than Cyril's.

Tuesday, December 14th, 1915.

Worked on canal bank in morning. In evening went up to firing line. Had to belly-flop in mud and water four times in half a mile owing to M.Gs. and rapid fire. Got over near Hooge when mine went up and then over came umpteen shells and rapid fire. I got into ditch, up past my knees in mud. Was helped out and we rushed across field over to support trenches with wire. I fell over a dead man. On way back we had to belly-flop again, owing to rapid fire and, going through Ypres, shells burst 10 yards away. I got hit slightly. Five men in another party wounded. Ugh!

Wednesday, December 15th, 1915.

Another day fatigue up near Hooge. No work done as no tools. Beaucoup tea, thanks to K. Shrops. L. I. who supplied us with everything. We got back safely but another party got hit. *Fourteen* men were wounded. Poor old 'C' Company.

I am feeling rocky, wrist hurting slightly and nerves going. Iodine for wrist and rum for nerves in evening.

Rum was useful in anaesthetizing the nerves, as well as helping to fortify them if men were about to go over the top. More usually, it was dished out on a day-to-day basis to reinvigorate those holding the line. With approval, it could also be given to men who had undergone a particularly onerous ordeal, such as a trench raid, or a fighting patrol in no-man's-land, but not ordinarily for men returning from a working party near the firing line such as described by Ernest Steele.

The rum was extremely strong and came in large earthenware jars, chunks of which litter the battlefields today, testament to its ubiquity. It was served out by a sergeant, who measured the dark viscous liquid into a tin mug, on to a spoon or simply tipped it into a soldier's mess tin. This was done in the presence of an officer, at least in theory, ensuring that each man took his tot and did not pass it on. Its medicinal effects were instantaneous, warming a soldier up from frozen toes to numb ears. To the young who had never taken rum, and to a few who had never even tasted alcohol, the effect was overpowering, as seventeen-year-old Ben Clouting found out.

> During the first cold snap we received our first rum issue which we were to drink straight down. The old soldiers showed no hesitation tipping their heads straight back, so following suit I downed my share. My goodness, my eyes nearly popped out of their sockets! I'd never tasted rum before in my life and this was neat navy rum; I thought my throat was on fire.

The over-consumption of alcohol was as much an issue for public concern in the Victorian and Edwardian periods as it is today. Alcohol was the cause of a great deal of social vice and family violence, and Christian organizations struggled to persuade all classes, with an emphasis on the poor, that the devil was in the drink and that abstinence was always best. Temperance was not just a principle, it was a movement, and thousands of boys who went to war had promised their parents that they would try to avoid the German bullet and the sins of the bottle in almost equal measure.

There was no sin in the way Smiler Marshall chose to use his rum. Trench foot was a debilitating condition brought on by living in alternately freezing and wet conditions. To combat the problem, whale oil was issued as a protection against the weather. It was not a popular remedy; rum, according to Smiler Marshall, was much better. Smiler was living proof that not all rum was dished out as stipulated in military manuals.

I didn't smoke much but you got plenty of cigarettes issued and someone would say, 'Who'll give me one or two smokes for the rum ration?' I used to give them my cigarettes for the ration so my water bottle was always three parts full.

Now, when we got in the front line the orderly officer and orderly sergeant came round twice during the night, once just before twelve and again between five and six in the morning. When they'd gone by I'd know they'd got a good distance of the front line to go, so as quick as lightning I unwound my puttees and took my boot off and my sock and poured some rum into my hand, took a little lick myself, and then rubbed my toes for ten minutes then put my boot and puttees back. You were not allowed to take clothes of any description off in the front line, not for three days. When they went by next time I did the same to the other foot and therefore I kept good feet. If you didn't attend to your feet, well, if the frost penetrates them and your boots are wet through, then your feet can go black if you aren't very careful.

Standing in a trench at night, peering across no-man's-land, was hard enough for anyone who was cold and craving sleep. Young boys, many of whom had not added the bulk or fat that came with maturing years, found frost, biting winds, and snow almost impossible to cope with. Sentry duty in particular was a job that would eat away at a man's very spirit, the cold seeping up the legs and into the body, making him ache from head to toe. It was also mind-numbingly boring and endlessly repetitive.

Nevertheless, every man on duty knew that to be found asleep was a serious matter and potentially a court martial awaited anyone who was caught as Royce Mckenzie well knew.

We'd been three or four days with nothing to eat and no drink, nothing, and we were buggered, absolutely buggered. We'd lost a lot of men, so we were stretched out, about twenty or thirty yards between each sentry, looking over no-man's-land and I was struggling to keep my eyes open and I must have fell asleep, anyway I felt this tap on my shoulder and it was Sub Lieutenant Newall and he says to me, 'Mckenzie, it might not be me next time, try and keep awake.' He was one of the finest gentlemen I ever came across, if it had been anybody else I'd have been court-martialled and shot.

Bristolian George Blanning was not so lucky. George was born in June 1898 and was sent out on a draft in 1916. According to Bill Pain, a private in the same battalion, he was still not quite eighteen.

He was in the front line and when the visiting officer came round they found him asleep and he got tried by court martial and Major Hawks – a proper old army man – was in charge and Blanning got sentenced to three years' penal servitude. We were all on parade and heard it read out as a lesson to other troops of course. That night, the commanding officer, Lieutenant Colonel Martin Archer-Shee, MP, came back from England and interviewed the chap and said, 'Now tell me your correct age' because he didn't believe that the boy was nineteen. George was stubborn and wouldn't give his age away at first, but eventually Archer-Shee got it out of him that he was going to be eighteen in two weeks' time, and he got him off. They put him in the cookhouse until he was nineteen, and that's where he finished up, doing the cooking behind the lines.

Court martial records indicate that George Blanning's sentence of three years' penal servitude was later suspended.

Sleeping on duty endangered everyone in the front line, but total exhaustion was total exhaustion and it took a hard-nosed officer to make an example of any man whose head had perhaps fleetingly slumped forward on to the parapet. Working at night, under the cover it gave, expending physical energy was in many respects preferable to standing motionless, watching shadows. Work generated body heat that kept a man awake and, if he was not warm, then at least he was less cold.

At night on sentry duty a soldier was expected to keep his head and shoulders above the level of the parapet to maintain a good field of view. In the darkness, he was protected from all but a random shot. During the day a trench periscope was used, revealing little other than barbed wire, earth and discarded rubbish. The enemy remained hidden, and it could be weeks, even months, before Tommy saw Fritz and then, perhaps, only a fleeting glimpse. Vic Cole had been in France throughout the summer of 1915 and had, as yet, seen no one.

> I was making my way along a much battered and little used trench, endeavouring to trace a broken telephone wire, when, taking a look over the top to see where I was, I saw a German about three hundred yards away digging at the back of a trench parados. I watched him for a moment and thought, 'Well, I'm entitled to have a shot at him.' I aimed, pulled the trigger and saw a piece of cloth or leather fly off the side of his coat – he disappeared – did I wound him? I shall never know, but it was my first shot at the enemy.

It was sniping, though not in the pure sense of the word. Other men, picked deliberately for their marksmanship, were the real snipers; the rest were happy to take potshots as the fancy took them.

Sniping was a perennial threat. A battalion's routine spell in forward trenches, especially in a busy sector, was punctuated by casualties from this deadly game of cat and mouse. The victims included a disproportionate number of those new to the line, oblivious to the dangers of a quick peek over the top, as well as the careless, tall or downright unlucky.

Seventeen-year-old Londoner Archie Gardiner belonged to the category of the exceptionally unlucky. During his battalion's three-day tour in the line close to Ypres he was the sole fatality, shot by a sniper as he inadvertently raised his head above the parapet.

Archie had enlisted in the Queen's Royal West Surreys with his best friend Edgar Lee. Both were aged sixteen and lived just a few doors apart in Greenvale Road, Eltham. They had grown up together, serving side by side in the 1st Royal Eltham Scouts. Archie was a little older than his friend and had gained a reputation for being mischievous, and it is possible his parents thought the army might do him some good, for neither objected when he went to join up.

Archie had been serving an engineering apprenticeship at Woolwich Polytechnic. He had never been the most conscientious student and his first year's training had been marked as only 'fair'. It was during his second year, coinciding with the outbreak of war, that Archie's work slipped badly. His attendance dropped and his tutors were not happy with his conduct, marking his report 'Unsatisfactory. Slack and inattentive'. It was to no one's surprise when, in early March 1915, Edgar and Archie enlisted. They were given the consecutive regimental numbers 5026 and 5027 and, being staunch friends, they sought to stick together, embarking for France on the last day of August 1915 with the 8th (Service) Battalion.

They had not been overseas very long when, one wet November night, the battalion arrived in the line near the shattered village of Dickebusch to find the trenches waterlogged and in desperate need of draining. In places, the sodden parapet had simply collapsed and it was while undertaking repairs that Archie was hit and killed.

Edgar Lee wrote a short note to Archie's parents.

> I am writing this in the trenches. I have just come back from seeing poor old Archie. He was killed by a sniper this morning about 10.30 a.m. He was shot just above the right eye with an explosive bullet and death was instantaneous. I am sorry there is no mistake about it because I went and saw him myself.

The depth of Edgar's loss was terrible. 'I miss him more than you at the time, being with him every day,' he wrote. The battalion war diary briefly noted: 'Quiet days, our snipers gained the upper hand easily.' Unusually, Archie's death was not recorded. His local newspaper, the *Eltham and District Times*, later published a farewell to its local lad, mourning the passing of 'a true British boy'. It said, 'He always played the game and he played it to the end.' Archie was buried in Spoilbank Cemetery, four kilometres southeast of Ypres. Two days after he was killed, his battalion left the line.

The sniper who killed Archie may have hidden himself in the ground between the German first and second lines. Alternatively, he may have been shooting from within the trench, carefully concealed behind an iron shield built in the parapet. These shields gave considerable protection to the snipers, who used just a small aperture in the half-inch-thick plate through which to shoot, knowing they were safe from all but the most accurate of retaliatory shots.

It took a steady hand and a keen eye to be effective and snipers were frequently young, although Second Lieutenant Stuart Cloete's 'best sniper' was perhaps something of a record. The boy turned out to be only fourteen years old.

He was the finest shot and the best little soldier I had. A very nice boy, always happy. I got him a Military Medal and when he went back to Blighty and I suppose school, he had a credit of six Germans hit.

Sniping helped counteract the unremitting boredom of daytime life, but it was not risk-free, for the hunted rarely stood their victimization for long. They retaliated by using their spare time in a meticulous hunt for their tormentor, trying to work out exactly where he was hiding. Once he was discovered, the men would wait. The next time the sniper fired, an instant fusillade would be directed at him by men positioned at different points along the opposing trench.

Cyril José had his 'closest shave' when he slid aside the metal plate that covered the aperture in the sniper's shield. Unbeknown to Cyril, a German had already pinpointed the position.

I was just taking a squint through the hole, intending to have a shot when, as I had it open – thud – plonk! A bullet hit the sandbag in front of the hole and ricocheted, hitting the iron plate. Another half inch probably and I should have had a little hole through my head. But thank God it didn't come off and I'm still alive and kicking.

Although the sounds of war terrified many, there were those, like Smiler Marshall, who found some enjoyment in the situation. He was always keen on a bit of fun and the noise of war, in particular, delighted him.

I loved to hear the artillery and the machine guns. I can't tell you why but I did. I used to sweep the Germans' parapet each night with a machine gun, just lift up the safety catch and press the button, brrrrrrrrrr brrrrrrrr and they done the same to us. That was a bit of fun, oh yes. Their bullets hit the top of the parapet and sent the dirt flying all the way along.

Smiler had arrived in France in November 1915 with a draft of men that included his best friend Lenny Passiful. Both boys had enlisted under age; Smiler had now turned eighteen but his childhood friend was still only seventeen.

In the line, snipers were active and Smiler and Lenny decided to while away the hours with a spot of retaliation.

Lenny was in a different troop from me but he had asked his sergeant if he could come and join me in the same bay of the trench. A German had been using a sniper's shield and we reckoned there was a chance of getting him because when he shot there was a tell-tale flame from the barrel of his rifle. So what we'd try and do is get ready and concentrate waiting for the next time he fired, although we still had to be lucky to get him through that hole.

I'd had five or six shots when Lenny said, 'Let me have a go, Smiler,' and he jumped up on to the fire step. Now I'm down in the trench watching and he had a shot or two when I saw him suddenly fall. The German had got him right through that little hole in the shield with Lenny's rifle still lodged up on the parapet. He lay at the bottom of the trench just coughing up a little blood. 'Don't worry, Len, you got a Blighty one,' I told him. 'When I get a chance, I'll write to your mum.' But he couldn't, no, he couldn't speak. I sent word by another chap to go and tell the sergeant, Sergeant Geoffrey Weir, that Lenny had been wounded. I begged this sergeant to let me take Lenny down the communication trench to a chalk pit where our dressing station was, but no, Sergeant Weir took him. I think he thought I was just trying to get out of the line.

I wrote to Lenny's mother and told her to expect Lenny home but a little time later I got a letter back to say she was sorry to tell me that Lenny had lived only three days and was buried not far from me at Bethune. Oh, that was terrible, terrible. That finished me as far as that went. I had got two or three other good mates but Lenny! I never really forgot it, not to this day.

With thousands of men fighting in close proximity, the quantity of ordnance flying around at any one moment would prove lethal to someone, somewhere. Ben Clouting had been in France for nine months. He was serving in the cavalry but, owing to the emergency in front of Ypres, his unit, the 4th (Royal Irish) Dragoon Guards, had been dismounted to serve as stop-gap infantry. On 10 May the fighting was heavy and Ben had been given a casualty to carry out of the line. A sergeant had been sniped through the face and was almost unconscious when Ben and three other stretcher-bearers got him down to a dressing station. They left him soon after to return to the line and were on their way when one of the team, Frank 'Mickey' Lowe, suggested they broke for a cigarette.

> We hadn't halted long when Mickey muttered, 'Anyone who gets through this war will be a lucky blighter . . .' Then, almost as soon as he had spoken, he grunted, half spun around and fell backwards. I caught him underneath his arms and slid him down to the ground, blood literally pumping out on to my riding breeches. And that was it. He never mentioned another word and within three or four minutes he was gone.

Mickey Lowe was killed by a bullet in the middle of the back, a victim of one of the vagaries of holding the Salient, the land that bulged out beyond the Belgian town of Ypres. This land was occupied by the British right under the noses of the enemy who, having failed to take the town during heavy fighting in 1914, had taken up position on the first in a series of low ridges outside. The enemy had not just the advantage of higher ground but the opportunity to fire on the British trenches from north, south and east, thus giving the impression of fire from behind.

It was just such a stray bullet that got sixteen-year-old Norman Crowther. A lad from Leeds, he had joined up in Halifax in November 1914. Like so many, he had given his age as precisely nineteen, although he was four years younger. At five feet five inches, with a thirty-four-inch chest, his enlistment papers noted his physical development as only 'fair'.

A year later, Norman was in a trench in Belgium. His fate was described in a letter written by a comrade, Frank Cocker, on 22 November 1915.

We had another lad killed the last day in the trenches and the circumstances are particularly sad for he was only 16 years of age. He was an Elland lad, Norman Crowther by name. On Monday night I was sitting warming myself by the cokefire which we had by the telegraph operator's dugout. Young Crowther was sitting there too and he looked so young and childlike as he nodded with sleepiness over the fire. Just then Mr Everitt came round to give a message to the telegraphist, and he stayed and sat with us round the fire. Mr E. is a nice, sensible man, who has been with us about two months. He looked across at the sleeping lad and a smile of pity came into his eyes. I said, 'This kid is going to give himself a blighty if he nods his head much closer to the fire.' 'Yes,' said Mr E., 'and he is a kid, too, is Crowther, how old will he be?' 'Oh, he is only just turned 16, Sir,' I said. Mr E. shook his head, 'Too young for this game but he sticks it very well.' The next day at noon, I was on duty and went round to change the sentries. Young Crowther was one of the sentries and I gave the usual order 'Next relief there!' I stood a moment to see that the next man came along and then turned and went back. I had only just got into the next bay when I heard a call 'stretcher-bearers'. I turned and rushed back and there was the poor lad face down in the trench reddening the water all round with his blood. I stooped at once to pick him up and inevitably I stooped in the nick of time for another shot came (from behind our trenches) and struck the parapet just above my head. I hoisted him over on to his back and the S.B.s having arrived, handed over to them. He only lived about ten minutes. It appears he was following me to sit by the fire again when the shot came across (from a long distance where the line curved round to the left) and entered his back piercing the lung and bursting the main artery. So ended another young life, in the twinkling of an eye.

After three or four days in the line, a battalion would be relieved and taken back into 'rest' although rest did not mean relaxation, and much work lay ahead, carrying supplies up to the men who were now occupying the vacated trenches.

Handing over always took place at night, exhausted soldiers trudging back to their billets and to sleep. An officer, Sidney Rogerson, who served with the 2nd West Yorkshire Regiment, recorded the stark picture.

That march was a nightmare. Not till then did I realize how tired I was nor how done the men. I had snatched less sleep than they, my total for the three days was no more than six hours, and had been more continuously on the go. They on the other hand were overloaded with sodden kit. We had not gone far before requests were made for a halt. I turned a deaf ear. Men so weary, I argued, would only fall asleep the moment they broke rank. It would be harder to get them on the move again. Besides, we were still in the shelled area. Requests turned to protests. Some of the younger men could hardly walk.

Back at the billet, the men would form up before they were quickly dismissed, whereupon an exhausted rush would be made for the best shelter available. Men shattered by long days in the line were battle-worn and surly, and younger soldiers were often forced to miss out on the best spots, as Norman Gladden knew all too well.

I looked into two or three shelters which were by no means over-crowded but was made to understand in no unmeasured terms that all the places were reserved. At last in desperation, for it was still raining, I pushed into one close at hand. Williams, a burly miner whose uncouth bullying manner I had already noted, occupied the end place. His raised fist moved to within a few inches of my nose as he told me to clear out.

Despite the threat, Norman persisted and managed to secure himself a spot. The camp was sited in a field of mud that oozed inside each bivouac when anyone clambered in and out. 'It is less difficult perhaps to imagine the utter desolation in our souls as we huddled under the clammy canvas,' he wrote.

After a good sleep, the men had a chance to clean up, scraping away the caked mud that clung on to uniforms and equipment, before having a wash and shave. Cecil Withers remembers the time:

Of course, you would get talking to one another. Lots of boys of fifteen and sixteen said they were eighteen and nineteen, shocking, you know, young boys, and the army took them as nineteen, they didn't ask any questions, no birth certificates, no identity required at all. You knew they were that age, they told you on the sly you see, we'd be getting ourselves cleaned up, talking about one thing or another and they'd say, 'Well, I'm only sixteen.' To my eyes it was obvious, they hadn't started shaving; they just had a whisker here and a whisker there, but you would never tell tales on each other, never betray each other.

Even though men would be 'volunteered' for jobs, there was always spare time to write a letter home, catch up on sleep, and, when the mood took them, sort through souvenirs found in the line or taken from bodies. Some picked up keepsakes either for themselves or, if they got the opportunity to realize a few shillings, to sell off to men of the transport who brought up supplies from the railheads.

'Souvenirs are all the rage just now and we are in a good place for them. After we are shelled we go and dig out quite a number of them,' wrote one soldier. Cyril José had collected 'a German bullet found in my dugout, a piece of shell exploded in the fort we were in, and a Nun's prayer book'. Ben Clouting collected a German knife and a Very light pistol from which he removed a severed hand. It was a collecting instinct that appealed to all, irrespective of age. The astute collectors only chose items of real value but boys new to the front, like Cyril, were less discriminating, and many continued to carry around hopelessly large amounts of junk instead of cherry picking.

George Coppard was out on rest near Gonnehem when he re-evaluated his collection.

I decided to jettison my souvenirs weighing nearly twenty pounds which I had been lugging around in my pack. German fuse tops, funny shaped bits of shrapnel and a rusty saw-edge bayonet were among this collection of old iron. Why I had been torturing myself with this agonizing load I don't know, just a boyish habit of collecting something out of the ordinary, I suppose. 'You're just a bloody twerp carting that lot around,' my pals scoffed. And so my eyes opened at last, I chucked the stuff away, not without regret but with substantial relief when the time came to move off.

It was a hobby not without its potential risks. Vic Cole was given leave in 1916.

It was night when we boarded the boat and the powerful lights turned on each man as he went up the gangway threw into instant relief any irregularity in dress or any bulge concealing forbidden souvenirs. I must confess to some apprehension at this point for tied to my rifle inside its dust cover was a German saw bayonet and in my pocket a Hun forage cap. The penalty for taking enemy weapons out of France was immediate cancellation of leave, but with luck I remained undetected and all was well.

Vic was more than glad to go home. By this time it was evident that war was not the glorious adventure anticipated, and there were those for whom the novelty had worn off rather quickly.

Alfred Cowell, who had enlisted in the Birmingham Pals aged sixteen, managed only a few weeks in France before writing home dejectedly:

> I got in on Dec 5th. I am fairly well in health, nothing to call ill, just fed up. We are in the trenches and I shall be very glad when we are out of them again as this mud is up to your neck, no swank. When I get to England again I bet you a quid I stop and I'll chance being shot as it is awful.

George Coppard was feeling the effects of trench life too.

> To tell the truth, deep down in me I was scared of the future. For the first few months trench warfare had been a kind of dangerous fun to me. Although only a boy, I had lived with grown men, sharing their fear and dangers. It was still fun when not in the trenches. Up in the front line, however, anything approaching merriment was dead.

There was a way out for those who were under age. A family could make an application for discharge or to have a son withdrawn from the firing line. It was an option that was not guaranteed to succeed and the boys themselves could not make an application, although a few wished that they could. Alfred Cowell did not hesitate to point out in a letter to his mother that three other underage members of the battalion were already due for discharge after their parents had written to claim them. They had corresponded with the War Office, enclosing their children's birth certificates,

and these boys were due to leave for England on Boxing Day. Alfred suggested that his mother, Mary, did the same for him. She did and a month later he was on his way home.

There was no question of Ernest Steele going home. He had once been given the chance when, in September 1915, an NCO had approached the under-age boys with a message. 'Sgt. Clifford said all under nineteen years of age could go back to England if they wished. After long discussion we decided to stay.' Ernest would stick it out and serve until the end, but his trench experiences had taught him a hard lesson and he was not about to let his younger brother make the same fateful decision. In a letter home, he warned him in no uncertain terms.

Belgium

Monday September 1915

Dear Harry,

I heard from Mater last night and she said you wanted to join up. Now I am going to talk to you seriously, or at any rate try to, so look out!

First, remember your age. You may be tall, and you may feel old and strong, but you are only 15; therefore you are too young to stand the strain of anything approaching this. Then, I have no doubt you want to do your duty. Well, do you think it would be your duty to join the army, and spend England's money in training you now, and then when you got out here, you would crumple up immediately? It would merely be wasted on you. Why, I am over three years older than you and even I am beginning to think I am not much use out here, although I think I shall be all right.

No matter how strong you feel, it takes more than a grown man's strength to survive this strain for long. You know how strong Ernest Cox was! Well, when I saw him, he told me his nerves were entirely gone and he starts immediately he hears a shell, even if it's merely one of our own guns. Don't tell anyone else that as he does not want Mrs Cox to know . . .

We *all* have to sacrifice something to do our duty. Your part is to carry on with business as usual *in spite of* all the recruiting sergeants in creation. Just grin and bear the things they say, and remember that by doing it you are doing your duty and that if you don't you are showing how weak you are. I have seen several kiddies out here; they have a pretty rotten time and don't survive it long, although they have cost as much as anybody else to train. So, if you are spoken to again by anybody, just tell them your age, and don't let me hear any more about your wanting to join. It makes me feel pretty rotten and I know it will make Mater feel worse.

Don't mind me saying this, and think I am trying to father you, it is for your own good, and also for the Country's good that you should not join, and having seen some of the results of youngsters joining, I think I am entitled to say this. You can see from this letter how your suggestion has made me feel, worse than I have felt since I have been out here.

Love to all
From your elder Brother who knows
Ernest

The letters home, and lengthening casualty lists, woke families up to the fact that the decision to let their sons enlist was not necessarily one that might iron out a few adolescent problems or make a man of a lad, but one that might rather be his end. Death was an ever-present backdrop to life, and lads like Smiler Marshall had plenty of time to ponder on that fact.

All the time, well, you were just wondering whether you were going to be the next one. All the time. Would you be the next one to be killed? The Padre used to reassure us. He used to say a little prayer and then say, 'However near you are to death, there's somebody nearer.'

One of those who witnessed the draining effect of life in the line was the Nationalist Member of Parliament for Galway City, Stephen Gwynn, who had temporarily set aside his life in politics for one on the Western Front. This erudite officer noted how soldiers knew that courage was a wasting asset. 'In the first weeks or months curiosity, the sense of adventure, and a mere lack of realization prevented the mind from dwelling on the thought of death'. Nevertheless in the end, the thought of death settled down upon the spirit of everyone, and, interestingly, 'perhaps all the more upon the very young,' he observed.

Corporal William Andrews, an older soldier serving with the Black Watch, witnessed how one boy's powers of resistance gave way after a particularly difficult time in the line. The boy, who is known only as Private X, had spent much of his time close to the battalion tailor, a South African veteran who knew what being under fire meant. But this older man was now deemed not fit for line and had been sent back to the quartermaster's stores and the boy was bereft.

The youngster, Private X, was a pathetic sight, his face swollen with crying. He had black hair, black eyebrows, and a round face, which normally would be cheerful, and perhaps comic. It was now childish and frightened.

'Don't take me back again to they shells, corporal,' he said, again and again. 'For God's sake get me out of this. I can't face they shells. I don't mind the bullets, but I can't face they shells.' NCOs had told him he must cheer up, or he would be shot for cowardice, but this did not steel his shattered nerves, nor did my reasoning with him, and my attempt to cheer him with chocolate.

It seemed to me the best thing was to take him to the medical officer and get a sedative. We had many youngsters in the battalion, though I believe, none as young as X, and I was afraid his hysteria might spread to others. So I reported the case to Captain Boase, and he, failing likewise to make any impression on the

boy's terror, gave me permission to take him to the medical officer. This was Major JSY Rogers . . . He seemed to have the priceless War gift of being able to do without sleep, and when casualties were heavy brought to his work a spirit of healing that made many forget their pain. He put a friendly hand on my shoulder when I went into his aid post. 'We're not going to have you breaking down, are we?' he said. I smiled back. 'No; it's this boy I'm troubled about. He gave a false age on joining, says he is only fifteen, and he simply can't stand the shelling. What am I to do with him, sir?'

At this X began crying again. Major Rogers offered him a cigarette, and lighted it for him.

'Now look here, my boy,' he said, in a kindly voice. 'I know you want your people at home to be proud of you, don't you? You wouldn't like your mother to think you were funking it?'

X admitted he wouldn't, but he said: 'I can't stand they shells. I don't mind they bullets, but I can't stand they big shells.'

The poor lad had no spirit left. He must have been knocked down or shaken by a big shell exploding near him. I had to leave him at the first-aid post, and I did not see him again. He may have been sent to hospital, or perhaps he was given some quiet job behind the lines, such as being servant to a chaplain. He passes out of this story.

In the end no cajoling or soothing words would help those lads who had had enough and simply walked away. Their youth would probably save them from the ultimate sanction for desertion, court martial and execution, but there was no absolute guarantee.

In 1916, Reverend Philip Clayton, better known to history as Tubby Clayton, went to see an old friend, Philip Gosse, a medical officer. Clayton, the co-founder of a rest home for soldiers in the town of Poperinge known as Talbot House, had a problem and sought out his old friend to see what he could do. Tubby had seen many boy soldiers on overseas service: he recalled seeing

one young hero aged sixteen sporting a Military Medal awarded for bravery, being frog-marched under escort back from the line for immediate dispatch to England. This time the circumstances were rather different.

A deserter had come to see Tubby. So scared was the lad in front of him that Tubby failed to recognize him but on hearing his name recalled that he had been an orphan brought up by two ladies in the New Forest, close to Tubby's home. This boy had enlisted aged fifteen or sixteen. Gosse listened to the case:

> He had been with his battalion nearly a year, during which time he had been blown up and buried by shells, and seen his friends killed and wounded, until at last, broken in spirit and sick in body, he had bolted.
>
> It was clear that if something was not done about it the wretched lad would be court-martialled for desertion and stand a very good chance of being shot. Instead the two conspirators arranged a plot.
>
> I admitted the deserter into our dressing station as a case of marked debility and shell shock, and put him to bed, where he slept for twelve solid hours.
>
> The difficulty was what to do next. After much discussion, a medical report was made out stating that we had found Private H wandering about, that he was not responsible for his actions, and that he had been admitted forthwith to the ambulance, to await dispatch to a hospital at the base. The plot was successful, and the lad at last got back to England, whence he ought never to have been sent.

Not every boy was treated with such compassion, though to be fair not every boy owned up to his youth to save his skin. If a boy was put on trial for a serious misdemeanour, it must have been tempting to reveal his age in mitigation, but how was the boy to know that owning up to yet another offence was not going to exacerbate the situation? Private John Tiernan of the Royal

Irish Fusiliers, a fifteen-year-old lad from Droghedd, Ireland, was caught sleeping at his post in July 1916. He was arrested and tried by Field General Court Martial (FGCM) being sentenced to serve five years' penal servitude, suspended for the war. It was almost two months later that his age was discovered and he was ordered home. Private Thomas Bomford, serving with the Essex Regiment, was another who chose not to state his true age at his FGCM. Bomford, who had served on Gallipoli, had been found, like Tiernan, asleep at his post and was sentenced to one year's imprisonment with hard labour. Aged just fourteen, he was taken to prison and released only after his father heard of the punishment and forwarded the boy's birth certificate.

Were these boys asleep because they were simply negligent, unaware of the seriousness of the offence or was their youth such that the burden of serving overseas was simply too much for their growing bodies? In Bomford's case, possibly not the latter. This lad was well-built, even at fourteen, and at five foot ten inches tall and a good chest size, he would have towered above boys his age and was easily on a par with his peers in the army. He had added five years to his age on enlistment, and questions were asked as to how he was accepted; all replies pointing to his unusual strength. He had easily passed for a nineteen-year-old.

But Bomford was an exception, and many of the lads who fell short of military expectations, to a greater or lesser degree, simply could not handle the strain of service especially during the winter. One can only guess why Rifleman William Buchanan, of the Royal Irish Rifles, shot himself in the arm in January 1916 but circumstantial evidence points to his inability to cope. He had enlisted in mid-October 1915 and was sent to France at the end of the following month aged sixteen and after barely six weeks' training, enduring freezing weather in the line. In January he was awarded a FGCM at a special hospital in Boulogne, reserved for those suspected of self-inflicted wounds, found guilty and sentenced to thirty days' Field Punishment No. 1 for his troubles. He rejoined his battalion in the line at the end of March 1916 and was only subsequently sent down to the base as under age.

By mid-1915 voluntary enlistment had dropped to a level where recruitment officers had to get out from behind their desks to challenge anyone they could find in the street who looked a likely candidate for the forces. Boys keen to join up found the standards for enlisting a recruit had, unofficially, fallen significantly. Enlistment in the summer months almost guaranteed service overseas by the end of the year when conditions on the Western Front were appalling. Private Donald Cheers was one example. He enlisted in mid-August 1915 and was sent to France with his battalion in mid-November, despite a formal protest by his mother, Isabella Cheers, to Donald's commanding officer. Donald had joined up on or about his fifteenth birthday.

These lads were volunteers, but not in the 1914 sense of the Kitchener volunteers, lads all part of the same battalion, destined for a year's training. These were lads who were frequently pushed into units that were short of men; units that had taken a battering, and required large drafts to bring them back up to strength. Three months' training, and sometimes much less, could see a boy in the trenches; a boy who had not built up the stamina and the fat to withstand the bitter cold, a boy ill-equipped mentally to cope with the rigors of active service in the army. 'It is a crying shame that a boy of his tender years, not fully formed yet, should be exposed to the rigors of winter in the trenches,' wrote Isabella Cheers by way of complaint to the Infantry Records Office in Hounslow.

Private Harry Allwood, 2nd Sherwood Foresters, is another good example. In March 1915 he had joined the Royal Scots Fusiliers but was discharged in mid-June, adjudged 'unlikely to become an efficient soldier'. He suffered, so a medical report made clear, from 'severe palpitations with frequent fainting attacks. [He] continually falls out on parades and [was] once brought to hospital in [a state of] severe collapse.' Yet this soldier had no problem re-enlisting the following month and, despite his frailties, was sent to France in December 1915. He lasted three months before being sent home. Another, Private Stephen Isaac, attested in mid-May 1915 and was sent to France that October just after his seventeenth birthday. He lasted less than a month for a report stated he 'found himself quite unable to do heavy marching in France and had to file out at once on account of pain'. Likewise, Private William Bain, 9th Devonshire Regiment, enlisted late June 1915 and was sent to France under age in October 1915. He lasted two months. He was 'Unfit to stand the strain of the campaign' and was sent straight from disembarkation in England to the 2nd Birmingham War Hospital to recover.

Thousands of men, not just under-age boys, succumbed to the effects of trench foot and other debilitating illnesses owing to the weather. Yet many boys, especially those with only short periods of training behind them, were the least equipped to adapt to their environment and many wrote home that winter desperate for release. One such was Private Barrass who had enlisted aged fifteen and went to France just after his sixteenth birthday. In asking for his discharge, his father recalled how his boy 'had been so keen and sure about it,' but now, after seven weeks overseas, 'he writes to me that he feels the work beyond his powers . . .' adding poignantly, 'He is a good boy and meant to serve his King and Country.'

5

Junior Officers

AS A SACRIFICE
GLAD TO BE OFFERED
A BOY
HE DIED FOR ENGLAND

Second Lieutenant Harold Cottrell
2nd South Lancashire Regiment

Killed in Action 30 September 1916, aged 18

THE OPENING MONTHS OF the war had been catastrophic for the officer corps of the small British Regular Army. Between August 1914 and the following March, some 6,000 of its officers had been killed, wounded, taken prisoner or were missing. This loss had to be made good, and replacements were found among the young temporary officers who had enlisted for the duration of the war.

Initially, there had been confusion about the appointment of temporary officers, with the War Office offering precious little guidance. Good luck or, better still, good contacts could win a commission, with a large number of appointments being made by commanding officers, adjutants and civil dignitaries before the system was tightened up.

Many of the new officers who were sent to France in early 1915 had come forward as the result of a Government advertisement in *The Times* the previous August. The appeal for temporary officers aged seventeen to thirty had elicited a good response, but there was no expectation that these men, especially the youngest, would see overseas action until they were aged at least eighteen. There was an assumption that, unlike most working-class boys of their age who needed to be nineteen to go abroad, these youngsters would be sufficiently well built to cope with overseas service and had innate officer qualities.

The war changed this expectation. While senior army officers and politicians knew that the war would last a long time, few predicted the number of casualties. In particular, losses from among junior officers proportionately outstripped those of any other rank.

Junior officers led from the front, but in 1914 and 1915 their distinctive dress had been a contributory factor in their undoing: the cut of the jacket, the breeches as well as the 'Sam Browne Belt' with a revolver holster made them stand out in daylight and silhouetted them in deepening gloom. Sword drill was still an important part of officer training and in 1914 officers took these outdated weapons to France. Although in the main they were dispensed with, right up to and including the Battle of Loos in September 1915 there were officers who made themselves conspicuous to the enemy by advancing sword in hand. Even then, when swords finally disappeared, officers were still to be witnessed attacking with a walking stick or cane in hand.

For all their bravery, these junior officers were marked men and German riflemen wreaked havoc among their ranks. To counteract the threat, officers began to wear other ranks' uniform with markings of seniority that could be seen only close up and, in time, this helped to cut the high proportion of casualties.

At the same time as the pre-war regular officer was becoming an endangered species, the BEF in France was rapidly expanding in numbers. The army grew almost four-fold in 1915, to just short of one million men by the end of the year. Territorial officers would help fill the void and, in time, Kitchener's new breed of junior officer would also arrive, but in the meantime a pool of officers was needed from which to draw in order to alleviate the current difficulties.

The boys who enlisted as regular officers, as Stuart Cloete did in September 1914, were, in the most part, thoroughly keen to serve. Their motivation was not identical to nor wholly dissimilar from those who enlisted as privates. The boys destined to be other ranks were mostly already at work, bored, and sometimes hungry. The boys of officer stock were frequently still at school and just as bored, and hungry too – but only for change. As Cloete wrote:

> The psychological force behind the idea seems to be of a dual nature. First, something was going on that was too big to be missed – adventure on a heroic scale; secondly, the eagerness of a young man to test himself, to try out, as it were, his own guts.

Cecil Lewis was a typical excited schoolboy. In the spring of 1915, he was on the stone terrace at his school at Oundle, with his great friend Maynard Greville. They were avidly discussing the war and their possible participation. Maynard was keen to leave at the end of term and enlist, despite the fact that both were still sixteen years of age. Cecil said:

> 'They won't let us.'
>
> 'Why not? We're almost seventeen.'
>
> 'But old King says you can't get a commission in anything until you're eighteen.'
>
> 'Rot! What about the Flying Corps? They'll take you at seventeen. They want young chaps . . . I vote we write to the War Office and see what happens.'
>
> 'All right! Oh, Maynard, wouldn't it be ripping!'

It took them a long time to get those letters right. 'We mustn't let it look too much like kids; but it wants to sound keen and all that.'

The decision to enlist in the Royal Flying Corps appeared to have been taken on a whim but, according to Lewis:

It was the last link in a subconscious chain of wish fulfilment. For, now I come to think of it, I hardly remember a time when I was not air-minded. At prep school I was already making gliders out of half-sheets of paper, curving the plane surfaces, improvising rudders and ailerons, and spending hours launching them across the room from chairs and tables.

But, in spite of this passion for 'aeronautics' – as they were then called – it never occurred to me that I might be actively concerned in them. That I myself might fly a real full-sized aeroplane was beyond the bounds of the wildest possibility. Then came the war and the importance of the air began to be realized. An immense impetus was given to aircraft design and manufacture. The opportunity opened, and the onlooker became participant.

The allure of flying was extraordinary. Only a decade had passed since the science fiction of flying had become science fact, and the thrill of taking to the air was out of all proportion to the potential dangers, which were very real and frequently fatal. With the war, aircraft design rapidly improved, offering would-be pilots new, faster, more aerobatic planes, but, while reliability was gradually enhanced, the stresses placed upon aircraft, pushed to the limits of stress and performance, made accidents prevalent.

One incident concerned the son of none other than the Undersecretary of State for War, Harold Tennant. Second Lieutenant Henry Tennant had just passed his eighteenth birthday when he enlisted into the cavalry early in November 1915 before transferring to the RFC, training with the 17th Reserve Squadron. In May the following year, he was badly injured when his plane unexpectedly stalled and nosedived seventy feet to the ground. Tennant suffered broken bones, a fractured wrist and ankle, a severely lacerated right cheek, impairment of vision, and numerous cuts and bruises. Not surprisingly, he also suffered 'severe shock' and required medical treatment for well over six months. He did not survive the war, though; he was killed in May 1917 at the age of nineteen.

The vast majority of young men who applied for temporary commissions in 1914 and 1915 did so with the full knowledge and cooperation of their parents. Almost all had previous experience in school, college or university Officer Training Corps and were therefore assumed to have certain leadership skills. In many cases, they were the sons of serving or recently retired army officers. Such fathers could be prevailed upon to find their boys a place in their regiments or, failing this, to use the network of friends from other units to gain a commission, even if it meant the commanding officer turning a blind eye to the age of the applicant.

George Llewelyn Davies was studying at Cambridge University in 1914. He was also a member of the university's OTC and so received a letter from the adjutant pointing out the duty of all undergraduates to offer their services to the country right away. His younger brother Peter, who was seventeen, noted in his diary the impact of the letter on both boys: 'This slightly disconcerting document – for great wars were a novelty then – was taken to apply to me also, as I had left Eton and was due to go to Trinity next term.'

In a matter of days, both Peter and George were on their way to Winchester to apply for a commission, their sense of duty overriding any hesitation on their part about going to war.

I think George as well as I had odd sensations in the pit of the stomach as we emerged from Winchester Station and climbed the hill to the Depot. At any rate George had one of those queer turns, something between a fainting fit and a sick headache . . . and had to sit for a few minutes on a seat outside the barracks. I would willingly have turned tail and gone back to London humiliated but free. George, however, the moment he recovered, marched me in with him through those dark portals, and somehow or other we found ourselves inside the office of Lt. Col. The Hon J. R. Brownlow, DSO, commanding the 6th (Special Reserve) Battalion of the King's Royal Rifles. [He] was busy writing, and looked up to ask rather gruffly what we wanted.

'Well – er – sir, we were advised by Major Thornton to come here to ask about getting a commission – sir,' said George.

'Oh, Bulger Thornton at Cambridge, eh? What's your name?'

'Davies, sir.'

'Where were you at school?'

'Eton, sir.'

'In the Corps?'

'Yes, sir, sergeant.'

'Play any games? Cricket?'

'Well, sir, actually, I managed to get my eleven.'

'Oh, you did, did you?'

The colonel, who had played for Eton himself in his day, now became noticeably more genial, and by the time he had ascertained that George was the Davies who had knocked up a valuable 59 at Lord's (which knock he had himself witnessed with due appreciation) it was evident that little more need be said.

'And what about you, young man?' he asked, turning to me.

'Please, sir, I'm his brother,' was the best I could offer in the way of a reference.

'Oh, well, that's all right, then. Just take these forms and fill them in and get them signed by your father and post them back to me. Then all you have to do is to get your uniforms . . . and wait until you see your names in the *London Gazette*. I'm pretty busy just now, so goodbye.' And the colonel waved dismissal to two slightly bewildered second lieutenants designate, and went on with his writing.

Stuart Cloete, who enlisted as a temporary officer aged seventeen years and two months, is an interesting case. Stuart was sent by his father to an establishment called 'Jimmy's' in Lexham Gardens. 'He was supposed to be the best army cram-mer in England, having succeeded in getting boys through the Sandhurst exam who were all but mentally defective.' Cloete was sure nevertheless that he would fail, even though he would study under Jimmy's tried and tested method of cramming defined by, and based upon, the age-old school method of question-spotting from past exam papers.

Convinced he would still be unsuccessful, Stuart tried instead for a temporary commission.

> These were now being offered to public school boys if suitably recommended by two officers. Here Captain Harvey, a retired naval officer, a great friend of my mother's, helped me. He took me to the barracks at Hounslow – a scene of indescribable confusion – and the colonel of the regiment who was a friend of his, signed my papers almost without looking at me . . . In addition to the colonel's recommendation, Allan Haig Brown, who commanded the Lancing OTC and whose ferrets I had looked after, gave me a letter saying I had served under him, as was required.

Hedging his bets, Cloete attended the Sandhurst exam and was surprised to find he could actually answer some of the questions but then, before the maths paper, he received an envelope marked OHMS (On His Majesty's Service). It contained his commission as a temporary officer. Cloete, having achieved his ambition, failed to turn up for his last Sandhurst exam. 'I later realized I had made a great mistake in not going through with it – because no one failed, so great was the need for officers in the new army now being formed.' He had missed out on two years' seniority, for no temporary officer could be made up to regular commission until he was nineteen, unless he had been to Sandhurst. In time, Stuart would serve as an acting captain on the Somme aged eighteen, then on his nineteenth birthday he was made a regular second lieutenant and a temporary captain. 'Had I gone to Sandhurst, so great were the casualties, I might have been a regular major. I might also have been dead.'

Influence and nepotism were rife, and boys who were just seventeen, and even those who were younger, were helped to get into the army quickly and with minimum fuss. A well-known case involved the son of the poet Rudyard Kipling. John Kipling, who had only just turned seventeen, had been rejected for military service owing to his extremely poor eyesight. When his father prevailed upon friends in the Irish Guards, a commission was offered. John was to be killed in action when he was eighteen. Ernest Lancaster, born in Southsea in May 1899, is one of many less-well-known cases. He enlisted as a private in the Hampshire Regiment and was recommended for a commission in 1915 by a family friend who was a retired colonel. Ernest later served with the 7th Dorsets, and then the Machine Gun Corps in France in 1916 and was killed aged seventeen.

There is also much evidence that a father could secure a commission for his son in his own regiment. Ernest Stream was headmaster of Grimsby Municipal College but had also been a major in the Lincolnshire Regiment. His son John Stream joined the same regiment shortly after his sixteenth birthday in November 1915. In fewer than ten months, John was serving as a second lieutenant on the Somme with the 7th Lincolnshires, still two weeks short of his seventeenth birthday; he was killed in 1918 aged eighteen. Similarly, Stanley Bates, the son of Lieutenant Colonel John Bates, was given a commission into the 1/5th King's Own (Royal Lancaster Regiment), the same battalion as his father; and Louis Broome, a lad from Brighton and the son of a colonel in the Indian Army, was granted a commission in his uncle's regiment, the 2nd Battalion Royal Scots. Both Stanley and Louis died, aged seventeen, during the early summer of 1915.

Unlike the enlistment papers that other ranks signed, an 'Application for Appointment to a Temporary Commission in the

Regular Army for the period of the War' had to be countersigned by the parents of the applicant if he was under the age of twenty-one, and then by at least one responsible person who could claim knowledge of the individual for at least four years. He would then certify to the good moral character of the boy in question. In theory, this would protect the army from under-age enlistment among its officer corps, but in practice it failed to do so.

One determined boy, Reginald Battersby, may have been vouched for by two 'responsible persons' but he would still make it to France while well under age. Reginald was born in February 1900 and, after the death of his mother on the outbreak of war, had enlisted in the Manchester Regiment. His relationship with his father, Walter Battersby, was strained, but his father's shock at his son's enlistment was reserved more for the fact that he had enlisted as a private than that he had enlisted at all. Walter was an influential man and his contacts were very good. Making enquiries, he was able to obtain a commission for his son and, although Reginald had to add four years and one month to his age, this did not appear to affect his chances of becoming an officer. Signing his application for a temporary commission and certifying to his good moral character were not only the headmaster of his grammar school, but the Lord Mayor of Manchester, Daniel McCabe. McCabe professed to knowing Reginald since birth and so, presumably, must have known his true age.

Once an officer was seen as being of the right calibre, commission papers were of secondary importance. Papers lodged at The National Archives reveal an applicant who changed his date of birth, on 'remembering' his correct age. Robert Batson could not decide whether his date of birth was 9 June 1897 or 1899, while in another glaring example, a date of birth, written in a completely different hand, was added only once the rest of the form had been filled in and countersigned.

Digby Cleaver from Hove in Sussex was just seventeen when he applied to join the RFC in August 1915. His application for a commission was completed with the exception of his age, which Digby, for his own reasons, omitted. His father, Howard Cleaver, countersigned that the information given by his son was correct on 20 August, the same day that a friend of the family, a lieutenant colonel of the RAMC, signed as to the applicant's good moral character. Only later, on 30 August, was Digby's age added to the application by an officer of the RFC. Whatever the reason for Digby's omitting his date of birth, clearly age was an issue of some kind.

Yet the award for most outstanding commission papers must go to Philip Lister. This boy remains something of an enigma. He had no clear links to the army and was the only son of widow Kathleen Davidson, and yet he was accepted for a commission in January 1915 by Lieutenant Colonel Pollock, commanding the 10th King's Own Yorkshire Light Infantry. Lister's application for a commission was so poorly executed, his handwriting so infantile, as to beggar belief, and it is remarkable that his paperwork passed even cursory scrutiny. His date of birth was given as 30 July 1895 although it is known that he was born four years later, in 1899.

The problem with commission papers was the question of who was technically certifying what. The boy signed the statement he had given, including his age, 'to be correct' and it was then countersigned by his father or mother.

The responsible person who also signed the paperwork would then add his details. In Philip Lister's case, A.A. Bull, a clerk in holy orders, living at the vicarage in Waltham St Lawrence, confirmed the boy's good character. Another boy, Ernest Lancaster, had his moral character certified by a Justice of the Peace for Portsmouth, while James Eason, Mayor of Grimsby, signed on behalf of John Stream.

Were these men signing simply to guarantee the boy's good moral character or were they also signing to guarantee the accuracy of the information given on the application form? It is unclear.

However, such ambiguity could help assuage the guilt that a clerk in holy orders might feel if he knew the boy in question was only fifteen years old. It is perhaps a moot point, but if a boy added four years to his actual age, would that not negate somewhat the notion of his good moral character?

For those whose progression to officer status was a little more formal than simple influence, there was a selection board to be faced. In Parliament, an MP and retired army officer who had sat on many boards regaled the House of Commons with stories of how they were bombarded with boys eager for a commission.

> Over and over again young fellows have come forward for commissions. They have been too young, and we have told them so. We have rejected them, and told them to come again in six months' time. They have pressed us, urged us, almost beseeched us to take them. That is not a single experience. It has occurred over and over again. I have had before me something like 300 or 400 of these young men. It is difficult sometimes to resist their appeals. They are well developed, they are keen upon work, and, instead of accepting them, you are going against their wishes.

Another MP, Colonel Greig, described the difficulties that commanding officers faced. They were confronted by

> the eagerness, heroism, and courage of these youngsters, who sometimes have the connivance of their parents in concealing their age. Personally, I had a somewhat remarkable experience of this. It was the case of a relative of a distinguished Member of this House. The boy turned out to be seventeen years of age. His father communicated with me, expressing a desire that he should go in for some other course of military training. I said to the father that I supposed it was not with his connivance that the boy had joined, but he replied that it had been done with his connivance, as he thought it was a proper and useful thing for the youngster.

The enthusiasm of these youngsters to see active service cannot be overestimated. Charles Carrington was one who chopped and changed not just battalions but ranks in his anxiety to get to France. He had originally sought a commission, but his keen interest was not reciprocated by the authorities and he had enlisted as a private in the Birmingham Pals. Once in the army, Charles and those around him became absorbed by one thought: when would they leave for France?

Everyone agreed that proper training was essential, but with no action on the horizon, Charles's friends began to desert, turning up in other regiments in the hope of an earlier date of embarkation. Their actions inspired Charles, not to desert, but to try once more for a commission, though his thought processes appear mind-boggling today:

> On the whole, the best way to jump the queue for France was to get yourself selected for an officer's commission, since young officers had the heaviest casualties and the highest replacement rate.

Displaying remarkable sangfroid, he contacted an influential uncle 'to pull strings' and shortly afterwards he was offered a commission.

Charles Carrington's logic was undoubtedly correct but, as his new battalion had yet to leave for France, it was unlikely to apply in his case. Charles Douie, another young subaltern, was in a similar position. He had suffered gut-wrenching disappointment when he was designated too young for overseas service with his battalion, the 1st Dorsets.

> My name had been high in the list of subalterns ready for service at the front, and I had just missed a draft for Cape Helles [Gallipoli]. The inexorable decree of the War Office in regard to age was brought to my notice and my name was removed.

The total rejection felt by those left behind was very real. In a moment of despondency, Douie looked for an alternative route abroad. Interestingly, his conclusions were diametrically opposed to those of Carrington:

> For months I haunted the orderly room and, in my bitter disappointment and my sure expectation of the early termination of the war, contemplated the resignation of my commission and enlistment as a private soldier. I had observed that the affairs of the private soldier and more especially his age were not subjected to the same scrutiny as the affairs of the young officer. Birth certificates were not demanded.

The problem for young men such as Charles Douie and Charles Carrington stemmed from the recruitment criteria for 'temporary commissions'. Many of those who had responded to the War Office appeal for applicants as young as seventeen were, within months, gazetted as second lieutenants in His Majesty's forces. They naturally felt humiliated when they were struck off the list for overseas service because they were not the right age. Charles Carrington was typical of this new brand of officer who, just because of his youth, was left to kick his heels when the rest of the battalion sailed for France at the end of August 1915. His rejection had been particularly cruel. Just two days before embarkation, he was ordered before the commanding officer.

> The colonel sent for me to say that in accordance with a regulation beyond his control I was to be left behind, even though he had given me a good 'confidential report'. Well, I was still only eighteen years old, and didn't look a year older, as I pretended to be. Anyone would have been disappointed but I was more than that; I was heartbroken . . . As my platoon waved their goodbyes, I felt finished, disgraced, and my war over.

Stuart Cloete had a very particular reason for being left behind and it was not directly connected with his age. Like Charles Carrington, he was due to sail with the regiment in August 1915 and, had he gone, would have taken part in the Battle of Loos the following month. The fact that he did not was due to an incident while he was sharing a billet with a more senior officer. The man made a pass at Stuart who in turn threatened him with a knife if he tried the move again. 'He did not try again but had no love for me after that and, owing to his influence, I was left behind as being too young and incompetent to go with the battalion.' If Stuart was right, then he had been left behind as a 'punishment', an interesting insight into attitudes of the time. His battalion was very badly mauled at Loos: if nothing else this officer had, as Stuart acknowledged, inadvertently saved his life.

Before Charles Carrington could go overseas, he was sent to Cannock Chase to a 'young officers' company' and was indignant at his temporary reduction to the status of officer cadet.

> My friends and I had one object only in view – to find a means of escape . . . we all pulled the strings we could get a grip on, with a fair measure of success, since the War Office was in considerable chaos. One of my friends overcalled his hand by appealing to a great-uncle whom he had never met, a very elderly field marshal, and received this reply or words to this effect: 'Field Marshal Sir Evelyn Wood acknowledges receipt of a letter from 2nd Lieutenant So-and-So, and begs to inform him that he (the Field Marshal) spent many years at the War Office combating the baleful effects of private influence.'

In early 1915 the first temporary officers began to appear in France, sent out as drafts to replace those who had been killed or wounded and their obvious youth was noted: 'In the streets of Havre one was struck with the boyish looks of the English officers, so different from the grave air of our more elderly French confrères,' wrote Lieutenant Wilfrid Piercy, who saw at close hand the reinforcements, officers and men, as they stepped off the boat from England or marched through the town.

> Our own boys are amongst the youngest: how many of them are below the age for Foreign Service it was wiser not to guess. In passing into our lines from those of the battalions recruited in the better districts of London, I have been struck anew by the simple immature expressions, the attitudes and bearing which mark the plasticity of minds still in the making.

In March 1915, two temporary officers, seventeen-year-old Lieutenant Willy Spencer, a boy from Highgate in London who was serving in D Company of the 2nd Wiltshire Regiment, and seventeen-year-old Second Lieutenant Maurice Beningfield, serving with the 1st Worcesters, were preparing to go over the top. Maurice already had some experience. In his enthusiasm to enlist in 1914, he had joined the Artists' Rifles and had gone to France in late October. In February he was given a commission in the field.

Both men would be among the leading waves in the proposed battle for the village of Neuve Chapelle, due to start on 10 March and to be led by two regular divisions, the 7th and 8th. It was, in part, designed to show the French the offensive capabilities of her ally as well as to seize the heights of Aubers Ridge. At 7.30 a.m., a lightning bombardment of the German front line was undertaken, 3,000 shells being fired in thirty-five minutes before the troops went over. The attack along a three-kilometre front was initially a great success: as the troops stormed forward, they took the German front line easily and then piled on towards the village, which also fell into British hands.

Unfortunately, the difficulties of supply and coordination rapidly escalated, while German snipers, lodged in the buildings that had been overrun, began to pick off the British soldiers.

Willy Spencer had gone forward and was soon killed; his body was lost. Maurice Beningfield had been more successful, leading his men across the first line of German trenches, but as he jumped on to the parapet of the second line, a machine gun was turned on the young officer and he was seen to be hit in the head and throat, falling into the flooded trench. A fellow officer and friend, Lieutenant Walter Whittle, attempted to find and retrieve Maurice's body but failed. Walter was himself killed two days later. In the end neither body was found, and both are now commemorated on the Le Touret Memorial to the missing.

Another battalion that took part in the fighting was the 2nd Middlesex. This unit was badly cut up by machine guns firing from a moated farm, several officers being killed. In the aftermath, new drafts were sent out, including four officers, one of whom was seventeen-year-old Second Lieutenant Brian Lawrence. The draft joined the battalion on 20 March near Laventie, a village west of Lille. Brian had been educated at Wellington College and on the outbreak of war had won a place at the Royal Military College in Sandhurst, just days before his seventeenth birthday. He had been commissioned into the Middlesex Regiment in early January 1915.

Barely ten weeks after arriving in France, he was dead, killed as he stood outside his dugout by a stray bullet glancing off the top of a sandbag. His parents, Arthur and Agnes Lawrence of Maidenhead, were informed of their son's death a few days later. The news was sent by telegram and included the express sympathy of the Secretary of State for War, Lord Kitchener. Such messages were changed later in 1915, extending the sympathy of the Army Council instead, an alteration probably made to depersonalize the telegram so as to forestall parents writing back – as Brian Lawrence's father had:

23.6.15

To The Right Hon. The Earl Kitchener of Khartoum K.G.

My Lord

I beg to thank you for your kind expression of sympathy, on the death of my only child Second Lieut. Brian Lightly Lawrence of the Second Batt. Middlesex Regt.

Please pardon me my Lord for saying, I do hope in future you will see your way not to send out such children, for what is 17??

He went gladly, and I would have had my tongue taken out, rather than have breathed a word to stop him; he has done his duty, and died a noble death, but the fact remains he was only a child, anyhow in years.

I have the honour to remain

Your Lordship's obedient servant
Arthur L. Lawrence

All these young recruits had taken on and ascribed to themselves the attributes of an officer and this had made an enormous difference to their self-perception and confidence. The boy suddenly had a job, a wage, a chequebook and an account at Cox's, the designated bank of an officer. With such accoutrements, 'the umbilical cord was finally severed', wrote Stuart Cloete. 'That it had been replaced by an iron chain of army discipline meant nothing to me, I could accept that much more easily; indeed I embraced it.' Keen to get abroad, after missing the first boat Stuart agitated to be sent on the next draft. When he finally went, his elation at stepping ashore in France was tangible. 'My address was 32nd Infantry Base Depot. S.17. c/o APO, BEF. France. I was very proud of this. I was with the British Expeditionary Force at last.'

All such boys had willingly joined to serve as officers and took on the responsibilities of men. Nevertheless, they were young to bear such onerous burdens as that of leading men into battle. Remarkably, they were not even the youngest officers – they were to come later in the war – but of those under the age of eighteen who led the way in 1915, more had been killed than would die in any subsequent year of the war.

6

The Beginning of a Campaign

A YOUNG LIFE
CHEERFULLY GIVEN
GOD MAKE US WORTHY
OF SUCH SACRIFICE

16201 Lance Corporal Albert Taylor
12th Royal Sussex Regiment

Killed in Action 13 November 1916, aged 17

ONLY AFTER THE FIRST offensives of 1915 at Neuve Chapelle and Aubers Ridge did the issue of under-age soldiering really begin to force its way on to the political agenda. Both Territorial and Regular soldiers were now abroad in force, in Belgium, France and, since April, on the Gallipoli Peninsula. Thousands of boys had been killed or wounded, lads who, just months before, were holding down civilian jobs in Britain. As the full extent of the losses started to appear in newspaper columns, parents began to have second thoughts about the wisdom of allowing their young sons to go abroad.

The War Office had first addressed this issue in late December 1914, in a memorandum reiterating the established principle that boys under the age of nineteen should not be allowed to serve overseas.

Complaints have been received that untrained and immature lads have been allowed to proceed overseas with certain Territorial

Force Units notwithstanding the orders that have been issued that no one in a unit of the Territorial Force is to be allowed to proceed to join the Expeditionary Force unless he is medically fit, fully trained and is 19 years of age or over.

GOs C.-in-C. should impress on all GOs C and OsC [Officers Commanding] Units the necessity of complying strictly with the instructions issued and so preventing a recurrence of these complaints.

This message was directed particularly at the Territorial units, which had recruited boys from the age of seventeen and allowed them to go abroad after just a brief spell of training. This created problems in giving boys the opportunity of serving at a younger age than with the Regulars. To rectify this, it was announced on 11 February 1915 that the age at which the Territorials could recruit for overseas service would be raised to nineteen, bringing them into line with the rest of the army. A week later, on 19 February, a reminder was issued by the War Office highlighting the fact that under-age Territorials were still being sent to France:

GOs C.-in-C. are asked to impress upon all OsC Units that they are personally responsible that no NCOs or men are sent either with their units or as reinforcements, who do not fulfil the conditions laid down for the time being by the Army Council and that it is the duty of such officers to ascertain the age of every man in their units as recorded on his attestation papers.

This was not a problem when boys had no reason to lie on their attestation forms before the war, but virtually none had given their correct age since. Duplicate attestation papers were not held at battalion headquarters, and so officers in charge of Territorial Force records were quickly asked to dispatch details of all men serving with units yet to go overseas, showing their date of attestation and their age on those dates. It was now the commanding officer who was made responsible for ensuring he had a complete record of the ages of every NCO and man serving under him.

The War Office was delegating an unfair duty to these commanding officers. Not only, as has been noted, was there no proper reserve for the Territorial Force from which to draw new recruits, but directives sent out only the previous month, January, had called on these same men to ensure that they held at 'least 200 men trained and ready to provide possible demands for drafts'. Just where officers were to find such men, all of whom would have to be aged nineteen or over, was not entirely clear.

The War Office appears to have sent out these memoranda with little thought as to how they might be implemented, and the suspicion remains that they were not interested in the outcome. In any case, there was as yet little pressure on them to deal with the matter of under-age boys serving overseas; these memoranda precede any of the 1915 offensives. A few battalions, such as the 1/10th King's Liverpools and the Queen's Westminster Rifles, responded, sending a few under-age boys home, but the fact that the War Office was forced to make almost identical appeals later that year highlights the extent to which commanding officers felt safe in ignoring them in the first place. There were far more pressing problems that required their attention.

The Government's handling of the war had so far gone largely unquestioned in the press and in Parliament, but by early 1915 the 'honeymoon' period, that political latitude given to all governments in time of conflict, was rapidly coming to a close. The war was going badly and there was increasing disquiet among politicians. Critics were starting to pass judgement on the dull and lethargic handling of the war by the Liberal Government.

Only a crisis would remove the general inertia and, in May 1915, one arrived. The Shell Scandal, as it became known, exposed through the pages of the press the apparent dire shortage of munitions available to British forces in the field. It was a scandal that was to push many leading figures into openly criticizing the Government's conduct of the war for the first time.

The storm broke on 14 May. An article in *The Times* by Colonel Charles Repington, a long-time friend of Sir John French, the Commander-in-Chief of the BEF, reported that he had seen for himself that the recently undertaken offensive by the British army at Aubers Ridge and Festubert had stalled owing to a lack of firepower, specifically a critical shortage of high-explosive artillery shells. Repington also revealed that British artillery had been rationed during the offensive, news that caused consternation at home. French himself condemned the Government for what he saw as an almost criminal apathy in the supply of munitions. Clearly, a far greater number of shells would be needed to bring the war to a successful conclusion.

The *Times* story put the Prime Minister, Herbert Asquith, under almost intolerable pressure, and on 25 May he invited leading politicians from the Opposition benches to join him in a coalition government. Lord Kitchener remained Secretary of State for War, but responsibility for the supply of shells was taken from his control and given to a new Ministry of Munitions headed by David Lloyd George. The Munitions of War Act passed soon afterwards effectively gave Lloyd George carte blanche to raise munitions production by whatever route he thought appropriate.

Lord Kitchener was an icon, his name synonymous in the public's consciousness with steadfastness and iron will. In 1914, he was admired almost immeasurably by public and soldiers alike, but he was never a politician. He was a loner, a man who inspired confidence in the public but behind the scenes was almost incapable of delegating authority. This was perhaps his defining weakness. He expected unfettered obedience to his wishes and plans, and, because of his prowess, regularly intimidated ministers. His far-sighted recruitment drive in 1914 had been remarkably successful on one level, bringing a million men into the army in the first few months of the war, but it had been a disaster for industry, stripping skilled workers from an economy that now found it hard to supply ammunition to the very men it had lost.

It was difficult, if not impossible, to remain ambivalent about Kitchener. He inspired respect and devotion in some, frequently those who knew him at a distance. In others, he inspired fear while, in a growing number, he brought to the surface repugnance for his style of management, and a distaste for his domineering tactics and his unwillingness to delegate. What was plain to many of his parliamentary friends and enemies were the gaping cracks in the great man's performance in office.

One MP who was highly critical of Kitchener and the War Office was a relatively unknown backbencher, Sir Arthur Markham, a wealthy forty-nine-year-old industrialist from Mansfield, with interests in mining, iron and steel, employing 25,000 people in Nottinghamshire. He had been a Liberal MP since 1900 and, from the start of his career, had chosen to concentrate his efforts in Parliament on his constituents' welfare and interests.

Often irascible and short-tempered, Markham tended to see issues in black and white, and individuals in the same way. Yet under 'a brusque and sometimes aggressive exterior' he was, according to his sister, the writer Violet Markham, 'extraordinarily sensitive to the sufferings of other people'. Markham's sympathy for others was framed by an acutely developed sense of morality and decency, one that eschewed compromise. No issue was too trivial for his attention if justice appeared to be at stake.

Markham's sense of right and wrong had been affronted by the bullying tactics of Germany and its invasion, against all international law, of militarily weak Belgium. It was this same natural compassion for the underdog that propelled him, months later, to take up the cause of the under-age soldier. Little did he realize how much the issue would come to dominate the following year, nor how significant a role he would play in the campaign to halt the enlistment of young boys into the army. Characteristically, Markham would throw himself into the campaign, exhausting himself in the process, and driving himself into an early grave.

An intensely patriotic man, Markham was never in doubt about the righteousness of Britain's cause, but his campaign would now require open and concerted criticism of the Government. He had the confidence, born of a lifetime in business, to attack the Secretary of State for War as directly responsible for much of the prevailing economic mess. 'In his opinion, the whole system of War Office administration was fundamentally wrong,' wrote Violet Markham. It was elementary to her brother that conflict called for 'an adjustment of effort between the claims of the armed forces and those of the industries which must supply every need of the fighting man'.

First-hand experience had brought the need for this adjustment to Markham's attention. At least five thousand of his own employees had left to enlist and, typically, he visited some of them. He said:

> They have always asked me the same question which I was unable to answer – why they were called away from their work before the Government were in a position to equip them.

It was concern for balancing these competing requirements and making the best use of resources that brought Markham to confront the iniquity, as he saw it, of under-age soldiering. The fact that the questions he raised in the House were met with ministerial indifference only helped to drive him on. He quickly became identified with the issue, and although other MPs framed similar questions in the House, it was Sir Arthur Markham who became the focus for public attention and in particular that of the families who had young sons serving overseas. As one correspondent was to write:

> You are becoming a Sir Arthur of the Round Table, redressing wrongs and succouring the distressed, and so you have to pay the penalty of getting constantly bothered.

Shortly before Markham took up the cause in Parliament, he wrote a thirteen-page polemic entitled 'The Conduct of the War', in which he attacked the Government, and in particular Lord Kitchener and the War Office, for their amateurism. It is not known exactly when he wrote this statement, although from certain allusions it was probably around July 1915. Nor is it obvious to whom the paper was sent, although it was clearly for wider consumption. It is infused with characteristic anger.

'Short of disclosing facts of advantage to the enemy I recognize no limits,' he wrote. His mission statement included advice, ideas and recommendations on how to improve the prosecution of the war. But it also included something else, his first known attempt to formulate, in writing at least, his dissatisfaction with the Government's handling of the issue of under-age soldiering. In it he cites no letters or particular cases, though he is clearly aware of the concerns voiced by parents:

> The most serious complaints come from women who declare that they applied for the release of their boys upon enlistment but were assured by the recruiting officer, the adjutant, or the commanding officer, that the boys would not be sent abroad until they were nineteen.
>
> Relying upon the word of honour of these English officers and gentlemen – a word which had never been known to fail in the past – these women were glad to leave their boys to 'do their bit' in the Home Defence Army.
>
> They now feel that they have been tricked, deceived, and lied to, in the most scandalous and un-English fashion. The 'word of an officer and a gentleman' no longer runs in these families or in the circle of their acquaintance. These people are convinced that the army is run and managed by a set of men who have no sense of honour, justice or truth.

The spring battles of 1915 and the stationary nature of the conflict highlighted the appalling conditions in which men had to serve. The number of casualties among boy soldiers had grown remorselessly, often caused not by injury but by succumbing to the effects of weather and disease. Until this point the Commons had not raised the issue, but for the next six months it was to become a hot political topic, as the full extent of the enlistment errors of 1914 and early 1915 came to public attention. The sometimes chaotic and amateurish way in which both recruiting sergeants and medical officers had not hesitated to enlist tens of thousands of boys into the British Army was at last being recognized.

It was another backbench MP, Barnet Kenyon, who first raised the issue of under-age enlistment with the Government, as Hansard transcripts for 22 June 1915 reveal:

Barnet Kenyon asked the Undersecretary of State for War, Harold Tennant, whether he is aware that numbers of lads between the ages of fifteen and seventeen have for patriotic reasons enlisted, making a false declaration of their ages; whether, seeing this is well known to the responsible authorities, he will say why the War Office permits lads of these ages to be recruited; whether he will instruct the recruiting officers to call for birth certificates in the cases of all young lads who desire to enlist; and whether he will dismiss any recruitment officer who enlists lads under the age laid down by the regulations.

The reply from Tennant was perfunctory.

The lowest age at which a man may be accepted for the Regular Army is nineteen. If any doubt exists as to the age of a recruit when he presents himself, the examining medical officer is referred to. If the medical officer is in doubt, the recruiting officer is required to make full inquiries before finally approving the recruit. I am afraid that the suggestion that every recruit should produce a birth certificate is impracticable. The Regulations give the parents of any lad below seventeen who has enlisted a right to claim his discharge.

It was a solitary question and the issue, at least on the floor of the Commons, appeared settled for the time being. Perhaps the enquiry jolted the War Office into action, for on 26 July it notified all general officers commanding

> to use their utmost endeavours to stop the enlistment of young men who are below the prescribed minimum age of nineteen, and to issue stringent orders to this effect. Where it is considered that there is reasonable ground for doubting the accuracy of the age given by the recruit, some proof should be required before his enlistment is proceeded with. It is of special importance to secure that no youth, even though of a physique superior to that of the average of his age, should be encouraged to say that he has attained the prescribed age when as a matter of fact he is below it.

The problem with voluntary enlistment was that it was always subject to the vagaries of public sentiment, swayed by duty, fear, patriotism, plain resignation or deep-seated anger. Recruitment figures were prone to rise in response to reports of desperate fighting on the Western Front or news of an atrocity, but they would subsequently fall. In early May, news broke of the sinking of the Cunard Liner *Lusitania*, with the deaths of 1,198 civilian passengers. As a direct result of the perceived outrage, the numbers of men who enlisted that month rose steeply. There was a similar response in October that year when the English nurse Edith Cavell, working in a Brussels hospital, was executed by the Germans for helping Allied soldiers escape to the Dutch frontier; lurid reports of her fate helped bring more volunteers into the fold.

For fourteen-year-old Albert Harvey, the son of a bricklayer from Hull, the stimulus was more directly personal: he reacted to an attack on his hometown. Albert had already attempted to enlist in 1914 and had been rejected, but now he was stirred once again into action after the first Zeppelin raid on his birthplace in June 1915. He was at home that night and had actually seen the Zeppelin from the top storey of his house. Later, he went out into the street to find many people roaming around, a number still wearing nightclothes.

> There were at least three big fires and much damage, including Edwin Davis' shop, near Holy Trinity Church, which was destroyed. There was much excitement and no doubt people were fearful and angry. It was Sunday night and a number of people attacked German pork butchers' shops, one in Charles Street.

A policeman who attempted to protect a German shop from the maddened crowd was chased down the street and was lucky to escape. In all, the bombing had claimed the lives of twenty-four civilians while another forty had been injured, enough of an atrocity in Albert's young eyes to make him want to enlist: 'I felt that I wanted to get at the Germans.'

Periodic and unpredictable atrocities could act only as a useful top-up to the monthly requirements of the army, but it was no way to run a recruitment campaign. The daily work of organizations such as the Parliamentary Recruiting Committee (PRC) was vital to pull in a steady stream of volunteers, but gone were the days when it was easy. Between 11 and 25 April the PRC held 852 evening and 124 dinner-hour meetings in London's fifty-nine constituencies, as well as 268 Sunday meetings in parks and open spaces, and sixteen in employers' shops, works and factories. A total of 150 speakers had been used. Again, between 27 June and 11 July another PRC campaign in the capital was launched: this time a total of 1,421 meetings were held, using a variety of bands and marches to stir men to action.

In June 1915, the Conservative politician Lord Derby published an updated summary of methods to be employed during a

recruitment drive in west Lancashire. Derby had been a prominent figure in the campaign. He had spoken at rallies across the
country and so felt sufficiently expert to offer advice to others.

> Do not forget that under the present system you are asking a free-
> born Lancashire man to offer his services, possibly his life, for his
> country, and that he is within his rights to refuse you. If he refuses
> do not threaten him with conscription. He knows that at present
> you have no power to enforce that threat, and will probably only
> be the more stubborn in his refusal. For the same reason, if you
> are unsuccessful, do not call the man 'a coward' and a 'shirker'.
> Experience has shown that a quiet explanation of conditions, rates
> of pay, terms of service, separation allowances, given courteously
> and tactfully, is far the most successful recruiting method. DON'T
> HUSTLE; DON'T THREATEN; REMOVE DIFFICULTIES.
> Talk personally, then you will bring recruits.

The public rally, the bread and butter of the recruitment drive,
still attracted huge attendances but was not always able to trans-
late spectators into volunteers. All too often, the new recruits
were the boys who, too young to enlist in 1914, were now a little
fuller in figure, a little bolder in attitude. One Tunbridge Wells
newspaper recorded such a rally in May 1916 when an enormous
crowd of 10,000 people gathered on the common to be addressed
by Captain Campbell Duncan, DSO, and other notables of military and civil life. An appeal was soon made for recruits to join
the colours.

> A tall, slight youth of fair complexion stepped forward, and
> numerous comments were made upon his extremely youthful
> appearance, but, boy though he was, Roy Upfold had the spirit
> of his fathers, a soldier family, still burning within him, and he
> stepped forward dauntlessly to do that which many older men
> hung back from.

He was fifteen.

George White, at the time of his enlistment, was even younger than Roy Upfold. George had not been driven to join up by news of atrocities or the loss of a friend at the front. Rather, as the son of an artilleryman and now the stepson of a man who had served in the 9th Lancers, it was his desire to serve that drove him on. Towards the end of May 1915, he saw a poster indicating that there would be an open-air meeting at Ospringe on 2 June. George and his friend Charlie went to the meeting in the hope of enlisting.

Charlie had no difficulty with his family about volunteering as he was seventeen but I was in a different position being two months away from my fifteenth birthday. Charlie supported me when I first broached the subject of joining up to my parents but, naturally, they said 'No'. However, I kept up the pressure with help from Charlie and hinted that I might run away to enlist, as lots of other young lads were doing.

I think Dad [his stepfather] sympathized with me as he had left home at the age of seventeen to join the 9th Lancers and he knew that I was well advanced, physically, for my age. This, and the fear of my leaving home, helped to persuade Mum to make, what must have been to her, an abominable decision to let me volunteer at the meeting. No doubt she felt and hoped that those doing the enrolling would see that I was too young and therefore refuse me.

The 2nd of June was a lovely day and Charlie and I proceeded to attend the gathering in an Ospringe field that evening. We listened to the speech followed by a powerful plea for the men to come forward to do their duty to God, King and Country. We two walked proudly forward to do just that and Charlie was interviewed first.

Much to George's surprise, Charlie was rejected by the recruiting sergeants as being under age.

I thought, 'Well, that's done it, they certainly won't take me.' However, I gave my name and my age as nineteen. Forthwith, I was asked further questions, the answers to which were written on a form which I had to sign. While this was going on, my disappointed colleague looked on and all the time I expected him to blurt out that they should take him as he was two years older than me. But he kept quiet and was so pleased that I had succeeded.

Derby's advice not to threaten or bully was all well and good, but threats and bullying had been precisely the tactics used by many of those charged with finding recruits, and they had often proved productive, especially among boys. In the late summer of 1915, Hal Kerridge was still sixteen years old when he was accosted by recruiting sergeants in Richmond in Surrey.

You had sergeants wandering about all along the pavements and anybody who looked a likely soldier they'd stop, positively stop you, and ask you to join up and walk beside you and try and pester you to join.

William Bagwell was one parent who became very annoyed at the tactics. In early October 1915 his son Clarence had been accosted on his way home from work by a recruiting sergeant. 'He was almost forced with others by a crowd to the recruiting office,' his father wrote. Despite telling the sergeant that he was only sixteen, Clarence was told to lie. 'The lad was quite disheartened when he came home. He is not a very strong lad, we have had quite a lot of trouble with him.' William Bagwell forwarded his son's birth certificate.

This form of coercion was becoming all too common. The Adjutant of the 4/10th Middlesex Regiment wrote to the War Office requesting to release not only Bagwell but another boy he named as Private Mills, aged fifteen. Significantly, the letter added that the recruiting sergeant had clearly acted with 'very misplaced zeal', especially as Bagwell's age had never been concealed.

The fullest enquiries are being made to find who the sergeant in question was with a view to withdrawing him from the recruiting staff if no satisfactory explanation is forthcoming. It seems that the approval and examination of recruits at the administrative centre must occasionally be carried out in a somewhat lax way as these letters from parents are very frequent now.

News of intimidation came to the attention of Sir Arthur Markham, who raised the issue in the Commons, challenging Tennant to give instructions to the recruiting sergeants to desist from insulting and intimidating persons living in the Mansfield division. Was the Undersecretary of State for War aware, he asked, that at recruitment meetings held in Mansfield, speakers had threatened to boycott tradesmen who, it was alleged, had refused permission to their sons to enlist? He also inquired as to whether Tennant knew

that a youth of fifteen years of age from New Annesley, in the Mansfield Division of Nottinghamshire, has constantly been accosted and insulted by recruiting sergeants in Nottingham, who informed him that he was a rotter and a slacker, and that he was not telling the truth when he told them his age was fifteen.

Such practices were 'contrary to the spirit of voluntary enlistment and the policy laid down by the Prime Minister'. In reply, Tennant stated merely that he had 'instituted an inquiry'.

The enlistment of some young recruits could scarcely be called voluntary. In September 1915 a county magistrate and MP, Sir Frederick Banbury, was sitting in court as usual, next to the chairman, when

a very small and sickly looking man, who looked as if he had not had anything to eat for a long time, and three small boys, suddenly appeared. The chairman turned to the magistrate on the other side and said something to him, and the three boys and the man disappeared with the magistrate through another door. I said, 'What did you do that for? If these boys are defendants in this case, why do they not go into the dock?' The reply was 'They are recruits.'

Although there is no evidence that either reformatories or borstals had a habit of sending miscreant lads into the clutches of the armed forces, nevertheless a small number of such boys did find their way into khaki. Of 336 boys released from borstal institutions in the year ending March 1915, 150 were in the forces, while in all some 600 former borstal boys were known to be serving. As the age of majority was twenty-one years, boys up to that age could be sent to borstal rather than to prison. This meant that many, but by no means all, were already of military age and were accompanied by borstal attendants to recruiting stations in exchange for their release on licence.

William Swift, a lad from Liverpool, had been convicted of 'shopbreaking' in January 1914, when he was sixteen. He had been given a three-year custodial sentence, but by June 1915 he had served half of it, and was discharged into the army. His parents, aware of his enlistment, cautiously wrote to the Borstal Association that they had no objection to his serving his country, but felt he was too young to serve in the front line.

William had no qualms about joining up. Almost as soon as he arrived for training, he wrote home saying that he was doing his best. Brief records kept by the Borstal Association noted that he had begun to run for the regiment and that he had written asking for money to buy shorts. By February 1916 he was winning races, but bemoaned the fact that, because of his age, he was being kept back from the front.

By July, William had his wish. Although still under age, he was sent to France to join C Company of the 8th King's Own Royal Lancaster Regiment. His letters home record that the 'grub' was better than that served in England, and overall it was 'all right down here'. The following month, his battalion was involved in an attack in which it suffered serious casualties, and his parents wrote to ask for his return. By September he had, to his disgust, been removed from the trenches until he was nineteen. His borstal report noted that 'he would rather have remained in the line as he was an acting sergeant and platoon commander, and he couldn't expect further promotion from his current position [behind the lines]'.

Little more was heard of William until the following year, when a letter was sent by the Reverend Martin Leonard, DSO, chaplain to the battalion, to the Borstal Association stating that William had been killed in the trenches on 29 May 1917. His casebook was closed.

Another borstal boy who hoped to make good in the army was Thomas Clarke from Wolverhampton. He had been convicted of theft and given two years' detention, but by April 1915 he had also been released under licence into the army, being walked to the recruitment office by borstal staff. By June, Thomas, like William Swift, was enjoying army life and he wanted to sign on for seven years. After receiving fourteen weeks' training, he was on his way to France and the trenches, aged just seventeen.

Not much is known of his service overseas until April of the following year, when his battalion, the 1st Royal Berkshire Regiment, was issued with orders to proceed up the line. It was at this point that Thomas absconded from his regiment, being picked up by the authorities shortly afterwards. The seriousness of his crime might not have become apparent to the teenager until his court martial, when he was charged not just with desertion but with an unspecified case of theft. He was court-martialled in the field on 28 April 1916 and sentenced to death.

In due course, details of the sentence were received by the Borstal Association back in England, as was the news that his sentence had been commuted: he was 'let off with ten years which he will have to do after the war as he was too young to be shot', noted a borstal official.

Thomas was returned to his battalion and was wounded soon afterwards. He was sent to England to recover and, when he embarked again for France, he wrote to his mother saying he hoped that his future would be a brighter one. It was not to be. Just days after rejoining the battalion, he was sent into action on 14 November and was killed. He was buried very close to the spot where he died. On his gravestone is the family's dedication: 'In cherished memory. Gone but not forgotten'.

There was, and remained, a dichotomy at the heart of the Government's stance over boy soldiering. Young boys, while not actively encouraged to join up by Government, nevertheless fulfilled a crucial role in recruitment by humiliating their elders into enlisting. It was no coincidence that uniformed groups such as the Boy Scouts and Boys' Brigade were frequently to be seen, and photographed by the press, at recruitment rallies organized by the Parliamentary Recruitment Committee, waving flags and leading marches: if young boys were shown to be doing their bit, what excuse a man? The newspapers, reflecting the mixed attitude, frequently revelled in stories of boy soldier endeavours. Roy Upfold had his moment of fame when a story appeared in his local paper under the dramatic heading, 'BOY OF 15 IN THE TRENCHES, Remarkable Spirit of Tunbridge Wells Youth'. In the article, he is referred to as a 'hero' twice, not least for his desire to avenge a brother who had been killed at the front. Most local newspapers ran stories of 'their' boys who had apparently 'made good' by enlisting under age. 'Winchester Stripling At The Dardanelles', tub-thumped one; 'The Fighting Spirit', thundered another.

Ben Clouting, who had been out in France from the start of the war when aged just sixteen, made regular appearances in his local newspaper under headings such as 'BOY SOLDIER'S EXPERIENCE':

> Yesterday morning Mr and Mrs W. Clouting of Littledene, Beddingham, received a letter from their soldier son, Private Ben Clouting, 4th Dragoon Guards . . . [he] intimates that he is still 'going strong'. Private Clouting, although only seventeen, is a fine big fellow, and has already had some exciting experiences, taking part in the Battle of Mons. He celebrated his seventeenth birthday at the Front. He was formerly a member of the Southdown Troop of Boy Scouts, and the training he then received is standing him in good stead. Ben's letters home are quite cheery, but, of course, it is not all honey out there. His many friends will wish him every success in his military career.

An article in the *Tamworth Herald* recounted the experiences of Private George Collett, who had enlisted at fourteen:

> So well developed was he that he deceived the doctors who accepted his statement that he was 19 and a half. Indeed, one army doctor passed him with the comment that he was 'a well developed man for his age (19 and a half)'. Young Collett was five feet nine inches in height and looked much older than he was.

In early 1916, his parents had tried to get their son released but he had refused to come home. In a letter home to a friend, printed in the newspaper, Private Collett gave his reasons for staying.

> I think it is my duty to stop out here. I assure you that the wet muddy trenches are no attraction, it is no delight to sit in two foot of water all night long. Nevertheless, why are we all sticking it so? Supposing all of us chaps were to give in, then the Boches would get through. We have seen and heard what the Germans did to the peasants when they advanced in the early part of the war, and we

know they would do their work just as well on the English civilians provided they got through and overrun England. That is the
reason we have got to hold out. So you can see the reason why I
am sticking it, there are plenty of chaps not much older than me
doing the same.

'This is the spirit that has made England what she is today,'
the newspaper preached to its readership, 'the bulwark of the
Allies.'

Even those boys who returned home severely wounded were
not necessarily cause for any press or public soul-searching or
introspection. When Private Howard Peck, a seventeen-year-
old lad from Nottingham serving with the 1/8th Notts &
Derby Regiment, was wounded in October 1915, his plight
was evident for all to see. His face 'was badly smashed', he had
lost three toes off one foot, and his other leg was also badly
damaged. The boy's obvious fortitude while in considerable
pain won the admiration of Mrs M., a visitor to Peck's hospital
in Leeds. In a letter to the local *Hucknall Dispatch*, dated 25
November, Mrs M. wrote:

> I visit the hospital very frequently, and have never heard young
> Peck murmur. He is a splendid fellow, and has won the admira-
> tion of the staff, and his fellow sufferers. If our boys possess such a
> spirit I think we need not worry about the future of our country,
> or the final decision of right against might.

Given the extent of his injuries, Peck's long-term future was quite
probably less rosy than the nation's.

It was not only local newspapers that took an interest in the
boys; national newspapers also ran stories about young soldiers,
asking just who the youngest serving soldier at the front might
be. The *Daily Mail*, which was periodically to campaign with Sir
Arthur Markham for the return of young soldiers, printed stories

that appeared to praise their military prowess. 'SOLDIER OF 14.
BOY IN SAME REGIMENT AS HIS FATHER', ran one article
in July 1915:

> Hundreds of boys of fifteen have enlisted, but a case has just
> become known of a lad of 14 who grasped an opportunity to enter
> the army. 'Isn't it time you young men did something for your
> country?' asked a recruiting sergeant of a group outside a music-
> hall some time ago. 'Rather,' said a sturdy lad named Priest (aged
> 14), who looked up eagerly. 'How old are you?' 'Sixteen,' said
> Priest. 'Sixteen! A fine young man like you would pass for nine-
> teen anywhere. Come along!' And young Priest went. He is now a
> private in the same regiment as his father, who is 41 years of age.
> Priest's old schoolfellows have sent him a five-shilling War Loan
> Voucher.

Parents at home or abroad wanted to share their pride in their
sons' patriotism. The father of fourteen-year-old Lance Corporal
Christopher Paget-Clark, the scout who had been on coastal patrol
in Devon before he enlisted, reacted to the Priest story by writing
to the *Mail* about his own son:

> Dear Sir
>   In your Monday's issue I note that you refer to the enlistment
> of a lad of 14 and another similar case may perhaps be of interest
> to your readers. It may also assist to stimulate the younger genera-
> tion to come forward and afford an example to the slackers of more
> mature age.

The *Mail* ran the story, as well as news of yet 'More Soldiers of 14',
printing names and information provided by proud families. Ten
days later the *Daily Sketch* ran a picture of Paget-Clark, noting his
lance corporal status, and also featured the picture of George Moor,
who had, at eighteen, just won the Victoria Cross at Gallipoli, his

child-like image appearing beneath the words 'BOY OFFICER WINS THE V.C.'. The over-riding impression given by all the newspapers, both local and national, was that none of these boys, though their names and units were publicized, would be afforded the indignity of being sent home.

At one moment the newspapers appeared to praise the actions of these young boys, the next they sounded words of warning. One correspondent of *The Times* wrote in 1915:

> We must not be too particular in seeking recruits at this stage of the war, but there must be a limit. And we think that limit has been reached in the case of what is known as the Bantam Battalion [men officially between five foot and five foot three; unofficially they were taken two even three inches smaller] of the Royal Scots. I have lately been in the Scottish capital, and could not fail to notice the unmistakable youth of some of the recruits of this corps. I am prepared to say that a considerable number of these lads were not more than fourteen. I spoke to them, and their manner, their physique, and voices were a sufficient indication of their real ages . . . The Recruiting Staff officers should be asked for an explanation.

It was a view entirely endorsed later by an officer, Captain Eric Whitworth, of the 12th South Wales Borderers, a Bantam battalion in the 40th Bantam Division. In France he had come across a tearful seventeen-year-old who could no longer stand the trials that overseas service presented. Whitworth managed to secure the boy a 'cushy job' with the Divisional Military Police. 'He [the boy] left the next morning smiling and grateful,' wrote Whitworth adding:

> But we ought not to have these boys with us . . . The genuine Bantam is a fully developed man of small height and most are very fine men; the Bantam was never meant to be growing boys, as

40% or 50% of ours are, in the eagerness to join up at the beginning of the war. One can only blame the authorities.

At the end of August 1915, the War Office had issued a memorandum forbidding the practice of enlisting boys for 'Bantam' battalions while, shortly afterwards, repeating its first order made in December 1914 that no boys under the prescribed age for overseas service should be sent abroad:

> Cases of men of the T.F. [Territorial Force] being sent abroad below the attestation age of 19 years are still being frequently brought to notice. GOs C.-in-C. should again impress upon all concerned the necessity of complying with the instructions . . .

The Government was finding it difficult to control recruiting sergeants who ignored directives either because they were patriotic and over-zealous, or because the financial rewards were too great an incentive to forgo. They were also failing to deal with commanding officers of home depots, who were under intense pressure to send to France drafts that were battle-ready. Ten months later, in response to questions in the House, Harold Tennant admitted that not only had no court martial ever taken place against a boy for 'fraudulent enlistment', but that no recruiting sergeant or officer had been prosecuted for deliberately accepting boys who were under age.

The *Times* correspondent continued:

> We may admire the enthusiasm and dash of youth, but war is not all battles, which are, indeed, but incidents of comparatively infrequent occurrence in what is often only a long tale of exhausting marches, exposure, and hardships. It is these which boys are little fitted to undergo, and it is these to which their physical strength and moral endurance will both alike succumb . . . If our authorities are labouring under the impression that boys of fifteen

can stand campaigning under modern conditions, they will, to their cost, find out their mistake.

Clearly the army had never wanted undernourished, poor-sighted weaklings, boys who would never reach a level of fitness that would allow them to proceed overseas or who would require such work to improve their physique that it would be nothing short of madness to take them. The problem was that the authorities were increasingly malleable when it came to accepting lads who were willing, and at least *tolerably* fit and able, at which time age was of almost secondary concern.

The army's attitude to the quality of recruits and their worth was reflected in the wider society, often in national newspapers such as *The Times* but also in local newspapers and pamphlets. In August 1915, for example, a short piece appeared in the magazine of Boots the Chemist, *Boots Comrades in Khaki*, under the title 'Juvenile Discharged':

One of our members has regretfully returned to civilian life. Originally he left Cheltenham without his father's consent to join the Royal Flying Corps, and though only 16 years of age was ordered over to France . . . He wrote to wish his father 'Goodbye.' The father, sensibly enough, did not respond with 'Good Luck,' but engaged a solicitor to procure the boy's discharge from the army, which he should never have entered. The youth has been inoculated twice, and vaccinated once. During his futile term with the colours he has cost the country as much for clothing, maintenance, training, and transport as a man of serviceable age.

The cost to the nation of discharging such boys was considerable, but this was the same magazine that only a few months before had unequivocally praised the actions of another former employee, Richard Pomfret, a fifteen-year-old private in the 2nd Coldstream Guards and former porter at the Accrington Branch of the chemist, who had been described as having 'a giant heart in a giant body'. Pomfret had been killed in action on his sixteenth birthday, exactly two weeks after landing in France.

The full significance of the conflict dawned slowly on many parents, a fact highlighted by the number who accepted, albeit reluctantly, the enlistment of their sons. They did not encourage fraudulent enlistment, except in a few cases, but chose instead to accept the situation on the basis that the war would be over quickly and in the meantime it would do the lads good to have some fresh air and exercise.

The reality of war undermined such composure and parents increasingly sought not only to withdraw their sons from the Western Front but to stop them from going in the first place. This endeavour became more pronounced as the army began placing greater emphasis on the need for fresh reinforcements after the major engagements of March, April and May, and markedly after the heavy fighting of September and October 1915. The work of MPs like Markham, and the spreading knowledge amongst parents that it was possible and legal to halt their sons' progression to the front, stiffened their resolve to get them home.

Senior army officers were going to get grumpy. Letters were arriving on the desks of battalion commanders, if not in a flood, then in a steady trickle. And nothing was more annoying than to have to pull a boy from the ranks as he completed his training. Overseas service was just around the corner and news that the unit was about to be sent abroad triggered a flurry of parental letters such as that sent by Mrs Ethel Andrews. 'As my son is up for four days leave, I have come to the conclusion that he is about to go to France. I am enclosing his birth certificate to show that he is under age.' Her son, Private Alfred Andrews, was aged sixteen and as a consequence he was withdrawn from the draft.

Another boy, Rifleman Albert Holden, King's Royal Rifle Corps, had enlisted at the age of fifteen without his mother's consent though not without her knowledge. He had served six months before his mother came forward. 'I should have given his age before, but I always thought he would remain here, but now I find they are sending them abroad and I cannot bear it . . . Mrs A Holden.' Private Holden's progress to France was also abruptly halted.

Letters such as these caused consternation amongst officers such as Colonel William Watts, who commanded the 20th battalion The Welch Regiment. In a note to his superiors dated 17 November 1915, he made his views abundantly clear:

> There are about 15 members of my Battalion who have been serving about <u>six months</u> – and their parents have now discovered <u>after that period of training</u> that they are under age of 18.
>
> I have no doubt there are many others in the same position but they have not made any application for discharge.
>
> I am of an opinion such cases are of a very great expense to the country – and if these men get their discharge, merely on asking for it, the nuisance will not abate, but increase.

Watts' frustration was evident in the case of a boy named Grainger. His mother had written asking for his release and supplying the usual documentary evidence as to age. Grainger should have been released straightaway, but by January 1916 he was still with the battalion, as official correspondence reveals, and Colonel Watts was gently chided for his delay in carrying out the order to discharge the boy. Colonel Watts replied that Grainger had not been released because it had proved difficult to find the boy who, as it turned out, had enlisted under the name of Edward Walters, another administrative complication the colonel could well have done without.

The 6th Battalion Worcester Regiment, a reserve battalion, was in a similar pickle. A travelling medical board had been sent to the unit in early January 1916, inspecting those lads deemed 'immature'. It had discovered a total of eighty-nine boys of whom

just seventeen were aged eighteen or over while the remainder
were aged seventeen or under and so were at least a year, perhaps
two years, off being sent on active service. The solution, born of
clear annoyance, was to enlist them into the Navy where recruits
could be taken on as young as fourteen, and where a lad could
legitimately be sent on active service at sixteen. Permission to
make this transfer was given in a War Office letter dated 10
October 1915, suggesting also that a Naval Recruiting Officer be
on hand 'at the time they are discharged, so that the man may be
enlisted on the spot'.

As a sign of the army's official disapproval of fraudulent enlistment, regulations were imposed maintaining that no under-age
soldier was to be released until he was 'in possession of sufficient
money to defray the cost of his journey home'. That was all well
and good, but the army was cutting off its nose to spite its face.
A lad under seventeen would only cost the army further sums in
training, accommodation and food, on top of the necessary vacci-
nations and inoculations. What was the point of keeping him
until he had been paid enough money to get himself home, other
than to serve as an exemplary warning to other would-be under-
age recruits?

On 15 September 1915, a letter was received by the
commanding officer of the 13th Scottish Rifles ordering him
to discharge No. 20187 Private Thomas Bambrick who had
turned sixteen two weeks before. The CO was reminded of the
regulations as amended by Army Order 402: Bambrick would
stay put until he had enough money to get home. The problem was that Bambrick was not anywhere near home; he was at
Maida Barracks, Aldershot and the cost of getting him home to
Glasgow was thirty-six shillings, five weeks' wages if nothing
was deducted for such things as breakages or for allowances paid
to his family.

News of the delay infuriated Bambrick's parents who pointed
out that the army had taken their son south: 'You took him to

Aldershot,' wrote Mr Bambrick, 'and you will surely have to bring him back again.' Mrs Bambrick was already angry. Her son's allotment to his mother had been stopped on the discovery of his age, and the book in which each week's allotment was noted had been withdrawn by the paymaster in Hamilton, Scotland. As Bambrick was still being paid, the money was presumably being set aside to pay for his ticket home.

> I have kept all the correspondence between us and as sure as I don't get a satisfactory answer to this I will write direct to Headquarters in London where I will surely get satisfaction. In conclusion there will not be a penny paid for my son's return. You are responsible for his return home to Sydney Street and I will expect him soon. Yours truly [Mr] W Bambrick.

Major Thompson, Adjutant of the 13th Scottish Rifles, wrote to the authorities asking if he could issue a free railway warrant 'forthwith' in order to get the boy off his hands, but his request was refused; regulations were to be obeyed and common sense ignored.

From detailed examination of the surviving records, it is certain that the army discharged or held back more under-age boys than it ever sent overseas, and to an unquantifiable but significant extent this was the result of appeals, either polite or vociferous, from parents.

Yet, to be fair to the army, how was it to know for certain that Private Joe Bloggs had lied on his enlistment papers, six or perhaps twelve months before? When Nellie Kings, distraught that her son had gone to France aged sixteen, wrote to the War Office, she added revealingly, 'We naturally thought so young a lad would be kept for home service, even though in build and health he has the appearance of a man.' Her son had enlisted in May 1915 and had gone to the firing line, to the family's 'utter astonishment and grief'.

Even so, it is sometimes hard to imagine how similar cases of a well-built but under-age boy being sent overseas did not receive closer scrutiny regardless of respectable height and an adequate chest measurement. Private Edward Barnett was of 'good' physical development according to his enlistment papers and was sent out with a draft of men to join the 20th Manchester Regiment in December 1915. He lasted nearly four months on the Western Front before he was brought home. He was born on 17 February 1902 and was therefore only thirteen when he went overseas.

In spite of the efforts of Sir Arthur Markham and the parents he supported, young lads were still enlisting, being sent overseas and facing the horrors of trench life; at no time on the Western Front was their youth and their courage more poignantly shown than, a month later, in one of the major battles of the war, the offensive at Loos.

7

The Attack

JESUS MARY AND JOSEPH
PRAY FOR HIM
AMEN

7937 Private Stephen Pepler
11th Royal Fusiliers

Killed in Action 1 September 1915, aged 17

IT WAS GENERALLY RUMOUR that first alerted soldiers to a forth-coming attack. Men looked for signs: subtle changes in routine, a longer time in rest, a greater emphasis on battle training, perhaps better food. Confirmation came when they were taken to see a battle plan laid out in model form, showing natural features, trench lines and machine-gun positions. They might not know when the battle would take place, but they knew it was coming. A visit from the brigadier to announce the attack would coincide with more rigorous training and orders for the men to pay special attention to cleaning rifles and ammunition, while specialists such as bombers, signalmen and machine-gunners ensured that all their equipment was in full working order.

The reaction to such news was usually silence and numbness. Most men could not help looking round, knowing that, regardless of success or failure, this would be the end for someone. Private fears grew: a number always believed that they could never face the bayonet, others that they would not be able to go over the top.

All feared the prospect of being mortally wounded, stranded in pain and alone in no-man's-land.

Inevitably, the incidence of sickness grew in the day or two before the attack, but the medical officer, attuned to every ploy in the book, gave most men short shrift, prescribing 'M & D' – medicine and duty. The medicine was usually no more than a pill taken from one of the squared-off and numbered compartments in his medical box. The No. 9 pill, a very mild laxative, was used as a virtual placebo, and the men knew that there was no escape on 'medical grounds'.

Before going up to the line, there was a chance to receive Holy Communion, then to fill in a field service postcard or, if they were very fortunate, write a letter home using one of the army's 'green envelopes'. These allowed the correspondent the right, on his honour, to send a personal letter with the knowledge that his own platoon officer would not censor the contents. Addresses would be exchanged, if they had not been already, with friends who would write in the event of one of their number being killed. Battle order was commanded, which entailed the men handing in their large packs and greatcoats to the quartermaster, carrying only their small haversacks into action. Two days' rations were handed out, along with extra ammunition and bombs as well as picks or shovels that could be used to dig in after an advance. Private business was attended to. Cash was pooled to keep it from the battlefield scavengers who searched the pockets of the dead. The survivors would divide the spoils between them, not as a reward for coming through unscathed, but as a gift from the dead and wounded, a departing commiseration for those whose war was set to continue.

Waiting to go into action was harrowing for everyone, but for boy soldiers there was an extra dimension to the tension that was hard to ignore. It tantalized the boy, gnawing away in the recesses of his mind, offering hope, yet promising long-term guilt: it was the chance to escape the carnage by using his age.

Second Lieutenant Charles Carrington, having himself enlisted under age, well understood the fears of a boy. His battalion, the 1/5th Royal Warwicks, was due to take part in an attack and he had been working feverishly to get everything ready. The companies had been assembled in less than two hours from the initial order to move and the battalion was about to get on its way. The sense of responsibility and duty concentrated Charles's mind and he was surprised at how little fear he felt.

One little incident reassured me still more. An NCO came up and said that Private Eliot wished to speak to me. The man was a mere boy, whom I had known in England . . . I found him crouched against a chalk-heap almost in tears. He looked younger than ever. 'I don't want to go over the plonk,' he flung at me in the shamelessness of terror, 'I'm only seventeen, I want to go home.' The other men standing round avoided my eye and looked sympathetic rather than disgusted.

'Can't help that now, my lad,' said I in my martinet voice. I was nineteen years and three months old myself. 'You should have thought of that when you enlisted. Didn't you give your age as nineteen then?'

'Yes, sir. But I'm not, I'm only – well, I'm not quite seventeen really, sir.'

'Well, it's too late now,' I said, 'you'll have to see it through and I'll do what I can for you when we come out.' I slapped him on the shoulder. 'You go with the others. You'll be all right when you get started. This is the worst part of it, this waiting, and we're none of us enjoying it. Come along, now, jump to it.'

And he seemed to take heart again.

In such circumstances, any decision by the officer in command to send a boy out of the line was a personal one, and he was well within his rights to refuse if they were about to go into action. The boy had lied about his age, and turning round at such a late stage to profess his true age might be met with sympathy but little leniency. There was, after all, no way of actually verifying the age of a boy, other than to look and gauge from his face, begrimed and mud-spattered as it well could be, concealing the softer features of youth. As a unit was about to go into action, it was difficult if not impossible to do anything anyway; much better for him to go over the top and sort out the problem later, should it remain to be resolved.

In the hours before an attack, few men would be able to sleep, other than occasionally nodding off. Wide awake, they might remember loved ones back home, or think of nothing in an attempt to empty the mind. There were few whose throats did not dry and whose stomachs did not turn over at the thought of the morning. In a few hours' time, they would have to fix bayonets and face the front wall of the trench, waiting for the signal to scale the ladders on to the parapet and advance.

Thomas Hope, the once enthusiastic sixteen-year-old, wrote:

I have one trump card – my age – but I can't summon sufficient courage to make use of it. I am torn between my natural fears and my anxiety to play the game. The others are in a different position altogether. They must go on; illness even, feigned or otherwise, would avail them little now. They are doomed as far as seeing this attack through is concerned, and they know it. When the door behind us is locked, it is easy enough to go forward, there is nothing else to do, but I, holding the key to safety, shrink from exposing my fear to my comrades by opening it, although every nerve and fibre in my body is crying out to me to avail myself of this opportunity to preserve my life.

It was possible to cope with despair when a soldier could resign himself to his fate and prepare accordingly. Where there was indecision, a possible exit, then that hope, however tenuous, could be torture. As the hours, then minutes, dragged inter-minably towards zero hour, there was plenty of time to think, to calculate the chances of survival and to wonder if everyone else was as scared. In an attack, comrades ultimately depended on each other, and there was a steely determination not to let anyone down, least of all the rest of the platoon. Successful train-ing instilled regimental pride and this could not be squandered easily – a subliminal thought perhaps, but one that was influen-tial nevertheless.

George White was going over the top, cavalry style. No trenches for him, but a mounted foray. His regiment, the 2nd Dragoon Guards, had been held in reserve during an infantry offensive, but had now been called forward, ready to go and exploit an expected breakthrough. As they waited, unmounted, they stood at their horses' heads, holding the reins and talking quietly, each reassur-ing the other. George said his prayers and then began to think about how he could be dead quite soon.

> I had no such thing as premonition and never thought I would be killed. On the other hand, I knew that it was quite possible, and got to wondering what it would be like in heaven. I could not comprehend existing forever in that ideal place. I suppose I considered I was fighting for a righteous cause and therefore if killed in action would, like a Red Indian who died fighting, go to the 'Happy Hunting Ground'. Funnily, it never entered my mind that if fatally wounded I might go to the other place, and therefore gave no thought to possible conditions there. Nor did I give any thought to the possibility that I might be badly wounded and perhaps maimed for life.

As they waited, George became aware of a flurry of activity to his left, where the Dragoons' C squadron was lined up. As he watched, he saw a young trooper ride forward from the lines to speak with some officers.

He seemed to be having a long discussion. Eventually, he rode back in the direction of our base and word filtered through to us that he had just informed his troop officer that he was only seventeen years of age. Apparently, he had lost his nerve and did not wish to take any further part in that day's operation. I suppose the officer concerned had no option but to report the matter to his seniors and they were then obliged to withdraw the man from the line.

To George, who was yet to pass his sixteenth birthday, the option of pulling out from the fight was anathema. 'I could just not understand why a young man should act as he had, with a chance to get into cavalry action in the offing.' The waiting had been difficult and the boy had seemingly played his 'trump card'. He was fortunate to receive a sympathetic hearing.

Honour, tradition, the threat of punishment, but above all comradeship forced men to face the unimaginable. Even so, it was a remarkable feat for any man to overcome natural instincts of self-preservation and go forward. In this regard, officers and NCOs with their burden of responsibility had an advantage over privates. The men serving under an officer were not encouraged to think independently but to react to orders and carry them out to the full. The officers who gave those orders had an enormous duty of care to the men under their command, and to break faith with them was a decision few would ever countenance. While there were certainly cases in which inadequate officers were 'quietly' removed to Britain, there was an acknowledgement too that they faced onerous pressures, and suffered disproportionate casualties, especially among junior, frequently teenaged, officers. Inevitably such pressures had to find an outlet. During the course of the war, of the 35,313 men court-martialled for drunkenness, one in twenty-five was an officer. To put this figure into context, fewer than one in 300 courts martial held abroad for offences such as cowardice, desertion, self-inflicted wounds or quitting a post were lodged against officers.

Before the attack went in, a bombardment would be laid down on the enemy front, to hit the support lines and so curtail the enemy's ability to re-supply and reinforce his front line; this bombardment would be lifted once the attack had begun. As the war progressed, different artillery techniques were developed not just to wear down the enemy but also to protect those about to advance. Then, as zero hour was reached, there was a signal given by an officer, usually a sharp whistle, followed by a mad scramble up the scaling ladders and out into no-man's-land to form up in lines. Enemy machine guns were always trained on the parapet and, mindful of that fact, some men raced up the ladders, preferring a bullet in the leg to one in the head or chest. Others chose to hang back for a second, judging the sweep of the enemy's machine gun, advancing the moment the bullets passed overhead. Everyone had, or imagined he had, a ploy to survive, although for most the moment of going, as described by one veteran, was akin to being dropped into ice-cold water.

The first offensive in which the regular, territorial and new Kitchener Army units would all play a part was the Battle of Loos, launched in September 1915. This was part of a wider three-pronged assault undertaken by the Allies in late summer to finally break the front and drive the Germans out of northern France. The Allied offensive had been agreed after much discussion in late July and involved a coordinated attack against the northern and southern flanks of the German Army, with the French attacking on two fronts, a small thrust immediately to the south of a proposed British attack and another larger assault in the Artois region. The British would simultaneously attack in the industrial and coalmining area of Lens.

The French, who had carried the greater burden of the war so far, were keen that Britain should commit herself to further offensives. If British troops took the initiative, the enemy's forces could be kept on the back foot, thwarting any ideas they might have of renewing offensive actions of their own. The Allied attack would, for the first time, give some of Kitchener's New Army divisions that had recently arrived in France a chance to cut their teeth in a major offensive.

The British commander-in-chief, Sir John French, and General Douglas Haig, commanding First Army, looked at the proposed area over which the British would attack and did not like what they saw: flat country that was covered in industrial workings, predominantly mines and their associated slag heaps. Dotted nearby were a number of heavily fortified villages protected by deep belts of barbed wire; it was country that the Germans would find easy to defend. Yet, notwithstanding the concerns of those at the front, Kitchener was keen for Britain to show France that she was willing to fight, and, after a meeting with the French C.-in-C. Joseph Joffre, ordered French to proceed with preparations, emphasizing that Britain had to do her utmost to help her ally even if that meant heavy casualties. On the ground, Haig would be directed to deliver the assault on a seven-mile front between Loos and La Bassée. Six divisions, numbering some 75,000 men, would take part in the opening attack.

A preliminary bombardment, the largest in the war to date, would begin on 21 September and would pulverize the enemy line until the morning of the attack. Firepower would, weather permitting, be backed up by the use of poison gas. This was the first time it would be used by the British and, with luck, would create havoc in the enemy trenches as British troops went over the top.

In preparation, the men were shown a model of the proposed battleground with earth, coal, bricks and chalk to represent hills, slagheaps, houses and trenches. Certain landmarks were already familiar. Heaps of coal, known as *crassiers* in French, could be seen from the British line, as could mine workings, including in

Loos itself the huge twin pylon linked by a walkway that the men named after London's famous Tower Bridge. Smaller idiosyncratic features also stood out, including the Lone Tree, a large cherry tree close to the German lines, which had somehow contrived to survive even with shrapnel and bullets embedded in its trunk.

Despite the initial reservations, confidence grew that the enemy defences would crumble under a sustained bombardment, with any surviving Germans overcome by the cloud of gas. It was known that the protective chemicals impregnating enemy gas masks were effective for only thirty minutes, after which they would need to be re-dipped. If the gas was released forty minutes before the infantry attacked, they should find the Germans overcome. So long as there were few casualties among the British infantry, they would quickly be ready to assault the enemy's reserves, while massed British cavalry waited to exploit the anticipated breakthrough.

Any discharge of gas would require accurate weather forecasts and constant monitoring of the wind direction. A final decision on the precise time for release could not be taken until a few hours before the attack. Even then, when it was taken, the news that the gas would be released at 5.30 a.m. was not communicated to commanding officers in the line until, in some cases, an hour beforehand.

Great coordination was required to bring supplies of ammunition and bombs into the line, as well as 1,500 gas cylinders that would need to be carefully positioned. Long iron pipes were also brought forward, through which the gas would be discharged into no-man's-land. Finally, to cut down the distance over which the infantry would attack, assembly trenches were dug, producing long white streaks of freshly turned chalk running laterally across the countryside. Progress was going well for all to see, Germans included; worryingly, they were observed displaying notice boards above their trench pointing out that they knew an attack was imminent and the date it would be launched.

The build-up to the attack was described by one of the under-age soldiers who took part. Private Len Thomas was serving with the 13th Siege Battery, Royal Garrison Artillery, on a 9.2-inch howitzer. He had enlisted at seventeen and had been serving abroad for five months. Although warned just before leaving for France that no one was to keep a diary, he – like Ernest Steele – had nevertheless written a daily account of his war in a small notebook.

21st More shelling of German lines at night. No 4 Gun dropped shells on cross-roads expecting to catch reinforcements.

22nd Best day's shooting since Festubert. Bombarded trenches and blew machine guns and trenches to blazes and also houses. Brigadier General very pleased with battery's shooting. Congratulates officers and men . . .

23rd Bombardment continuing. Trenches heavily shelled. At night called out on ammunition fatigue at 1 a.m. Shelled cross-roads.

24th Still on trenches. German lines on the ground [flattened]. Cavalry expected to charge. Infantry have orders read out to them about the charge. Gas to be used.

Private George Adams was understandably nervous. He had enlisted in March and, after fourteen weeks' training, had been sent abroad as part of a draft to a regular battalion, the 1st Middlesex. He had been in France for two months and had been rapidly accli-matizing to trench life. With the news that he was going to go over the top for the first time, nerves took hold. The battalion was to attack the Prussian Guard, they were informed, and the men were to 'give them the bayonet'. At sixteen, he was well aware of his lack of height and strength and was not particularly encour-aged by the idea of 'running up against a bloke armed with the same tool as myself and standing about six feet four inches in height and weighing about eighteen stone'.

The night before the attack, torrential rain poured down on the troops moving into position. With so much transport on the roads, progress was slow and it took battalions many hours to arrive. One boy struggling forward was sixteen-year-old Dick Trafford, a private in the 1/9th King's Liverpools, a Territorial battalion. When Dick enlisted with his mining friends, he thought little about what war meant, and although he was kept back when the battalion sailed for France in March, he soon joined them when, in August, he was included on a draft. He was not the youngest boy on the ship. George Woolfall was also sixteen, a couple of months younger than Dick, while other lads, such as Glenny Hale and Robert Carr, were only a matter of months older. This would be the first time over the top for all of them, news of which would later be a great worry to their parents back home. George Woolfall was the exception. His mother was already dead and his father, serving with the 1st King's Liverpools, was already in France.

George had enlisted in January 1915 but, ever since the battalion left without him, he had been more in than out of trouble, with a series of charges laid against him. He had been absent without leave, had broken out of billets and on more than one occasion refused to obey orders. He had also been charged with being insolent, and had absented himself from parades. This bundle of trouble was finally sent abroad and since then his behaviour had changed for the better and he had committed no further offences. His wish to serve abroad having been granted, he would go over the top with the battalion. Whether he was aware of the fact or not, he would be fighting less than three miles from his father, Richard Woolfall, who was himself preparing to go over the top close to the La Bassée Canal with his battalion, part of the 2nd Division.

Dick Trafford was full of apprehension at the thought of going over the top but he was excited, too. The day, however, did not start well.

We were going up in the early hours of the morning. It was dark and we passed through a battery of guns just as it opened up to start the final bombardment for the attack. I was near one of the guns and as it fired the noise burst my eardrum, blood squirting out of it, and I was deaf straight away. The sergeant took one of the little dressings we always carried in case we were wounded and packed my ear with cotton wool to plug it, and of course we were expecting to go over the top in an hour or two, so I would have to go over the top with my ear already wounded. I wasn't allowed to turn back. There was only one way – forward.

The final frantic British artillery barrage was designed as much to cut the enemy wire as further to destroy their trenches. The weather, which had been foul all night, began to abate at first light and with it the breeze that would be needed to push the gas towards the German lines. Frantic messages were sent back to headquarters asking for further instructions, but the decision to proceed had already been taken and the order came back that the cylinders must be opened on time. It was clear to the gas officers positioned in the front line that in places the poisonous cloud would drift back on to the troops. The prognosis proved correct. When the gas was released at the northern end of the attack, the cloud lingered in no-man's-land, then, to the horror of the front-line troops, it began to drift back towards the British lines.

The troops attacked at 6.30 a.m., and at the southern end met with considerable success. The breeze here was strong enough to take the gas over to the German front line and the attacking divisions stormed the German trenches with such success that within two hours they had entered Loos and were fighting in the town, overwhelming all before them. Surviving Germans were seen to run away, followed by jubilant Scotsmen of the 15th Division. All appeared to be going well, and such tangible evidence of success helped build a sense of euphoria.

Len Thomas's battery had opened fire at 3 a.m. The infantry had gone over, and in his diary he noted the good news filtering back from the front.

Infantry charge and didn't meet much resistance. Germans demoralized with heavy shelling. First line easily taken. Prisoners captured easily. Rough looking lot of villains. Plenty of our wounded back laughing and joking. Mostly London Terriers. Everyone in the best of spirits. Chaps wounded in three places joking with German helmets on their heads. By 8 [a.m.] infantry take Loos and press on. Refugees come over from Loos and tell terrible tales about the Germans. English 'tres bonne'. Field artillery move up. Cavalry reported on the go.

The success near Loos was in contrast to utter devastation five miles away to the north. George Adams had been lucky to survive, and he knew it. Days later, he wrote to tell his parents of his experiences.

On Saturday morning we went over the top and out of 700 who went over, 180 came back. I was one of the 180. It was not a real attack, it was a sacrifice to let the French get through on our right . . . We sent our gas over at ten past six, and at twenty past we went over and I am sorry to say that nearly all the fellows I knew have gone – and, Dad, Jack Badrick, the bricky who used to work for Harry Rooney, has gone as well. I turned round to speak to him and I saw him lying dead, shot through the head. The attack was a mess up from start to finish. We got over the top and walked across behind our gas, and then the Germans sent their liquid fire into the gas and set fire to it and when it cleared they were standing on the parapet in their shirtsleeves waiting for us.

The Germans, anticipating the use of gas, had prepared their defences. No one, George included, got further than 100 yards from their front-line trench, cut down by withering machine-gun fire.

Supporting the Middlesex Regiment was the 2nd Battalion Royal Welch Fusiliers, which included the poet Robert Graves. According to Graves, the bombardment, for all the gunners' endeavours, surprised everyone by its relative slackness compared to the firing that had preceded it. Then, half a mile from the firing line, Graves reports hearing

> a distant cheer, confused crackle of rifle fire, yells, heavy shelling on our front line, more shouts and yells, and a continuous rattle of machine guns. After a few minutes, lightly wounded men of the Middlesex came stumbling down Maison Rouge Alley [a communication trench] to the dressing station. I stood at the junction of the siding and the Alley.
>
> 'What's happened? What's happened?' I asked.
>
> 'Bloody balls-up,' was the most detailed answer I could get.

A little to the south, the 2nd Gordon Highlanders had gone over the top at 6.30 a.m. in the direction of the heavily fortified German village of Hulluch. Their gas helmets had proved of limited use against the gas that enveloped them as they attacked, and they found it hard to breathe. Matters were not helped by the sheer weight of equipment that they had to carry. Each man had been issued with two days' rations, 220 rounds of small-arms ammunition, a pick or a shovel and two sandbags, and they had laboured in crossing 550 yards of open ground to reach the enemy line. It had been tough going, and they were thankful to have met only light resistance, finding the German front line almost empty. After a break, they had been ordered on to the German support line where they had had to fight before digging in to await further orders.

Among those who waited was the fatherly figure of Corporal Charlie Parke. He had been out in France for nearly a year, and

was now involved in his umpteenth action. He had joined the
army aged sixteen and now considered himself an 'old sweat' at
twenty-two, a view endorsed after he saw the latest crop of reinforcements to join the battalion. It was plain from their faces that
they were young and Charlie had sympathy for them all.

> One young-faced newcomer, no more than sixteen years of
> age, started chatting nervously to me; dark-haired and of aver-
> age height and slender build, it transpired he hailed from the
> Birmingham area. He was clearly on edge. I dwelt on the thought
> how many young kids were seen now in the front line, all having
> lied about their ages . . . These kids were pitched straight into this
> catastrophic carnage and the stark fear in their eyes reflected my
> own terror at the First Battle of Ypres.

Like Charlie Parke, Ernest Fitchett of the 1st South Wales Borderers
was an experienced campaigner – he had been over the top at least
twice before, and had already been wounded – but he was only
seventeen years old. He had enlisted soon after the outbreak of
war and had been sent to France in October 1914, when he had
been bayoneted during hand-to-hand fighting. He was back in
France early the following year, and on 9 May had taken part in
a disastrous attack at Aubers Ridge, when his battalion had been
annihilated. At Loos his battalion was placed in support, moving
into old French trenches in the early hours of the morning in front
of the village of Vermelles. There they awaited the outcome of
the initial attack by the 1st and 2nd Brigades before being called
forward, as Ernest remembered.

> We sent over great clouds of gas and when we thought it had
> taken effect, we mounted the parapet but only to be met by a
> perfect hail of bullets + shrapnel under which we had to advance
> over 1,000 yards of open ground, and when we got about half way
> across, we were obliged to stop, for the machine gun, rifle, and

shrapnel fire was so heavy that it was impossible to advance any further just then. As we laid there we could see other regiments advancing on our right and left, and saw them take the first line but we could not advance until both flanks had advanced and cut them off.

The 1/9th King's Liverpools had been awaiting instructions from early morning. They had been held in support with the London Scottish on their left, the first Territorial unit that had seen action in France in October 1914. They formed part of a two-battalion reserve behind the attacking battalions of the 1st Division. At 9.10 the order was sent to attack but it was nearly two hours before it arrived and a further hour before they were ready to move forward. The Germans, suspecting an assault, called down artillery on the trenches opposite and had already caused casualties. Dick Trafford recalled:

It was just one noise, one big noise, the guns of both sides banging away at each other. Well, you could always see the shells bursting 'cos you could feel them, you could feel the shrapnel falling. There were no steel helmets in those days, and the shells burst close to the trenches and these bits of shrapnel were dropping around you and bullets flying past. You could feel the whistle of the bullets.

It was obvious that the trenches directly in front of their line of attack were still full of Germans, and the commanding officer of the London Scottish repeatedly asked for a further bombardment of enemy trenches.

Private Alec Stringer of the London Scottish was on tenterhooks. Barely a year earlier he had been enjoying the sun on Australia's Bondi Beach, but when war broke out he had cut short his tour and patriotically returned home to enlist. He had stretched a point with the recruitment sergeant in March 1915 when he had claimed to be nineteen years and eleven months when he was only fifteen years and eleven months, but that did not seem to worry anyone. He had turned sixteen in April and embarked for France five weeks before Dick Trafford in July. Two months later and here they both were, neighbours on a battlefield, both of them soaked through, cold and covered in mud. They watched the gas attack in the early hours and witnessed the terrible effects when the wind veered round, sending the gas back on to the men in the front trenches, choking some who came streaming back, their faces yellow, and the brass tunic buttons turned green. Now they were due to move forward; the London Scottish were about to attack with the King's Liverpools filling the gap between the 1st and 2nd Brigades. The London Scottish's right would rest on the Lone Tree, the Liverpools' left on the same famous landmark. Alec was always to remember that as they advanced past the 1st Battalion Black Watch, they were cheered on their way, while Dick remembered:

We went over in sections, and as soon as the German machine guns started, we dropped down. You feel like in a race, you're waiting to start, waiting for the signal, then the sergeant would shout, 'Right, lads,' and you're over the top. It wasn't always nice getting out of a trench because you didn't have footholds or any steps, you got over the best way you could and then you ran like hell to get to the German trenches as quick as you can. I remember thinking that if my time came I hoped it was a bullet and let it be sudden; I never wanted to be a cripple or to be robbed of my senses.

In a sense you relied on the Germans to give you orders, it was a case of hide and seek, you drop in what we call the prone position, you're on your face, then when the German machine guns stop firing for a moment you're up and as fast as you can go towards the German wire. If a man dropped, he dropped, that was it, whether they were killed or not you were not allowed to stop. You could hear men calling, 'I'm wounded, I'm wounded, will you come over here?' It was the stretcher-bearers' job to come along in due course and pick them up, but there were some horrible sights all the same, men with their arms hanging half off, some with their legs badly wounded; nasty casualties.

The London Scottish had suffered severe losses getting to the German wire, which remained uncut in many places, but the enemy's position became increasingly untenable as men from other units began to surround them. The Germans' ammunition was running low and they were threatened with annihilation. Alec Stringer was there and watched while attempts were made to get the Germans to surrender. These attempts failed. Then:

While lying out in front of the German barbed wire and looking to our left we found to our amazement the Royal Field Artillery was galloping up the road from Vermelles towards Hulluch and the German front line. On swerving to the left, they unlimbered the guns and started to bombard the German front line and the uncut wire in the area in which we were to attack. Unfortunately, many horses and men were killed in this operation but it was a sight never to be forgotten. As a consequence, the Germans realized that they would eventually have to surrender: a German officer with 400 men surrendered to the regiment.

The marvel of so many men surrendering at once was commented on by everyone who was close by, including Ernest Fitchett:

When they found that they were defeated, they all walked out of their trenches with their hands above their heads, several hundred of them in all, we then went on and took their second line quite easily but they hung on to their third like glue.

Just as astonished was Dick Trafford.

When we got to the German line, the whole lot gave themselves up – they came over with their hands up. They were marched down together with one or two of our fellas, as they would have done on parade in their own regiment, amazing.

It was early afternoon when the surrender came. The Germans at this point in the line had held out for around eight hours. The net result of the morning's attacks in the centre of the line had been satisfactory, if costly. A hole had been punched through the enemy's defences that they were frantically trying to repair. Although the attack a couple of miles to the north had failed almost completely, there had been considerable initial success to the south, where the gas had been blown across the German trenches; not only had Loos fallen quickly but Scotsmen of the 15th Division had been seen to charge up and down the far side of Hill 70, the best part of a mile beyond the town.

The fighting in the town of Loos was over by mid-morning, when all that was left was mopping up last-ditch resistance. Snipers were still active and casualties were being brought into a first-aid post set up by a medical officer of the Black Watch. He was treating the wounded in a house belonging to a Madame Moreau, one of many inhabitants who, amazingly, still occupied the town during the fighting. She lived there with her seventeen-year-old daughter Emilienne, and the pair of them spent the day helping to bring the wounded in, boiling up coffee and preparing food. Two German snipers, lodged in a house next door, had been firing at stretcher-bearers, and in her annoyance Emilienne seized a pistol from an officer. As soldiers attempted to dislodge the snipers, the teenager went round the back of the house and fired twice to cause a diversion, allowing the soldiers to enter and clear the building. She is reputed to have said, 'C'est fini,' as she returned, handing the pistol back to an astounded officer. Two months later, Emilienne Moreau was awarded the Croix de Guerre and the Military Cross.

Above and left: Private Walter Williams enlisted in the 8th Northumberland Fusiliers aged sixteen. He served on the Somme in 1916 at seventeen and was wounded in September 1918. The bottom image was taken after just two years' service at the front; the strain of war is etched on his face.

Above: Alfred Anderson *(front row, arms folded)* on summer camp with the Territorials just days before war broke out. To his right are his friends Jim Ballantyne and John McKenzie. All three boys went to France at the end of October 1914. Alfred was badly wounded in the neck in 1916 and John also survived the war, but Jim was killed.

Left: Father and son pose for a picture during the patriotic pre-war years. The son has all the trappings of a pukka soldier, making Boy Service his likely future.

Left: Fifteen-year-old Philip Lister's application for a temporary commission. A year after its approval he was on the Somme serving as an Acting Captain. Lister was killed on the opening day of the Arras offensive in April 1917.

"WHICH IS THE WAY TO THE WAR GUVNER?"

Right: This postcard was widely reproduced for sale during the war. Lord Kitchener himself was door-stepped on occasion by eager boys many years below enlistment age.

OFFICER (to boy of thirteen who, in his effort to get taken on as a bugler, has given his age as sixteen): "Do you know where boys go who tell lies?"
APPLICANT: "To the Front, sir."

Left: All too often, lying proved the most effective passport to service on the front line, as illustrated by this 1915 *Punch* cartoon.

Above: A newspaper advertisement placed by the father of Cecil Withers in *The Times*, dated 10 March 1916. On receipt of this proof that his father would not remove him from the army, Cecil gave them his real name.

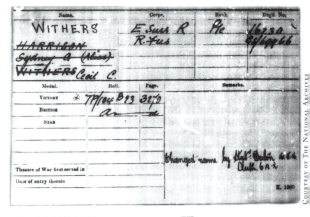

Right: The microfiche record of Cecil's medal entitlement as held by The National Archives in Kew, the false name that he gave the army crossed out but still visible.

Left: September 1916 and sixteen-year-old Private Hunt looks through a trench periscope opposite the German lines near Beaumont Hamel, on the Somme.

Courtesy of Anthony Battersby

Temporary Commissions in His Majesty's Army.

2,000 Junior Officers (unmarried) are immediately required in consequence of the increase of the Regular Army.

TERMS OF SERVICE.

To serve with the Regular Army until the war is concluded. Ages, 17 to 30.

An allowance of £20 will be made for uniform and of £5 15s. for equipment.

HOW TO OBTAIN HIS MAJESTY'S COMMISSION.

Cadets or ex-Cadets of the University Training Corps or Members of a University should apply to their Commanding Officers, or to the Authorities of their University. Other young men of good general education should apply in person to the Officer Commanding the nearest depot. Full information can be obtained by written application to The Secretary, War Office.

God Save the King.

Above: Second Lieutenant Reginald Battersby aged fifteen, shortly after he was commissioned into the 11th East Lancashire Regiment – known as the Accrington Pals. At sixteen he led his platoon into action on 1 July 1916 and was shot in the leg while engaging a German machine gun. In 1917 he was wounded again in the leg, which was subsequently amputated.

Left: The appeal made in *The Times* of 19 August for young men of the right upbringing and education to apply for a temporary commission as an officer.

COURTESY OF JOHN MARKHAM

20 Buckley Road
Broadesbury. N.W.
12th Oct. 1915

Sir Arthur Markham,
    Dear Sir
        Re. your question in the
House to-day, it may interest
you to know that my Nephew, who
was 10 years of age in June Last,
was enticed to join the forces, & was
advised by the Recruiting Sergeant,
to falsify his age.
    His Parent, whose only other
son, had already enlisted, applied
without result, for his release, & he
is now, still kept, tho' his employer
has also applied for his release.
    Should you require further
particulars I shall be most happy
to obtain definite & full details.
    His name & address is
Eric Truscott, of 19 Baker Avenue
Harrow,
        Yours Respectfully,
            John K. Pearce

COURTESY OF GEORGE FLINT

Top Left: Sir Arthur Markham, Midlands industrialist and Liberal MP. Markham fought for over a year to secure the release of under-age soldiers serving at home and abroad.

Top Right: One of the few surviving letters written to Sir Arthur Markham by a relative of an under-age soldier, appealing for his help. The MP received as many as 300 letters a day from distraught parents.

Left: Former Private John Flint *(sitting)* was a constituent of Sir Arthur Markham's. Aged fifteen, he enlisted in the 11th Sherwood Foresters and went to France to serve in the trenches. Sir Arthur campaigned vigorously for his discharge and eventually he was sent home. This picture was taken just after the war.

SOLDIER OF 14.

BOY IN SAME REGIMENT AS HIS FATHER.

Hundreds of boys of 15 have enlisted, but a case has just become known of a lad of 14 who grasped an opportunity to enter the Army. "Isn't it time you young men did something for your country?" asked a recruiting sergeant of a group outside a music-hall some time ago. "Rather," said a sturdy lad named Priest (aged 14), who looked up eagerly. "How old are you?" "Sixteen," said Priest. "Sixteen!" A fine young man like you would pass for nineteen anywhere. Come along!" And young Priest went. He is now a private in the same regiment as his father, who is 41 years of age. Priest's old schoolfellows have sent him a 5s. War Loan voucher.

PRIVATE PRIEST.

Above: Fourteen-year-old Private Priest as featured in the *Daily Mail*. The newspaper ran short articles on the youngest recruits and appeared to condone the enlistment of under-age boys.

THE LITTLE CORPORAL.

Christopher Paget Clarke, an Exmouth lad who enlisted last year, is only fifteen, and already a lance-corporal. He is now with his regiment in India.

Above: Lance Corporal Christopher Paget-Clark enlisted in 1914 into the Devonshire Regiment. His proud father sent the boy's picture to several national newspapers in response to the Priest article.

Above: Vic Cole training with the signals section of the 7th Royal West Kent Regiment. In September 1914, aged seventeen, he enlisted with his sixteen-year-old friend George Pulley. Vic was wounded twice during the war.

Above: Frank Lindley enlisted at fourteen, hoping to avenge the death of his elder brother early on in the war. Two years later Frank went over the top on 1 July 1916.

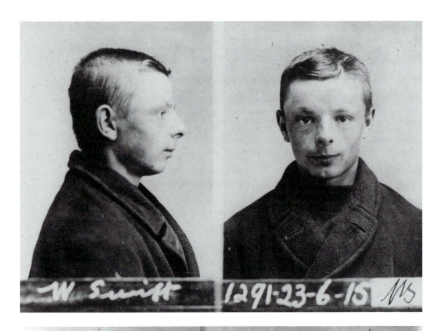

Top and above: William Swift *(top)*, sentenced to three years' youth detention for theft, was released on licence into the Army in 1916. He liked the life and proved to be a good athlete before being sent to France under age; he was killed in action in 1917. Thomas Clarke *(above)* was also sent to borstal for theft but was later allowed to join the Army. He was sent to France at eighteen and deserted, being court-martialled, sentenced to death and reprieved. He was killed in action on the Somme in November 1916 and is buried in New Munich Trench Cemetery close to where he fell.

News of the success around Loos had to be exploited quickly. Haig required the reserves to attack in order to keep up the momentum, but they were nowhere to be seen. The reserves, comprising two New Army Divisions, the 21st and 24th, and the newly formed Guards Division, were being held the best part of five miles behind the front line and under the command of Sir John French. Haig would have to appeal to the commander-in-chief to release the men, and French was worried about committing inexperienced troops to the fray unless a breakthrough was evident. The news from the front was good and consent eventually given, but not until well after 1 p.m. were the reserves placed at Haig's disposal, and then it was too late. The reserves, once ordered to move, would take many hours' hard slog to get into position, by which time the Germans would be able to reinforce their lines and even counter-attack. Nowhere had success been greater than at Hill 70, and even here the gains made were rapidly lost. The men of the 15th Scottish Division had been brought to a standstill on the reverse side of the mound by the rifle fire of the hastily reinforced German third-line trench. German gunners had then blazed away at the slope on which the Scotsmen lay helpless and now German counter-attacks were retaking the summit. Not only were the British losing the upper hand, they were handing it directly to the Germans. Instead of being ready to go at midday or early afternoon, the two divisions of New Army men were not in a position to attack until the following morning, and the delay was irreparable.

After the German surrender of their first and second lines around Hulluch, relative peace suddenly reigned over the battlefield in front of the village, to the extent that men could scamper around looking for souvenirs. Then at dusk, the London Scottish had been reorganized and pushed on a little further, as Alec Stringer recalled. 'We advanced up towards the Hulluch–Lens Road and D Company crossed over but could not hold it and had to come back over the road to join those of us that were left.'

The men finally dug in until relieved in the early hours of the morning. Returning to their old front line, a roll call was taken and Alec discovered that of his platoon only three men were left to answer their names.

During the hours of darkness, considerable confused fighting continued with the Germans launching several counter-attacks. Shortly before 10 p.m., the line held by the 2nd Gordons came under an increasingly well-directed bombardment, as Charlie Parke recalled.

The shelling was building up appreciably but there was no sign of movement from the other side; the usual pattern of German attacks involved an increasingly heavy barrage landing ever closer to the British line and, when it reached its maximum intensity, the German infantry would make its charge. The bombardment built up into a deafening crescendo but everyone still heard the 'alert' order from the Platoon Commander, an old sweat who might have had one or two shortcomings but whose vocal cords were never found wanting. To this order everyone responded immediately by mounting the ledge and fully manning the line; the enemy hadn't made a move but the fantastically heavy barrage meant the charge was probably only minutes away.

As the 2nd Gordons prepared to meet the German attack, Charlie remembered the sixteen-year-old boy he had allowed to rest in a small recess dug in the rear wall of the trench.

Suddenly I remembered the newest and youngest member of the section was still in the parados wall. 'How the hell could the kid sleep midst all that din?' I asked myself. 'Hey kid, get out here at the double!' I screamed, using every decibel at my command. Still no movement from behind the sandbag material; I stepped down quickly from the ledge. 'The kid'll be in trouble if he doesn't move fast,' the thought flashed through my mind as I reached for the coarse curtaining.

The sight I saw I just couldn't take in and for a split second was dumbstruck and, whatever I was, I was rarely at a loss for words. The lad was on his knees, his back to me, frantically tunnelling with his bare hands into the earth in a futile attempt to escape from the mayhem that was developing all around us. 'C'mon lad!' I shrieked, tugging at his tunic; the young soldier resisted with strength born of fear and all the time his two hands were clawing feverishly at mother earth. Blind panic, so terrifying to behold for even a hardened soldier, had not even allowed his common sense to select his entrenchment tool for the purpose. I forcibly grabbed him by the shoulders and pulled him back into the trench. The sight of that brave under-age boy lying on the duckboard shook me rigid. In less than half an hour, his entire head of hair had changed from close to black to virgin white; the horrendous sight was well-nigh unbelievable . . . The ravages of fear and terror had bleached his young looks in minutes and turned the boy into a frightful sight of half old and half young; everyone in the front line knew fear but to see it, visually, so stark and unhidden, was horrible.

The Gordons fought off the German counter-attack, the first of many that would eventually carpet the battlefield of Loos with bodies of friend and foe.

On the night of 25/26 September it had poured once again and brigades of the two New Army Divisions made their way forward into the fray. They were sodden, tired, hungry and heavily laden, and on their way into the line they were shelled and machine-gunned, causing casualties and confusion. Vague orders ensured that by the time morning broke, many New Army units were not where they were supposed to be. It was a recipe for disaster.

A new attack on Hill 70 would commence at 9 a.m. followed by renewed attacks around the village of Hulluch. A short bombardment hitting the German trenches on top would precede the assault but there were too few men to take and hold the Hill and, when the attack came, it was repulsed with heavy casualties. It was the story of the day: time and again attacks went in only to be beaten back; late orders, vague orders and even vaguer objectives created confusion, a situation compounded by the inexperience of many units attacking for the first time. Battalions that had already been mauled were called on to renew the offensive but had too few men to make a difference. Ernest Fitchett went into the attack again with the South Wales Borderers.

> We lost so many men, for three times in succession we charged at their lines and at last we broke through and advanced right into the village of Hulloch where we had to retire after some very fierce hand-to-hand fighting in which I lost my rifle and bayonet, and found a sword on a dead German officer. But we made another grand assault at dusk, and were fighting like tigers.

It was an impossible situation, even for experienced troops. Too often, men thrown into the attack had come up against the German line to find deep belts of uncut barbed wire with the ground in front swept by enemy machine-gun fire. Of the six New Army battalions that had attacked with the South Wales Borderers, over 2,500 were casualties by 12.30 p.m., only ninety minutes into the attack.

An hour later, and some surviving men of the New Army battalions were seen to retreat in disorder, casting away arms and equipment, much to the disgust of the regular units nearby. Ernest Fitchett wrote to his family.

> I daresay that you have read in the papers of our big attack and advance and how 'Kitchener's New Army' carried Hill 70. Well, it was not the New Army at all but the Old 1st Division that done the work and the New Army that got the praise.

He was rightly proud of his battalion, but after they were finally relieved later that night by men of the Guards Division, the numbers were greatly depleted. Ernest estimated that out of his brigade of four battalions, perhaps 3,500 strong, only around 850 were left, and in his own battalion only 125 were still standing when they were left the line.

With the British forces spent, localized counter-attacks by the Germans were organized. That evening, the 26th, the Germans launched a counter-attack against the line held by the King's Liverpools. An exhausted Dick Trafford helped fight one of the enemy's attempts to regain lost trenches.

The Germans counter-attacked the day after when it was dusk. We couldn't see them until they were almost on top of us. We only had one machine gun per company and this was positioned to kill as many Germans as possible. I knew the little gunner, Bob Grantham, he came from Ormskirk and he was in what we called the power pit, in the trench, and he had the machine gun trained to swing over and catch the Germans as they came over the Loos–Hulluch road. When they crossed the road the machine gun got most of them, but of course Bob couldn't have watched the road all of the time. I was watching the machine gun when I suddenly looked up and this German was stood on the top of the trench ready to jump down with his bayonet, which would have gone well into me, but instead Bob must have opened fire and instead of falling into the trench he fell the other way, luckily for me. He was a big man with a beard, a Bavarian Guard, I was told.

Not long after, one of the chaps shouted, 'Hey, Dick, will you come over here and reach me a cigarette?' I went over and saw that half of his shoulder was missing, well, he'd no arm left. He couldn't get to his cigarettes so I got them from his pocket, looked for some matches, and lit one for him and put it in his mouth. A wounded man would always crave a cigarette and he'd had what he wanted, to help ease the pain. But he hadn't two puffs on it when he conked out – he died there and then because the loss of blood must have been terrible. That was the end of him and my second shock. I couldn't say or do anything. I wouldn't say that he was a close friend but he was a chap that I knew well.

On 29 September George Coppard, who had now turned seventeen, entered the battlefield. He was on his way to the Hohenzollern Redoubt, on the left flank of the British offensive, a place with a terrible reputation for vicious fighting. The shell-fire was intense.

Our artillery – the howitzers at our backs, and the field guns on both sides of us – was firing flat out. Its deafening thunder threatened the eardrums. It was inspiring, though uncomfortable, for the eighteen-pounder shells were screaming just over our heads, an experience to which we were not yet accustomed . . .

At last we reached the top of a slope where the German front line had been before the attack. And there, stretching for several hundred yards on the right of the road, lay masses of British dead, struck down by machine-gun and rifle fire. Shells from enemy field batteries had been pitching into the bodies, flinging them into dreadful postures. As they mostly belonged to Highland regiments there was a fantastic display of colour from their kilts, glengarries and bonnets, and also from the bloody wounds on their bare limbs. The warm weather had darkened their faces and, shrouded as they were with the sticky odour of death, it was repulsive to be near them. Hundreds of rifles lay about, some stuck in the ground on the bayonet, as though impaled at the very moment of the soldier's death as he fell forward.

George was carrying two boxes of machine-gun ammunition. He had been posted to the battalion's machine-gun section and 'I was anxious to show that I could cope,' he wrote. What he saw at Loos made him realize that everything he had witnessed hitherto had been nothing more than simply 'playing about'.

Days after Len Thomas had bombarded the German lines he

too was given the opportunity to walk forward and look at the damage wrought by the guns. In his diary he wrote:

> Went down to the trenches. Got in our old first line and into theirs. Dead lying all over the place. In one German trench two dead lying on ground and we have to walk over them. In a machine gun dugout came across dead 'un and cut buttons off his coat. Bags of small ammunition. Fine dugouts with electricity in. Our artillery played hell with trenches . . . One gun of RFA went galloping into new position and got shelled, one shell blew a wheel off the limber but still they went on past Loos Towers. Behind came a heavy cart pulled by two horses and the driver got hit and fell off and horses went on on their own.

In time the bodies were cleared in places where the advance had captured and held fields that had formerly been no-man's-land. Where the land remained in dispute, this battlefield clearance was much harder. After the battle had officially finished in mid-October, sixteen-year-old George Adams was back. Hundreds of bodies still lay rotting and, if for no other reason than the smell, they had to be dealt with. George was one of those sent to collect the dead for burial.

> As soon as we got in last time we had to go out the front and fetch the bodies in, them from the 25th, and there were some terrible sights. Some as soon as we got hold of them fell to pieces, the first night we got eleven of them in and I was as sick as a dog for the stench was awful, but when we finished we got a good tot of rum and that pulled me round. The next night was a lot worse, we got nine in and four of them had no heads and they were nearly all eaten away by the rats and maggots and they were quite black and you could just see their skeleton showing through their skin. We were taking the last one out of the trench when we lost ourselves and we were wandering around for about four hours before we found ourselves where we started.

The first day of Loos had been costly in human life, and in young life too. It is officially known that at least eighty-six boys aged seventeen and under were killed that day, including Glenny Hale and George Woolfall, both of whom had sailed to France with Dick Trafford. Robert Carr had also been killed; he had just celebrated his eighteenth birthday. Their bodies were found at the time and personal possessions, including letters, photographs, a watch and chain, a Bible, and even penny stamps, were sent home to the next of kin. Richard Woolfall, George's father, survived the Battle of Loos but was informed in the field of his son's death and was granted a short leave to return home. The 1/9th King's Liverpools had got off relatively lightly: they had lost just thirty-nine who had been killed outright or died of wounds. The ages of just over half – twenty-two – are known, of whom five were under age, and a further eight were aged nineteen when they died; five of these had been abroad for over six months. Sadly, the bodies of four out of the five under-age soldiers were subsequently lost and their names appear today on the Loos Memorial to the missing – four of over 20,000 missing officers and men killed in the area during the war. Apart from those who died on the day, many more would have died of wounds.

Among the youngest boys known to have died were two aged fifteen: Private Richard Flynn of the 9th Welsh Regiment and Private Ernest Pitman of the 9th Royal Sussex, and another ten boys aged sixteen.

By the time the battle petered out in mid-October, around 15,800 men had been killed or were missing and a further 34,580 wounded. For all the first day's hopes, the line had advanced only two miles at most, while the village of Hulluch and Hill 70 remained in German hands. The intensity of the fighting on 25 and 26 September was recognized by the subsequent confirmation of ten Victoria Crosses, seven of which were earned on the first day.

*   *   *

The failure at Loos was blamed on Sir John French, whose handling of the reserves was deemed to have been the principal reason why the offensive failed. Haig vehemently disagreed with his C.-in-C. about where the reserve should be held, having told French before the battle that he would be committing all available troops in the initial attack. Haig's battle plans had been compromised and, from early October, he felt he had little option but to highlight the deficiencies of his commanding officer to their political masters back home. Haig wrote in his diary:

> I have been more than loyal to French and did my best to stop all criticism of him or his methods. Now, at last, in view of what had happened in the recent battle over the reserves, I had come to the conclusion that it was not fair to the Empire to retain French in command.

Disillusionment with French's overall competence was growing at home and abroad, and it was only a matter of time, and no little intrigue, before a replacement was made.

George Adams would soon be on his way back to Britain too, for, unbeknown to him, his sojourn at the front was about to be cut short. His parents were in the process of reclaiming him from France. However, there was no recall for other boys who had survived Loos, such as Dick Trafford, Alec Stringer and Ernest Fitchett. Ernest had even managed to pick up some mementoes, including a fine silver watch and gold chain taken from the body of a dead German. 'I have been offered 100 francs for it by one of our officers, but I would not sell it, for it will be a nice souvenir to keep after the war,' he wrote to his sister.

While Ernest had come through Loos, he would not live to see the end of the year, never mind the end of the war. For all his luck in surviving full-blown battles, he was wounded doing the everyday chores of trench maintenance, jobs that all men undertook while in the line. A shrapnel wound in his left thigh, while serious, did not at first appear life-threatening and brief letters sent from No. 2 Stationary Hospital kept his family informed of progress.

26.11.15
Dear Madam

Your brother, Private Fitchett, was brought into this hospital on the 24th with a very bad wound in his left thigh. He had a slight operation yesterday and we hope his wound and general condition will improve.

29.11.15
Dear Madam

I am sorry to have to tell you that your brother's condition this morning is very serious. It was found necessary to amputate his leg two days ago, and not being very strong at this time, it is a hard struggle for him to get over the effects of such an operation.

29.11.15
Dear Miss Fitchett

Your brother who is in hospital is under my charge, & has asked me to write and tell you about him. He had to have his left leg amputated on Friday last as gangrene had set in. It is very serious still as the infection is still there, though they amputated as high up as they could.

In fact, I do not think he can get well – in God's mercy he *may* be spared & everything possible is being done for his recovery. I have told him that he might not recover. He is very patient and very resigned to the suffering which he has to undergo when his wound is dressed. I am going to give him Holy Communion, tomorrow morning, St Andrew's Day.

I do pray that God may spare him. He seems such a nice and such a *good* boy. I am sure your prayers will be the same.

With much sympathy
(Rev) H. J. Watney

2.12.15
Dear Madam

I am very sorry to tell you that your brother died last night. We all feel his death very much, for he was such a sweet dear boy. He was conscious up to the end and had a happy peaceful death. The chaplain was with him a short time before, and I hope that it will be some consolation to you to know that everything possible was done for him.

With every sympathy
M. C. Corbishley (Sister)

December 11th 1915
Dear Miss Fitchett

My sincere sympathy in the loss . . . He passed away very peacefully about 6.30 p.m., I was with him till 5.30 and did not think he was to be called so soon. He was quite conscious till five minutes before he died, he did not suffer acute pain, but a dull ache all over . . . I will send you a PC [postcard] Photo of the Cemetery, including your brother's grave, in the spring. Just now it is all too muddy, and heaps of soil from the next row of graves, but they are beautifully tended. Some ladies put flowers on them every week.

Yours very sincerely
H. J. Watney

PS. I meant to tell you, Ernie said 'give my love to both my sisters and tell them I have not suffered much, and they must not grieve too much for me, I know I am safe in the arms of Jesus'.

Seventeen-year-old Ernest was buried in Abbeville Communal Cemetery on 2 December. Three days later, his Commander-in-Chief was told that his resignation was imperative and that General, soon to become Field Marshal, Haig would take command. Sir John French left for London.

8

The Winding Road to Conscription

ADIEU DEAR LAD
WHAT NEED OF TEARS
OR FEARS FOR YOU

2512 Private Leslie Sheffield
17th Battalion Australian Infantry

Killed in Action 26 July 1916, aged 17

JUST AS MILITARY SHORTCOMINGS were increasingly evident in France, so the political situation at home was in need of serious reappraisal. The recognition that the British economy must be organized for war had dawned only slowly on the Government. It had become imperative for politicians to get involved in the day-to-day running of the wartime economy, no longer leaving its direction to just one man, Lord Kitchener. The initial break-through at Loos had shown the importance of a good reserve of munitions, and it was essential to keep the supply flowing if future campaigns were to be successful. Labour, skilled and unskilled, would have to be mobilized and factory production massively expanded.

At the same time, the 'wastage', the euphemistic term used to describe losses at the front, had to be replaced by new recruits. The monthly returns showed that a rapidly declining number of men were volunteering for service. Over 1.34 million men had volunteered in the first six months of the war. This figure had fallen by over 50 per cent in the following six months, with July, August and September 1915 seeing further dramatic falls. Just 16,500 men had been recruited each week in September, at a time when the army calculated that it required the enlistment of 30,000 men every seven days for the infantry and a further 5,000 a week for ancillary services such as the Army Service Corps and the Army Ordnance Corps.

As laudable as voluntary enlistment was, essential war industries had to be protected or else manufacturing would be robbed of skilled labour, ultimately undermining the war effort. A contemporary memorandum showed an awareness of this:

> It is realized that measures must be taken to secure a supply of recruits sufficient in number to meet the ever-increasing demands upon the army and at the same time drawn from sources which would produce the least possible dislocation of the vital services and industries of the country generally, and in particular of the supply of munitions.

Central control was critical, and for this to be efficient there was an overriding requirement for the Government to compile an accurate record of the human resources of the nation. A National Register of both sexes aged fifteen to sixty-five was proposed. It would be a snapshot of the nation's available manpower, taken on a day yet to be decided. The memorandum speculated:

> The very fact of the compilation of such a national record would stimulate patriotism and bring home to everybody the duty of doing something for the public good.

Apart from indicating to the Government who was patriotically serving the country and who was actually doing work 'essential to the stability of the community', the scheme would point out 'slackers', the public's favoured term to describe those who, though old enough and fit enough, steadfastly refused to don a khaki uniform.

It would be a legal requirement under Registration for everyone liable to fill out a form in full, giving specific details such as address, marital status, number of dependants, occupation and skills. Failure to comply, or supplying false information, would result in a hefty fine or imprisonment or even both. The results would create an inventory that would enable recruiting officers to compile returns showing all the men available for enlistment in each county, city or borough.

The bill was quickly passed and given Royal Assent in mid-July 1915. Exactly a month later, on 15 August – Registration Day – forms were distributed by a small army of 150,000 patriotic citizens who gave their time freely to deliver and subsequently pick up every form over the following three days.

The Government had been careful to present Registration as a proudly patriotic measure, but inevitably there was considerable public anxiety as to the actual and immediate ramifications of revealing all to the authorities. The vast majority of civilians were utterly unused to central Government impinging so directly on their lives, and the effect must have been unnerving. The Reverend Andrew Clark, a country vicar living in Essex, was a good barometer of local feeling. He kept a daily diary throughout the war and never missed an entry. Three days before Registration, he jotted down the remarks of one well-respected parishioner who had told him that 'in his part of the parish the women were terribly afraid that the Register was the beginning of a plan to take away their men-folk'. In fact, their fears were well founded. The Government was taking its first step towards conscripting by legal means men who were deemed fit to serve in one capacity or another, but who had not yet volunteered.

As politicians turned their attention to the competing needs of the army and of industry, so Kitchener's profound limitations as Secretary of State for War, especially his inability to delegate, became apparent and his power gradually began to wane. Although fearful of his influence, Cabinet ministers increasingly sought to work around him, leaving his status intact despite the fact that some, such as Lloyd George, believed him incompetent.

Senior politicians accepted that in order to prosecute the war successfully, central control of labour was an imperative. This meant that the hitherto somewhat amorphous relationship between subject and State had to be changed for the common good. Registration was tangible evidence of that change. Suddenly, individuals could be compelled to serve the cause of the nation in time of war, and the State, with detailed information on every adult, could enforce compliance. It was a classic case of knowledge equalling power, but it was at least democratic. The vast reservoir of information that made compulsion possible could also be used to curb fraudulent enlistment.

It would take many weeks for the results of the national survey to be even tabulated, let alone examined. In the meantime, the enlistment procedure would remain as vulnerable to fraud as ever; at the same time Government policy towards the boys already serving in the army ensured that tens of thousands of boys would remain in khaki.

A month after Registration, on 22 September, Parliament returned to the issue of under-age soldiering when Sir Arthur Markham addressed the Prime Minister.

> There is one point I want to mention. I do not know whether I shall be strictly in order in doing so . . . In my own Constituency, boys of fifteen and sixteen have been and are being recruited, and the Government are perfectly well aware of it. In fact a boy of sixteen was recruited in my Constituency, and his father and mother went to the headquarters of the Sherwood Foresters and tried to get him back, but the authorities refused to allow him to go back . . . Are we to understand it is the policy of the Government to take

immature boys of fifteen and sixteen when they have set down a definite military age at which boys may be enlisted? I am told that these young boys are unable to stand the fatigue of a campaign, and many of them have to return from the War after the country has been put to the expense of training them.

Once again there was no direct response, and MPs moved on. However, a few days later, on the 28th, Harold Tennant, in reply to further questions, made a statement to the House. He informed MPs that instructions had been issued to commanding officers that a boy over the age of seventeen would be held to serve, even if an application for discharge had been made by the boy's parents and a birth certificate proved he had enlisted fraudulently. Furthermore, if the medical officer certified that a boy was physically up to the standard of eighteen and a half years, he could be sent overseas. Tennant told Parliament:

> A man's actual age is not always a true measure of his physical efficiency, and I think that adequate security against youths who are immature being sent overseas is provided by the requirement of a definite medical certificate of fitness for service abroad.

As a matter of military efficiency, the army did not want physically 'immature' boys going to the front; it was, after all, a waste of resources. Nevertheless, thousands of under-age boys reached the front line only to be exposed as inadequate. If a lad looked the part, he invariably was assumed to be able to play it. The fact that he was aged seventeen years was of singularly less importance.

The evident weaknesses in the enlistment process had been exposed for all to see. In 1914, under-age recruitment was, if anything, seen as a public expression of patriotism and there was little thought that these boys would go overseas. With growing numbers of casualties, the mood had changed. The Government had reacted to increasing concern at the number of boys embarking for the Western Front, as well as other theatres of war, by issuing instructions that recruitment officers must not turn a blind eye to fraudulent enlistment. The boys who had enlisted had nevertheless lied, and the Government's decision to hold those boys over the age of seventeen, and even to allow their service abroad, was seen by some MPs as punishment by indifference. In effect, the boys' plight was of their own making.

The Government was, nevertheless, partially responsible for the problem. During the war there was a policy of awarding to civilians various insignia, such as the 'On War Service' badge, to signify to the public at large that a man wearing civilian clothes was not necessarily a shirker. This was done to protect men essential to the war industry who had suffered abuse for not being in uniform. Incidents in which well-intentioned if misguided women had handed an un-enlisted man the white feather, signifying cowardice, were common. Such humiliation was usually indiscriminate as most feathers were given without knowledge of the recipient's status, age or occupation.

The effect of issuing badges to protect key workers also helped to isolate those who, for no good reason, were not playing their part. Inevitably, a great many of these were under-age boys who may not have been eligible for such badges. Boys of sixteen and seventeen were therefore exposed to the sly comment or the withering stare of those around them. The Government was, even if unintentionally, encouraging boy enlistment through embarrassment.

Recruiting sergeants now proactively sought out likely volunteers, openly pursuing and pestering boys like Hal Kerridge and Tommy Thomson to enlist under age. News of such tactics was received by Sir Arthur Markham from his constituents, and led him to believe that the men in charge of enlistment were either deliberately ignoring the instructions issued by the War Office or, worse still, were acting under the umbrella of some other hidden agenda. On 12 October, he sought answers in some of the bitterest exchanges yet heard in the Commons.

Seeing that under the present system of voluntary enlistment, numbers of boys are being recruited, will he say why no steps have been taken by Lord Kitchener to see that the regulations that the Government has laid down as to age limits are adhered to, and whether confidential instructions have been given by the military authorities that the regulations as to the age limit are to be ignored.

Harold Tennant replied that clear and precise instructions had been issued in June and that further clarification had been sent out as recently as the previous week.

My Hon. Friend is mistaken in suggesting that these instructions have been ignored by the military authorities responsible. Since these instructions were issued, no cases of under-age enlistment have come to the notice of the War Office, but if my Hon. Friend knows of any and will furnish particulars, enquiry will, of course, be made.

Markham, clearly unhappy with the response, pressed the Undersecretary of State for War once again. Was the Cabinet aware the War Office had 'deliberately connived' in the enlistment of boys under the prescribed age in breach of the Regulations, and if so, had the Cabinet sanctioned such an action?

Tennant remained unflustered.

In this country no boys under the prescribed age, as laid down by Regulations, have been enlisted with the knowledge of the War Office, and I regret the imputation of deliberate connivance, which is wholly unfounded. Boys under that age are not wanted, either with or without the consent of their parents.

Markham asked:

Does my Right Hon. Friend seriously tell the House that the Government and the War Office do not know that boys under the prescribed age have been enlisted from the time of the outbreak of War onwards? Does not the War Office know that? Does it know anything?

Tennant stuck resolutely to the Government line that the War Office's policy was to take only boys of nineteen. 'If boys under the proper age have been enlisted, it is their own fault for having made a false declaration,' he contended.

The argument continued back and forwards until the Speaker intervened. Markham's exasperation was evident for all to see. He did not take kindly to being stonewalled, and the inference that the Government saw the trouble of under-age soldiering as one of the boys' own making was galling.

In Markham's eyes, unfettered patriotism and uncontrolled enlistment had combined to create a mess that the War Office showed no signs of tackling. In reality, the imperatives of war, particularly the increasing shortfall in recruitment, would mean that voluntary enlistment, as the predominant method of recruitment, was coming to an end.

Dispensing with the voluntary system was no easy matter for a Coalition Government resting on a consensus of politicians of the political left, right and centre. Asquith was uneasy about opening up a political rift between those ministers who supported compulsion, such as Lloyd George, and those who were against, mostly die-hard liberals who saw the right to choose as an inalienable freedom, such as the Chancellor of the Exchequer, Reginald McKenna. If strong feelings existed within the Cabinet, it was likely that there would be some public aversion to compulsion too.

By early autumn, voluntary enlistment had reached an all-time nadir but, before conscription could be fully considered, one further scheme was introduced to increase recruitment. If it was successful, the need for conscription might be deferred, in the short term. If it failed, then the Government could argue that it had pursued all feasible alternatives and that if Britain were to win the war, conscription was the only solution.

The man charged with the task was Lord Derby. On 5 October 1915, he was given the post of Director-General of Recruiting as a prelude to the launch of his Derby Scheme just days after his appointment. In a secret War Office memorandum of 8 October, the role of the Scheme was spelt out.

> It is not intended that the voluntary principle should be abandoned, even though it fails, as it does now, to produce the number of recruits required. The proposal is that the *balance* not forthcoming by voluntary effort should be called up, under special arrangements, from those available for service.

Derby's idea was couched as 'an appeal to the people' but it was, in effect, an appeal to men aged eighteen to forty-one who were in reserved occupations to attest in the knowledge that they would not be called up until they were actually needed. All men between these ages would be classed in one of forty-six groups, according to age and marital status. The first twenty-three classes were occupied by unmarried men, class one being an unmarried eighteen-year-old, class two an unmarried nineteen-year-old, and so on. The second group was occupied by married men in the same age range, class twenty-four representing a married man aged eighteen, and so on. These men would be automatically transferred to the Army Reserve until they were required, whereupon they would be called up in ascending group order. There was one exception: any boy aged eighteen who attested under the Derby Scheme could not be called up until, at the earliest, three months before his nineteenth birthday.

There would be ample opportunity for Derby men to ensure that their work was covered during their absence. For married men, the scheme held out the incentive that they would not be required until all unmarried men had been called up first.

Privately, Derby had already become convinced of the need and merit of compulsion. Feeling like a 'receiver who was put in to wind up a bankrupt concern', he nevertheless felt compelled to try to make his scheme work.

> I believe the moral effect of showing to our enemies that England is perfectly determined by the voluntary method to put into the field all that could be got by the compulsory method will be such that it will bring the war to a far quicker conclusion.

It was a bullish proposition and one not heard again during the debate on conscription three months later, the logical flip-side of his argument being that news that Britain had had to resort to conscription would give Germany fresh resolve to fight.

Lord Derby may have hoped that his scheme would provide the springboard for a new wave of recruits as in 1914 but, if the architect of the scheme himself was in doubt, it seems likely that sensible money was already backing compulsion. In the meantime, while the Derby Scheme was played out to its conclusion, the real battle, for national conscription, was well and truly under way.

The resistance to forging an army built on conscription was based on two main arguments. First, there was the liberal ideal that the decision to fight for one's country should remain the inalienable right of the individual; secondly, that the forced employment of men in the army who had no wish to be there would undermine good order and discipline – indeed, many had argued that a conscripted man was not worth his salt against a man who enlisted willingly. The problem came when politicians and the army had to face up to the fact that continued reliance on voluntary enlistment would almost certainly cost Britain the war. The call for conscription could only become louder as the numbers enlisting voluntarily dropped in equal proportion. During 1915 those calls were heard coming from many sources, not least from a highly influential pressure group that had campaigned since 1902 for compulsory military training.

Conscription might have won the recent support of a number of well-known politicians, but the organization that could lay claim to starting the campaign was the National Service League, a group set up for the sole and express purpose of waking the country up to the need for National Service. The League had attracted many prominent figures among its 100,000 members, including Lord Milner and Field Marshal Lord Roberts VC. In 1915 the conscription debate breathed new life into the movement.

As part of the campaign, the League's honorary secretary, George Curnock, had begun a flurry of correspondence with Sir Arthur Markham, pointing out through the use of poignant examples the iniquitous nature of the current voluntary scheme. Curnock worked for the *Daily Mail*, a newspaper under the ownership of Lord Northcliffe, a vocal supporter of conscription. It was no coincidence that Curnock's letters to Markham appear to have started in October at a time when Lord Derby's scheme offered a possible reprieve for the voluntary system and Markham was involved in some of the frankest exchanges in the House on the issue of under-age soldiering. The letters were sent as Curnock looked to ratchet up the pressure on the Coalition Government, with Markham the willing political conduit for the League's aims.

Just as the League was writing to Markham, Markham in turn was in correspondence with Lord Derby. Ironically, Derby had written to him in the hope of enlisting his sister Violet to help in his campaign. Markham diplomatically made no mention of his contacts with Curnock, but one has the impression that a delicate political game was being played out by all three men, each with his own agenda.

28th October, 1915

Dear Lord Derby

I had intended asking a question in Parliament next week about your recruiting campaign, but perhaps you would rather I wrote to you about the matter. The point on which I wish information is whether under your campaign you are going to continue to take boys of 15 and 16 years of age as has been done under the old system.

Since I raised this matter in Parliament I have had quite a snow-ball of letters [up to 300 a day] from people all over the country saying that their sons have enlisted against their wishes, and in some cases boys of 14 have actually been enlisted. I think it would be very much better to reduce the age limit to . . . if you wish 17½, but I do not think it is right to continue taking these young lads who for patriotic reasons make false declarations. Before the war is over, these boys will probably be wanted and you are, there-fore, destroying useful material.

I do not think any voluntary system which openly connives at taking young lads while others remain at home can be justi-fied or defended. Now that you have the Register there ought to be no difficulty in ascertaining the ages of the recruits you are enlisting.

I hope now that the matter of recruiting has passed into your hands, you will put a stop to this scandal.

Yours sincerely
Arthur B. Markham

Derby's answer arrived the next day:

Dear Sir Arthur

I am in receipt of your letter. I am entirely agreed with what you say about enlisting boys and very strict orders have been sent out to recruiting officers that they are not to do so. It is quite young enough to take them at 18 and then not send them abroad for a year and anything I can do to carry this out I shall most certainly do.

Yours sincerely
Derby

Curnock's first letter to Markham was dated the next day, and pursued the idea that the War Office should insist on the mandatory examination of birth certificates on enlistment, not only to prevent so many young boys joining up but also to stop men over the current maximum age of forty-one trying to enlist fraudulently.

I estimate that scores of thousands of useless under-age boys and over-age married men have been taken into the army and are still being taken by recruiting officers with the result that the Nation pays for a worthless article, and the article when bought is a continual source of trouble to the War Office and the army. All this might be avoided by insistence upon a birth certificate . . .

His letter concludes: 'If you like to take the matter up in Parliament, I can give you any number of sound cases to proceed upon, including a "Gunner" of 14!'

30th October 1915
Dear Lord Derby
     I am glad to have your letter saying you have issued instructions to recruiting officers not to enlist boys, but I would remind you that the War Office have repeatedly given the same answer in Parliament that boys would not be enlisted; nevertheless the recruiting officers totally ignore the instructions.
     The form of declaration the medical men have to make does not even permit the doctor to say a recruit is under age. Some doctors

say they well know the recruits who have been enlisted are under age.

Now that you have the Register and all people of military age have registration cards, it seems that the sensible thing to do is to instruct the recruiting officers that they are not to enlist any person unless he produces his registration card . . .

The country is under a very great debt of gratitude to you for all you have done and are doing in the matter of recruiting, and I do not desire, therefore, in any way to criticize or make any suggestions in Parliament which might in the smallest degree cause you any annoyance . . .

Yours sincerely
Arthur Markham

The suggestion that birth certificates ought to be produced on enlistment continued to be rejected by the Government. It was a decision that Markham appears to have accepted. His reply to Curnock has not survived, but his proposition to Derby of the alternative use of the Registration card had been recognized, as is evident from Curnock's next reply to Markham:

2nd November
Dear Sir

Very many thanks for your letter and the most practical suggestion that the Registration Card should be produced by all recruits, an obvious and easy precaution against the enlistment of immature boys and old men; if, as I presume, the 'Class Number' is an indication of age . . .

I shall be very pleased to give you all the time necessary to a full examination of the cases brought to my notice.

Yours faithfully
George C. Curnock

Despite Sir Arthur's tendency to exaggerate at times, his letters to Derby indicate that he was an adept political player, praising and cajoling, respectful but mildly threatening.

He already knew the answer when, on 10 November, he rose in the House and asked the Undersecretary of War:

> Seeing that all persons who desire to join the army have now in their possession a registration card, will he, to prevent boys being enlisted, give instructions to the recruiting officers that no recruits are to be enlisted who do not produce their registration cards?

Tennant replied:

> Recruiting officers have already been instructed to examine the registration cards of recruits presenting themselves, and their attestation is being directed specifically to the question of age.

This was a breakthrough for Sir Arthur. Even if the change was not of his own making, his persuasion might well have brought the concession that recruiting sergeants were to pay special attention to a recruit's age. The truth was that the Government had every intention of ordering the scrutiny of registration cards. A great effort had been expended in generating an accurate record of the nation's available manpower, and there would have been no point in subsequently losing track of thousands of individuals by ignoring registration cards and permitting continued fraudulent enlistment.

With registration came rules governing where a man could enlist. For administrative purposes, the country had been divided up into areas and sub-areas. While a man could enlist anywhere in the country, area commanders accepting a recruit had to register the address against each man's name, as well as full particulars regarding his enlistment.

In the case of men who have been registered outside the recruiting area in which they present themselves for enlistment, it will be necessary to notify all particulars regarding the man's rejection or enlistment to the area commander concerned, i.e., the commander of the area in which the place where the address given by the man on his registration form is situated.

This information would also be passed on to the sub-area, making it far harder to enlist and harder still to disappear into the army. The days when boys ran away from Kent to Scotland to enlist incognito had largely gone. As it was a legal requirement to carry a registration card, there could be little excuse for a volunteer not to present one, and, just as importantly, little excuse for the recruiting sergeant not to look. A boy's enlistment in the past had often relied as much on the willingness of the sergeant to turn a blind eye as it did on the boy to lie convincingly; it would be harder now for a sergeant to ignore the instructions.

The information carried on the card was basic. Each card had the name of the holder, his profession and address. Perhaps surprisingly, there was no designated place to write the owner's class number, and it was usually – but by no means always – written next to the recruit's job description. Another apparent weakness was the absence of an identifying photograph, opening up the potential for a recruit to use someone else's card. This was an offence taken much more seriously than merely falsifying a birth date in a flash of patriotism.

Registration would do nothing to help the thousands of boys who had enlisted before 15 August. Release would remain dependent on families making an application for their son's temporary removal from the firing line, or, if he was under seventeen years old, his probable – but not guaranteed – discharge.

The linking of the registration card to the enlistment process must have pleased Markham, but he was still driven by his distrust of the War Office and Government to tackle the whole problem head on. He was well aware that the majority of those he had set out to help were already in the army, and their immediate future was far from being settled other than by shell explosion or bullet. It is clear from Markham's letter to Derby that, reluctantly, he would countenance seventeen-year-olds serving in France, but that boys as young as fifteen or sixteen were still soldiers remained a disgrace.

The Derby Scheme, originally intended to finish in November, was extended to December in a final effort by the Government to procure the numbers needed through the voluntary system. In the light of this extension, George Curnock wrote to Sir Arthur again. Curnock was concerned that Markham should not rest content in the knowledge that recruiting sergeants would now examine Registration cards. 'I hope you were not satisfied with the answers on November 10th and will continue to interest yourself in the under-age enlistment question . . .' wrote Curnock on 15 November.

Conscription was so close that Curnock was unwilling to relax for a moment. Throughout November, he continued to feed Markham information on boy soldiers, encouraging the MP to raise their harrowing stories in the Commons. Curnock highlighted two battalions of the London Regiment, one the 'Wandsworth Regulars' as he called them and one raised in Bermondsey, which, he claimed, were inundated with under-age recruits. He wrote:

I have written to the Mayor of Bermondsey, asking him if it is a fact that he has many boys of 14 to 16 in the Regiment, including two who enlisted on the day after they left school at the age of 14.

He also raised the pitiful case of a boy badly wounded at Gallipoli.

The enclosed notes will I trust be useful to you and your friends in the House. They summarize the case against the War Office in the matter of boy soldiers. I hope you will see in 'The Daily Mail' tomorrow a little article I have just sent to the Editor, describing one of the boy victims. As you may wish to refer to this case in the House I send you the following particulars:

Pte James Henry Robinson, 1st Lancashire Fusiliers.

Enlisted at Fleetwood, Lancashire, when 17 years and 3 days old.

Told by recruiting sergeant, who knew him well, to say he was 19.

Allowed to volunteer for Dardanelles after *1* month's training.

Shot in both legs and right hand on landing.

Sent back to England.

Left leg amputated above the knee after six months' agony.

Now at Westminster Hospital where Members of your House can see him and hear his story.

Hopes to work again as a grocer's assistant 'when I get my wooden leg' . . .

It is perhaps a sign of Markham's impetuous nature that he took the story of Private Robinson direct to the floor of the Commons on the very same day. In what was one of the most rancorous exchanges in the House, he addressed his fellow MPs:

I do not like to use strong language, but when the facts are strong, strong language is warranted. I do not think that there has ever been a period in the whole history of the British Army, except under the direction of Lord Kitchener, when the word of a British officer has not been synonymous with that of a gentleman . . . There has been fraud, deceit, and lying practised by the War Office. You have taken boys of the ages of fourteen, fifteen and sixteen rather than face the issue of Conscription . . . You have taken these boys knowing that they were boys, and then the War Office have said that they did not think they were under age. You have said that you would not send them to the Front until they have reached the official age, but you have time after time broken this promise and sent little lads to the Front.

I have here hundreds of letters of cases where the War Office, knowing that the ages of these boys are fifteen, sixteen or seventeen, and after they have received the [birth] certificates from the parents, have written back saying the age of the boy [on the enlistment papers] is the official age, knowing what they are saying is untrue. Yet they have the impudence to write to the parents saying it is not their wish or intention that boys under nineteen should go out.

There is a boy in Westminster Hospital today who was sent, when seventeen years of age, to the Dardanelles. He had only one month's training. He has had a leg amputated, and is now within two hundred yards of this House.

The honest and right thing for the War Office to do is to reduce the age limit, and to say so now. What is the objection to taking youths of seventeen and a half or eighteen? Let boys go at that age to serve their country, if you like, but do not put it forward in your official papers that nobody will be taken under the age of nineteen, and then take little boys of fourteen, fifteen, and sixteen, who are totally unfitted to fight for their country when older boys are not doing their duty.

Rising, Harold Tennant replied, as he had on so many occasions, with equal force:

He [Markham] said that we at the War Office had, in fact, employed these boys of fourteen, fifteen, and sixteen years of age, knowing them at the time to be of that age, and had deliberately sent them to the front. What are the real facts in these cases? Frankly, I regret them. I have told my Hon. Friend, both privately and officially in this House, that the War Office do not desire to recruit boys of that age, and that it has been done by overzealous recruiting officers who, of course, are rewarded for it. I regret these circumstances, and I say that the colonels of these regiments, when they really become acquainted with the facts, ought to send these boys back to their parents. They are very often returned and discharged. In some cases they are not returned, because not only have these boys cost the country a certain amount of money, but they have been given training and uniforms, and in some cases these boys of sixteen, seventeen, and even fifteen years are very efficient soldiers.

Markham riposted:

Why not reduce the age; why not say quite definitely, that you will reduce the age?

Tennant replied:

The answer is that we do not want these boys. We do not want them because, in a large number of cases, they are not able to withstand all the hardships of active warfare, and they only fill our hospitals.

It was a powerful defence but within Tennant's statement there was an admission that ran to the heart of Markham's argument. Was it right to keep under-age boys in France simply because they were deemed fit enough to stand the conditions, or should their age, regardless of fitness, preclude them from fighting? The Government line was clear. Officially they did not want under-age soldiers, but those who had deceived the military authorities and were strong enough to survive were acceptable, provided that the boy was willing to continue fighting and the commanding officer was ready to have him in the line.

After this debate, Markham drew Curnock's attention to his part in the debate: 'I did not mince matters about the lying and deceit of the War Office,' and asked for the journalist's continued help.

PHOTOGRAPH BY GEORGE PANKHURST © MARTIN BOOTH

COURTESY OF TREVOR ILES

Above: Brandenburg Prisoner of War Camp, Germany. Boys who fought under age and were captured were brought together and given tuition behind the barbed wire by other educated soldiers.

Left: Horace Iles aged fourteen. Having enlisted into the Leeds Pals soon after the outbreak of war, he went to the Somme aged sixteen. In May he was wounded and two months later he was killed in action.

Below: The front and back of the envelope used when Horace's sister, Florrie, wrote to her brother to persuade him to come home. It was stamped 'Killed in Action' and returned.

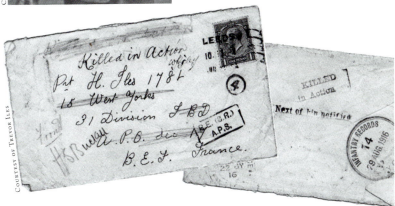

COURTESY OF TREVOR ILES

Right: Private James Walters. James had previously served at Gallipoli and was fighting on the Somme when he was killed aged sixteen. His mother had already begun the process of applying for her son's discharge.

Below: The memorial card printed to mark James's death.

Bottom: The pass for France issued to James's mother, Hannah, so that she could visit his grave in 1935. The pass was valid for nine days only, and it is believed that this was the only trip she made. She died soon afterwards.

In Affectionate Remembrance of

Pte. JAMES WALTERS

(Machine Gun Section, South Staffs.).

The beloved son of the late James Walters and
Hannah Gertrude Walters,

BORN SEPTEMBER 15th, 1899,

Killed in Action, AUG. 9th, 1916,

SOMEWHERE IN FRANCE.

His toil is past, his work is done.
And he is fully blest.
He fought the fight, the victory won,
And entered into rest.

But the hardest part is yet to come,
When the heroes all return.
And we miss among the cheering crowds,
The face of our dear one

THIS PASS permits the holder to enter France and or Belgium for the purpose of visiting

CE LAISSEZ-PASSER permet au titulaire d'entrer en France et/ou en Belgique à fin de visiter

Plot IV   Row F.   Grave 6.

at DELVILLE WOOD CEMETERY, LONGUEVAL, FRANCE. the grave of a late member of His Britannic Majesty's Forces.

le tombeau d'un des feus membres des forces de Sa Majesté Britannique.

It is available for a continuous period of ten days only.

Il est valable pour une periode continue de pas plus de dix jours.

from August 1935   until August 1935
du   2nd   au   11th

On or before the latter date the holder must either leave France and Belgium, or obtain a National Passport endorsed with permission to remain.

Le porteur devant quitter la France et la Belgique avant ou sur cette dernière date, ou se faire fournir d'un passeport national l'autorisant de rester.

Granted at the Passport Office, London.

Donné au Bureau de Passeports, à Londres.

on the
le

C. P. Wakefield.
Chief Passport Officer.

Surname
Nom   WALTERS,

Style or Title and Christian Names
Qualifications et Prénoms   Mrs Hannah Gertrude.

Nationality
Nationalité   British   Age 60.

Profession
Occupation

Home address
Domicile   62. Vernon Avenue, Basford, Nottingham.

Photograph and signature of holder.   Photographie et signature du porteur.

H. G. Walters

FOREIGN OFFICE
30 JUL 1935

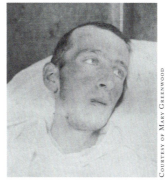

Right: Private William Plant aged seventeen, wounded and in hospital after nine months in France. On the back of this picture was written 'Don't send this home'.

Right: Sixteen-year-old machine gunner Percy Marshall *(second right)* with friends, recovering in a London hospital from injuries received on the Somme.

Below: 'Having made a mis-statement as to age on enlistment,' Percy Marshall was discharged in September 1916.

John at Kingston Red + Hospital 1916

Above: A group of soldiers in France on Christmas Day, 1916. All were under the age of eighteen, and had been removed from the line. Several had been overseas since 1915.

Below: Major Cardinal Harford *(middle left)* with some of the boys at Etaples. He had been badly wounded in the Boer War and fought in the trenches before being ordered to look after a thousand lads removed from the line in 1917.

Top and above: These two photographs show the same group of under-age and physically immature boys at Etaples camp on 18 July 1918. All had served in or close to the front line. It is only when they remove their uniforms that their youth becomes really evident, especially compared with the mature soldier in the foreground. They were kept at Etaples until fit or old enough to be sent back to the trenches.

Left: VAD nurse Marjorie Grigsby returned to England from France after serving six months at both a Base Hospital and a Casualty Clearing Station, caring for the wounded and dying while she was still only eighteen years old.

Below: Great Yarmouth, February 1918. At eighteen, Harold Lawton *(far left)* and his friends were sent to France to help stem the German advance. Just seven weeks after this picture was taken, he was captured, days after arriving at the front.

Top Left: Seventeen-year-old Ernest Steele, a decorative box maker by trade, shortly after enlisting into the Queen's Westminster Rifles in 1914.

Top Right: Ernest was killed during fighting in September 1918. He had served over three years in France and been commissioned into the Machine Gun Corps. He is buried in Heudicourt Cemetery.

Above: After Ernest's death, his father began a book of remembrance in which he wrote short notes and poems for the next thirty years. This page shows a picture of the newly commissioned officer in 1917 alongside a typical entry made by his grieving parents.

Right: The last letter written by Ernest the night before the attack at Epéhy. Within hours he was shot by a sniper as he reconnoitered a position for his machine guns.

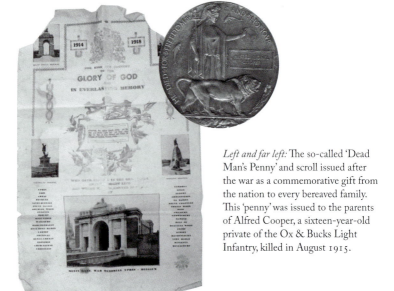

Left and far left: The so-called 'Dead Man's Penny' and scroll issued after the war as a commemorative gift from the nation to every bereaved family. This 'penny' was issued to the parents of Alfred Cooper, a sixteen-year-old private of the Ox & Bucks Light Infantry, killed in August 1915.

Below: Albert Harvey, aged ninety-seven, holding the image of himself as a fifteen-year-old soldier in 1915. Albert served with the 1/4th East Yorkshire Regiment at Ypres before being 'claimed' by his family and discharged as under age in early 1916.

Markham supported conscription first and foremost because it would help the cause of the under-age soldier; Curnock supported Markham's crusade because it would help the National Service League's battle for the introduction of conscription.

In reality, Curnock's help was hardly needed. So impassioned was Markham by his crusade that he simply was incapable of turning away fresh evidence of what he had firmly come to believe was a scandal of outrageous proportions. One case he raised on several occasions was that of John Flint, a local constituent from East Kirkby in Mansfield, and therefore one close to Markham's heart.

In October 1915 Sir Arthur had asked the Undersecretary of State for War why John William Flint, No 19370, D Company, of the 11th Battalion of the Sherwood Foresters, had not been discharged from the army. The boy's parents, on hearing that their son had enlisted, went immediately to Derby Barracks taking along a birth certificate that proved that John was only sixteen years of age, and asking for his discharge. The application was refused. Markham asked:

> Will he say whether it is the policy of the War Office to refuse to discharge boys of sixteen years of age who have entered the army by making a false declaration of their age unknown to their parents?

Tennant replied that inquiries had been made into the case and that

> it appeared that Private Flint should have been discharged in November 1914, when his father first made application. At that date when my Hon. Friend brought the case to my notice, namely in August last, Flint was serving Overseas, and instructions were sent explaining the case and asking that Flint should be sent home for discharge, if there were no good grounds to the contrary. May

I ask my Hon. Friend if he will abstain from founding general charges upon individual cases?

It seems doubtful that Markham genuinely believed that such actions were part of a wide conspiracy but, to a man who hated inefficiency and waste in business, such incidents when they occurred to a young boy were inexcusable.

Flint could at least be brought home. Another boy, Edward Bailey of the Monmouthshire Regiment, could not, for reasons Markham indignantly presented to the House. Edward's father, Isaac, had three sons at the front and had written to the commanding officer of the battalion when he heard that his fourth son, Edward, was due to embark for France, despite being just seventeen years old. Isaac Bailey had received a reply, the details of which were now presented before MPs.

In February of this year, I received a letter from the commanding officer informing me that my son was to be transferred back to the reserve battalion on account of my objection. On 18th April he was sent to France, with the result that he was wounded on 22nd April and died on the 29th.

Markham thundered:

That was a case where an undertaking had been given that he should not be sent to the Front. What did the War Office say upon that case? I cannot use the language I should like to use, because I should not be allowed to use it. I will just read the words, and let the House put its own construction on the value of the word of the War Office. The letter is dated 10th October, 1915:

'The Army Council desire me to say that every precaution is taken by them to prevent immature boys being sent to the front, and they desire me to express sympathy to you in the loss of your son – a keen young soldier.'

The father, not being satisfied in the case I have mentioned, writes again to the War Office. What do they say on the 22nd October?

'It is a great pity your son was allowed to go out under age, as it is not the intention of the War Office that young men under nineteen should be taken. Mistakes will inevitably happen and in your son's case efficient supervision does not appear to have been taken to ensure his not going out until he was nineteen.'

It may not have been the 'intention', but the War Office did not appear to rule out scenarios by which under-age boys might go abroad. A War Office Instruction (No. 46), dated 6 September 1915, reminded army officers that

the age given by a soldier on enlistment is his official age, and battalion and company commanders should not make promises to parents that their sons will not be included in drafts for service overseas until they are 19 (real age).

Was this instruction anything more than an acknowledgement that mistakes happen and that it was better not to make promises that could be broken?

The existence of a National Register at least held out the hope that errors would be cut to a minimum. The results of the nation-wide survey were to be supplied to the Parliamentary Recruiting Committee, with access given to the coordinators of the Derby Scheme. All the information gathered was checked and corrected before the statistics were sorted and tabulated. The results were finally submitted in early October, to coincide with the launch of the Derby Scheme. The returns had shown that the total number of men aged between eighteen and forty-one was 5,011,441, of whom single men numbered 2,179,231, and married men 2,832,210. In all, 1.5 million men were 'starred', their civil work deemed at that time too essential to the economy for them to be recruited. Of the remainder, at least half were found under the prevailing rules to be unfit for service, which left just short of 1.8 million men nominally available for the army. Three months before conscription was finally introduced, the British Government had the information it needed to mobilize the nation's manhood for war, weeding out 'slackers' from desk jobs and thinning out workers not essential to war production.

Using this information, it was possible to send a letter explaining the scheme to every eligible man in the country, followed by a visit from an appointed canvasser who went from door to door enquiring about men who had not enlisted. Almost all men, except those who were 'starred', were chased and harried. This met with indifferent success, for men who were riled at being doorstepped now dug their heels in and refused to attest, while some actively sought work in munitions to escape the threat of compulsion. In early December, the Reverend Andrew Clark recorded the feelings of one canvasser:

> Major W. Brown said that much against his will he had had to undertake the recruiting duty for Lord Derby's Committee. It was 'the most unpleasant job he ever took on, to recruit your neighbours' sons, your neighbours' men, your own men; but no one else would touch it.' Not a single married man had expressed willingness to serve. Five unmarried men had assented.

News of canvassers' heavy-handed tactics reached MPs, as did reports that young boys were being approached to enlist. On 18 November, Philip Snowden MP asked why, and by what authority, Lord Derby's letter had been sent to boys under seventeen years of age. Why were such boys being canvassed and threatened with a summons before the local tribunal? Was this done, he asked, 'with the knowledge and sanction of the War Office'?

Harold Tennant replied that if Lord Derby's letter had been sent to boys under seventeen years of age, 'this has been due either to a mistake on the part of those sending out the letters, or to the fact that the boy gave his age as eighteen or older when signing the registration paper'.

Suspicions among MPs such as Snowden and Markham persisted. They felt that the lessons of the past few months had given them reason to suspect the Government's motives, but their fears were probably unfounded. Undoubtedly, genuine mistakes were made, for it transpired that Lord Derby's missive had been sent to Lord Kitchener himself as well as to a Cabinet minister, though both men had yet to be door-stepped by canvassers.

Voluntary enlistment was becoming decidedly less an act of free will and much more a case of resignation in the face of harassment and threat. Rumours circulated that men who did not attest and apply to be 'starred' could not expect the chance to make such an appeal if they were subsequently called up. As a result, believed the Reverend Andrew Clark, there had been something of a rush to attest among local farmers.

> This is not voluntary recruiting, but compulsion in a dishonest form. The officer who attended at the council school on Wednesday evening this week said that, if men hung back, they would be hauled out with a rope round their neck. This is voluntary enlistment!

The rush to get 'starred' or to be registered as unfit for service brought forth a plethora of reasons for individuals seeking exemption. A Government report noted the more absurd responses given to canvassers. One man said he was suffering from 'Fiscal Decay', another from 'various veighns'. A third stated that while he could not enlist, he might nevertheless 'Sell new laid eggs to the Government at 3/- per dozen'. There were also those still keen to fight but whose physical restrictions made service problematic, including 'a dwarf from Nottingham who had asked to be enlisted as a mascot'. Youth, too, were still keen to share the national burden. 'A boy of eighteen, rejected on account of bad teeth, had had all his teeth out and a new set put in,' it was noted. The boy was still rejected because he had a twisted toe. To rectify the problem would require an operation. 'This he agreed to, on the condition that he should have a certain guarantee of acceptance on convalescence. He was in hospital seven weeks . . . and has now joined the ranks.'

Humorous and spirit-lifting examples apart, the Derby Scheme still failed. Altogether, 840,000 single males attested and were placed on the Army Reserve, although just over a third of these were later rejected on medical grounds. Excluding those who were 'starred', over a million men had ignored the appeal altogether. Of those who were married, 1.35 million had also signed, around 65 per cent of those nominally available, most in the belief that they would not be called up for a long time.

By launching the Derby Scheme, the Government had signalled to the public that recruits were urgently required and there was a noticeable if brief increase in the numbers who enlisted directly into the forces, from a low of 71,000 in September to 113,000 in October and 121,000 in November. Thereafter the number dropped once more. Voluntary enlistment had shaken out of the population almost all those who were keen to go, as well as those who did not wish to fight but who had enlisted out of patriotic duty. The rest were deemed either to be in jobs vital to the economy, or unlikely ever to enlist voluntarily, no matter how great the threat to Britain's security. Why should these men, it was argued, be allowed to enjoy the benefits of citizenship without being willing to share the costs? Conscription was the only alternative to this intractable problem and most people, reluctantly or not, accepted that it had to come.

Cecil Withers was one of the 121,000 recruits in November. Although aged only seventeen, he had felt the tangible pressure:

My four sisters used to bring their girlfriends to tea, and on occasions these girls would bring their brothers along and all of them boys who, without exception, were officers with their pips and Sam Browne belts. It was all swank, bloody swank, because girls liked that stuff. They would never ask why I wasn't in uniform, they were brought up educated, too polite, oh no, it was purely implied. They made me feel second rate, second class, they would look at me as if to say, 'When are you going to join up?' and their girlfriends would give me derogatory looks, it was humiliating. I was coerced by this pressure of circumstances into the army. I got so fed up with it all that on the last day of November 1915 I thought 'Blow it!' I drew my month's salary from work and went straight out of the office to join up.

Taking the train to Tooting, Cecil met an obliging recruitment sergeant who was patrolling close to the railway station on the look-out for recruits.

He came up to me and asked if I wanted to enlist, then he took me to an office where I gave my name as Sydney George Harrison. I'd heard that the editor of *The Times* was a Harrison and the name went through my mind – nice name that, Harrison, so I stuck with Harrison. I then gave a wrong address, wrong age, so that my parents could not find me. I went before the doctor and, no fuss, passed.

Despite the instructions from the War Office that were issued before he signed up, Cecil was adamant that no one asked to see a National Registration Card, and therefore the only details taken down were those he falsely supplied.

I kept my name Harrison all the way through training but when I'd finished and thought I was going over to France, I decided, 'Right, before I go over there I want to make sure that my people know I'm all right and in the army,' so I sent a letter to my father and got a chap who was going on leave to post it in London, a bit of artfulness on my part to make it look like I was in town. In the

letter I said that father should place an advert in *The Times* saying
he would not apply for my discharge if I gave him my address. I
couldn't stand the idea of being discharged; it would have been so
humiliating.

I bought *The Times* several days later and read the advertisement
in the personal column, 'Right that's me, that's good enough,'
and there and then, I went into the Wesleyan Chapel, sat down
at a table, and wrote to father on some blotting paper, giving my
address, and sent it home.

The failure of the Derby Scheme had served a useful purpose. It
had made conscription more palatable to the public by demon-
strating that all avenues for the maintenance of voluntary enlistment had been exhausted. Public antagonism towards 'shirkers',
periodically whipped up by the newspapers, also helped conscription pass on to the statute books with less opposition than many
politicians had once feared.

MPs were also widely reported as berating those who would not
serve. One, Colonel Charles Yate, told the House:

> I say that men who are not slackers have all attested, or will attest,
> under this bill. In this bill I want to bring in the men who have
> not attested, who will not attest, and who are slackers. Every one
> of them is a shirker.

It was a widely held view. The Military Service Act of January
1916 was passed by the Commons without rancour, leading
campaigners against conscription being, in the end, placated.

As far as the issue of young soldiers was concerned, the conscription debate centred on whether it was right to enlist boys at the
age of eighteen, and whether guarantees were in place that they
would not be sent abroad until the age of nineteen.

Under the Derby Scheme, boys could not be called up until
eighteen years and nine months; with conscription, boys would

be brought into the fold a full nine months younger and a core of worried MPs believed this age was simply too young. There was an awkward contradiction in their argument. They resisted all attempts to lower the age of conscription. Yet if boys could be sent abroad after the age of nineteen, would it not be better to accept them earlier into the army so that they would have a full year's training, equipping them better to withstand the rigours of trench warfare?

Few if any of the dissenters had any military experience, and they were arguing against the weight of opinion influenced by MPs with military careers behind them, whose anecdotes gave credence to their views of trench warfare and how it affected soldiers of all ages.

The burden of war had proved remarkably egalitarian. A large proportion of MPs had sons at the front, including at least one serving under age, while Members themselves had shown an admirable willingness to serve. A number had gone to France in the first year of the war, and during its course several were killed. Perhaps the best known was John Redmond, the Irish Nationalist MP who was killed in 1916, while among other notable victims was Conservative Member for South Oxfordshire Major Valentine Fleming DSO, father of the author Ian Fleming, who was killed in May 1917.

For a long time, the Government had argued that when it came to serving in the trenches age mattered less than the physical strength of the soldier. This argument had many advocates among those MPs who had served abroad and found that healthy lads had proved adept at soldiering in difficult conditions. If age was the issue, they argued, it concerned those who were older rather than those who were younger.

A forty-four-year-old MP and army officer, Major John Newman, could substantiate such a belief. During the conscription debate in January, he supported the view that boys of eighteen were more than capable of serving in the trenches.

I have served for the last few months at the front, and as a simple captain of a company, I walked with my men, and I can tell the Hon. Member that in all our long marches both in this country and in Flanders I never saw any young men in my company fall out, nor have I ever seen any of them helped along, though that occurred in the case of men of about forty.

'Are they eighteen?' asked a backbench MP.

Major Newman replied:

Yes, and some one or two in my company were not actually eighteen. I had a letter from the mother of a lad in my company who stated that he was only sixteen years old, that he was too young to serve in the trenches, and that he should be sent home. I sent for the lad, a very well-grown young fellow, though he is certainly not nineteen, and I told him, 'Your mother says you must go home. Here is your birth certificate showing that you joined under sixteen.' The lad said he did not want to go home and that he wanted to serve . . .

In Flanders, of which I have had experience, it is not the young who suffer but the middle-aged, men of thirty-five or forty years, who undoubtedly do get rheumatism in the trenches. Young men, I find, go through their duties splendidly . . . To my mind, the class of men you want in Flanders are young fellows of eighteen years of age.

Major Newman's argument was hard to refute, although his repeated claim to authority based on his trench experiences was, fortunately for him, not contested in the House. Before becoming an MP, Major Newman had served as an officer in the 5th Royal Munster Fusiliers and on the outbreak of war he had patriotically re-enlisted, joining the Middlesex Regiment. However, his subsequent service overseas had been a little more truncated than he suggested in his speech. His 'few months' were in fact no more than a 'few weeks'. Indeed, his eloquent words to the House were made less than two months after he had first gone to France.

A medical report on Major Newman noted that: 'He found that life in a dugout increased his pain and stiffness and on sudden alarms he found he could not get out of his dugout without help.' It was clear he could not continue to serve and on 4 January 1916 he was on his way back to England, reinforced in his belief that young men were more capable of sticking life in the line than someone more than twice their age.

Newman's service record had another limitation. His short sojourn in France had been with the 17th Battalion Middlesex Regiment, known as the 1st (Football) Sportsmen's Battalion. It was full of young men unscarred by industrial sickness and injury – indeed, many were athletes, including the first black officer in the British Army, Walter Tull, who played for Tottenham Hotspur. The battalion was therefore hardly representative of the rank and file of British soldiering.

Stephen Gwynn, the fifty-one-year-old Nationalist MP for Galway, had also been to the trenches, serving for two months in the ranks in January 1915 before receiving a commission in the Royal Dublin Fusiliers. Gwynn, whose standing as an MP rested on the highest standards of probity, had blatantly lied in order to enlist and by all rights he deserved censure similar to that directed at under-age soldiers by the Undersecretary of State for War.

Gwynn's application for a temporary commission hardly attempted to conceal his dishonesty. He stated his occupation as a 'Journalist' and although he was born in 1864 he claimed to be just thirty-seven years old. He then went on to state particulars, including his marriage to Mary on 17 December 1889 and the dates of birth and names of his six children, beginning with Edward, born in November 1890. By his own admission he must have been eleven when he married and twelve when he fathered his first child. Despite the evident fraud, Gwynn was commissioned in March 1915.

Unlike Major Newman, Stephen Gwynn had fought valiantly for several months in the harsh environment of trench warfare. In October 1916, a fellow officer, Roland Fielding, serving with the 6th Connaught Rangers, recalled the MP's arrival in the line.

> Stephen Gwynn arrived today. He has just been in to lunch . . . He is old for a Company Commander – fifty-two. All the more sporting therefore to have come out in that capacity, especially since he seems to have had a tussle with the War Office Authorities before they would consent to send him.

What is particularly interesting about Gwynn's case is the remark that there had been a tussle over his enlistment and who had apparently resolved it. In a note written on 9 June 1916, Gwynn thanked the Undersecretary of State for War for his help: '. . . you yourself gave me preferential treatment because I was a Member of Parliament in allowing me to join the army at an advanced age . . .' It was six months since Tennant had stood up in Parliament and stated that it was 'the policy of the War Office only to take those who are of proper age'.

Tennant's action tarnishes the record of his words when, displaying moral indignation at the behaviour of those who would fraudulently enlist under age, he berated Sir Arthur Markham for his struggle on their behalf: 'He [Markham] ought to remember that these boys, about whom he has been complaining for a year or more, were, on their own showing, liars.'

Conscription finally came into force in January 1916, and with it, under-age enlistment and the need to lie about age largely disappeared. The problem of boys who were already serving remained. In March, Harold Tennant reiterated the Government's policy as it stood, but, in answer to a specific question, stated that whether or not a boy embarked for service overseas was one for the medical authorities to decide on the medical facts of each case . . . There is no minimum age at which youths are sent abroad; they are sent when their physical qualifications are such as to make it suitable that they should be sent.

This was surprising. While the return of an under-age boy serving abroad was 'left entirely to the discretion of the commanders-in-chief', the rule, according to the last War Office instruction, was specific: for any boy serving at home and under seventeen years of age, 'Discharge will be carried out by his CO under King's Regulations.'

A few weeks later, on 9 May, Colonel John Gretton, during a further debate on the extension of conscription, quoted the explicit War Office orders:

No man, whatever his physical development may be, has to go out until he is nineteen years of age. Those orders are carried out in this way: Every man taken out for a draft has to pass a physical and a medical examination. The medical officer who conducts that examination is ordered to put on one side the young man who has any doubt about his age . . .

It was not that the instruction was unintelligible; the problem was that no one seemed fully in tune with the details. So it came as something of a relief to everyone when the regulations were simplified. On 13 June 1916, a War Office Instruction (No. 1186) was published that appeared to clarify once and for all the Government's view on the protracted issue of under-age soldiering. Everyone knew that there frequently had been a gulf between the age stipulated by a boy on enlistment and his actual age. Now there was broad agreement that birth certificates would be accepted as *the* key piece of evidence when deciding whether to remove a boy from the front or not.

No one, least of all Sir Arthur Markham, was under any illusion that the issue would be immediately and painlessly rectified.

The new instruction was, nevertheless, a vindication of the campaign he and his colleagues had waged. It indicated a change of Government heart, and, unofficially, the Undersecretary of State for War was gracious enough to write a letter to the MP for Mansfield outlining the details, a copy of which Sir Arthur released to the press. Nine days later, the *Daily Mail* was one of several national newspapers to publish the story.

BOY SOLDIERS OF 17
MR TENNANT SAYS THEY ARE TO BE DISCHARGED.

Sir Arthur Markham has received a letter from Mr Tennant stating that the long agitation on behalf of lads in the army has at last been successful.

The War Office has issued new instructions that boys under 17 are to be discharged and boys over 17 and under 19 are to be placed in the reserve.

The previous War Office instruction of September 1915 would now be superseded. All ambiguity regarding the rights of under-age soldiers to be discharged or temporarily removed from the fighting appeared to have been resolved. The simplicity of the new rules mentioned in the *Daily Mail* report appeared to promise unequivocal action for families who could prove that their sons were too young to be serving at the front.

The newspaper had printed only a précis and, although the contents of its brief report were in essence accurate, a couple of clarifications had been missed. While a boy already serving abroad under the age of eighteen would be sent home, the instruction added a crucial rider: it would occur only 'if he be willing'. If the boy were not 'willing', then the issue became unclear. 'If not sent home, he will be dealt with as in section (b) of this paragraph,' read the instruction. In short, he would be transferred to what was known as Class W. Reserve where he would be kept out of harm's way, probably at a base camp, although this was not made explicit. These boys would be joined by those aged between eighteen and nineteen who, under the instruction, could not be returned home but were sent for further training until old enough to go back into the line.

There was one other rider to the announcement. 'Boys' was taken to mean not *all* who were under the age of nineteen, but only NCOs and other ranks, not officers. The long-standing rule that allowed officers to serve abroad over the age of eighteen would remain for the time being. It is curious that in parliamentary debates this issue was not raised nor was the difference ever made overt. The continued lack of clarity led some parents to believe, after reading newspaper reports, that their young officer sons would not see action until at least their nineteenth birthdays. When these boys were later sent overseas, and hundreds died in the Battle of the Somme alone, anger was directed at the War Office in no uncertain terms.

The new rules had also changed the position of other ranks. Where once commanding officers had decided whether to keep an under-age boy at the front, now, once the parent had applied, it was up to the boy himself to make the final decision. The question remained. Would a boy be allowed to make the choice of his own free will or would he be subjected to undue pressure from his commanding officer? It was another example of how the issue was unnecessarily clouded for both politicians and the public.

Further clarification was still needed. MPs wanted to know, for instance, whether, in considering a boy's release, the age used would be the one that was 'real' or 'official'. Tennant replied:

It was to overcome the difficulty we found in accepting the given age [on attestation] as the real age that we have made this departure from our previous custom. We are now having recourse entirely to the birth certificate.

To speed up the whole process, Tennant recommended that parents should send their applications, including the birth certificate, to the officer in charge of records rather than direct to the War Office, which would only lead to delays. 'Would it not be quite as well for parents to write direct to commanding officers?' asked one MP. 'Yes,' replied Tennant, 'I think it would be quicker.'

Ironically, commanding officers had had the power to refuse a boy's discharge in the past and had not always known or chosen to use it. George Adams, who had fought at the Battle of Loos when he was sixteen, had become exhausted by his experiences at the front, and was increasingly anxious to get away. His parents had written requesting his discharge in late 1915. The following month, George was sent for, and medically examined. George wrote to his family:

A report was sent away, and today I had to go up in front of the CO. He asked if I was still willing to serve and tried to coax me to say I would, but my answer was 'No,' so he said he would send me back, so I am expecting to get away at any time. I don't know if he meant the Base or Blighty. I hope he meant the last.

Six days later, George was sent to the base depot at Rouen and, soon after, back to Britain where he was discharged.

One rule remained the same. Other than in cases of 'extreme youth', no boy in the front line could be the architect of his own salvation. Even if lads suddenly changed their minds and decided they wanted to get out, the best they could do was to write and 'encourage' their families to make an application, and then await due process.

Like George Adams, Private Claude Damant was exhausted. He had gone to France aged sixteen in November 1915 and had suffered in the winter weather. In desperation he had written to his mother who forwarded his birth certificate so that he could 'make use of it' and he had been pulled out of the ranks for further training at St Omer. He was not a boy with the strongest constitution, and in January he had come down with enteric fever and been hospitalized before being returned to duty. However, days later he was transferred to England. Yet, to his mother's surprise, he was not sent home but kept in the army until a formal procedure of discharge was undertaken whereby Claude's mother sent a now rather grubby, Western Front soiled birth certificate as proof of age and requested his discharge.

Claude's father had died when his son was still a baby and his mother had remarried. Mrs Diprose, as she became, was keen to get her son home. Claude was her only son and she knew he was not strong. Her letter dated 12 July 1916, requesting her son's discharge, was processed quickly. On 28 July he gathered up his belongings and made his own way home to Clapham in London, to be greeted by his delighted parents. And by the morning he was dead. His death, certified by a civilian doctor Richard Jaques, noted that 'suppurative meningitis' had been the cause.

When fifteen-year-old Albert Harvey – the Hull boy inspired to join up after a Zeppelin raid on his home town – was called before the CO, he was given no opportunity to keep up any pretence, for the officer was holding a copy of his birth certificate, proof that he was born on 4 July 1900, and not 1896 as he had attested. Albert was concerned only that if he was discharged people would consider him a 'mother's darling' for coming home and, with this in mind, spoke to the CO.

> I still implied that I would like to stay out. I gathered that if I still wished it, they would arrange for me to do some job miles behind the lines. Smiling, the CO told me to think it over and report the next morning.

Albert's friends in the platoon were in no doubt what he should do. 'You young fool, get back home,' said one. 'What do you think? He has the chance to go home and isn't taking it!' scoffed another. The opinion of his friends settled Albert's mind. 'When

I reported at the office the next morning, I accepted the idea of discharge.'

Instruction 1186 was just one of forty-eight emanating from the War Office that June week of 1916, and although it made a key change in the way boy soldiers would be handled in future, it was not front-page news. The whole issue had never become one of fundamental importance on the political stage; there was, after all, a war to be won. Yet under-age soldiering was a protracted problem, if a lesser one, that had proved contentious and difficult to resolve. It had been a thorn in the side of the Government when other, more pressing, issues had come and gone.

It was perhaps a pity that the announcement of Instruction 1186 received only passing attention. The national news, under-standably, had concentrated on recent events, not least the death of Lord Kitchener, drowned aboard HMS *Hampshire*, which had sunk after hitting a mine. The Prime Minister had temporarily assumed responsibility for the War Office until a replacement was found, Lloyd George becoming the new Minister for War in early July. The death of the national icon produced an enormous sense of shock. By the time this had begun to abate, minds were turning to the offensive about to break on the Somme. If the public had been able to foresee the enormous casualties of that first day, perhaps the cause of retrieving so many young boys from service overseas might have been given greater urgency.

9

The Big Push

A BOY IN YEARS
A MAN IN DEEDS

18/596 Private Willie Whitaker
18th West Yorkshire Regiment

Killed in Action 1 July 1916, aged 18

IN JUNE 1916, THE British Army was in the final stages of preparation for a major offensive. Nicknamed the 'Big Push', the assault was designed to smash the enemy's defences and allow the British to decisively break through the stalemate of the Western Front and relieve the French Army under pressure from the German offensive at Verdun. The attack would begin a general advance by the Allied armies that would send the Germans reeling all the way back, it was hoped, to Berlin.

Until July 1915, the Somme region had been held by the French but, as part of the BEF's expanding commitment to the war, it was agreed that British troops would take over and occupy the area to the north of the river Somme, while the French would remain on the ground to the south. Both armies would serve side by side and, largely because of this, the region was chosen for a symbolic joint attack: Allies together, shoulder to shoulder.

One of the first battalions to arrive on the Somme in 1915 had been the 7th Royal West Kents, and among their number were teenage friends Vic Cole and George Pulley. Vic had been sent to the Signals Section of the battalion and the two had been parted, but their paths still crossed, giving them a chance to catch up on news from home. The signals station was housed in a ruined flour mill near the village of Suzanne. Vic recalled:

> This sector, being on the extreme right of the British line at that time, was full of interest. Across the narrow millstream our right-hand company made contact with the left-hand company of the French Army, which stretched from here to the Swiss Alps.

The planned assault on the Somme was to be delivered in the main by troops of Kitchener's New Volunteer Army, including Vic's battalion. Throughout May and June, huge columns of these keen but largely untested men had made their way to the region, while hundreds of guns of all calibres were brought up and concealed from enemy eyes. Huge stockpiles of ammunition were prepared so that on 24 June these guns could launch the heaviest bombardment of the war to date. For five days, twenty-four hours a day, the guns would blaze away at the enemy trenches that stood before eight fortified villages. As a finale, five enormous mines, laboriously dug beneath strong points in the German front line, would be blown. These mines had been constructed by the Royal Engineers, and prepared with great care and precision. Once detonated, they would send a huge column of earth into the air and, if all went according to plan, hundreds of yards of enemy trench and everyone who sheltered there, too.

Shortly before the offensive began, Vic was granted home leave. He was about to depart when, at the bottom of a hill, he spotted George Pulley on a fatigue party. George was digging a trench and after a few moments he looked up. Seeing Vic, his face broke into a broad smile and he waved vigorously. Then, as he waved, a stray shell appeared to land flush with the very section of trench that George was digging. For a moment the scene was covered with smoke and dust and as it cleared Vic looked on, expecting the worst. Then there was George again, still smiling, still waving.

Vic himself was soon to have a stroke of luck too. After eleven months of war he was rather less enthusiastic than he had been and at the end of his leave he had had to drag his young body back to the war. It was late June and the bombardment was well under way. On arrival in France, he was sent to the village of Meaulte, well behind the lines on the Somme, although 'The continuous roar of heavy guns here was overpowering and air activity was considerable,' he recalled. He was due to sleep one night in an old barn before rejoining the battalion. About midnight, he was awoken by the shattering noise of an explosion and a gaping hole appeared in the far wall. 'Several men had bruises or cuts from the flying splinters and my trousers were wet with blood from a gash in my side just above the hip-bone.' It was a small wound, but Vic would not take part in the coming offensive when his battalion, George Pulley included, would go over the top to attack Montauban, one of the eight fortified villages.

The air activity that Vic noticed included Cecil Lewis's No. 3 Squadron RFC. A pilot's most vulnerable time was in the first few weeks of service, but after two months on the Somme Cecil was still going strong and had been given orders to photograph and re-photograph enemy trenches, as shells saturated the enemy's front and support lines. These images would help senior commanders determine the success of the bombardment. Only after this would the troops go over, supported in part by 185 aircraft of the RFC. These planes would monitor the progress of the advancing troops, acting as contact patrols, passing on information between the front line and headquarters.

One of those manning the guns was Len Thomas, serving with his battery of 9.2-inch howitzers. Despite orders, Len continued to record day-to-day events, his frequent scribbling unseen or ignored by those around him. The number of shells available to the battery, he had noted, was out of all proportion to those held behind the guns at the Battle of Loos. Then they had had 100 rounds; for the Somme they had been allocated 3,000, each shell weighing 290 lb.

> On the 26th we were firing all day and night and plenty of infan-
> try were marching down. The 27th was wet, but it didn't stop us
> sending plenty over. Very many guns around here. The food was
> very poor. Never do I remember getting any food when we were
> firing all night, nothing after tea till breakfast, about fifteen hours.
> I used to nibble one of the very hard biscuits for hours. The 28th
> was again wet, and the attack was postponed for a day or so . . .

The bombardment had been extended too, to seven days, and the advance postponed until 1 July. Rain and heavy cloud had made reconnaissance difficult, so pilots were ordered to fly low to take pictures. This put them directly in the line of fire, as Cecil Lewis well knew.

> At two thousand feet we were in the path of the gun trajectories,
> and as the shells passed, above or below us, the wind eddies made by
> their motion flung the machine up and down, as if in a gale. Each
> bump meant that a passing shell had missed the machine by four or
> five feet. Grimly I kept the machine in its course above the trenches,
> waiting, tense and numb, for a shell to get us, while Sergeant Hall
> worked the old camera handle, changed the plates, sighted, made
> his exposures. I envied him having something to do. I could only
> hold the machine as steady as possible and pray for it to be over.

It was the eve of the attack, and the infantry prepared to move up into their positions. They were addressed by commanding offic-ers who pronounced words of encouragement and warning. The attack was to be pressed home, and there was to be no falling back.

The 7th Royal West Kents had paraded to hear their pep-talk. It finished with a Special Order sent by the brigade commander:

I wish it to be impressed on all ranks the importance of the operation about to commence. Success will mean the shortening of the war, failure means the war prolonged indefinitely. Success or failure depends on the individual effort and fighting spirit of every single man. The Germans are now outnumbered and outgunned, and will soon go to pieces if every man goes into the fight determined to get through whatever the local difficulties may be.

I am confident the 55th Brigade will distinguish itself in this its first battle. Let every man remember that all England and all the World is watching them.

GOOD LUCK. WE MEET AGAIN IN MONTAUBAN.

T. D. Jackson, Brigadier General

Commanding 55th Infantry Brigade

Further north, sixteen-year-old Frank Lindley listened to a similar pre-battle speech forearmed with a healthy dose of scepticism.

On the eve of battle a bloke came, I believe it was Lieutenant General Hunter-Weston. We were in this clearing in the wood and we all crowded round and he started talking to us. He looked like he'd just stepped out of a bandbox, all polished up with red tabs. He says, 'Now, you men, you will get on the top and you'll walk across with port arms and go straight into the German line.' There was a rumour that a bloke said to him, 'Where will tha be?'

The two battalions of the Barnsley Pals had been in and out of the line on several occasions and the men, including Frank, could not help but notice the wire in front of the German lines which would have to be cut if the attack was to be a success. Frank remembered:

Their wire was about four times as wide as ours. The quantity of wire they had, heavens, you couldn't have got through that in a month of Sundays. Our wire was narrow compared to theirs. When they were saying, 'Our guns will tear up the wire so that you can get through', I thought, 'By God, I hope so,' but no. We knew all the time we were in for a bashing and we couldn't do anything about it. We weren't daft.

Len Thomas had also heard the optimistic predictions. On 30 June he wrote:

In the evening our officer Lt Paine told us a breakthrough was expected, the cavalry would go clean through and at 5 p.m. next day, 1st, the guns were to be dismounted and taken to a position about seven miles up the Bapaume Road but not expected to be put into position as the war would now become mobile. We hoped so, but many were very dubious, especially about moving . . .

As part of the final preparations, battalions such as the Barnsley Pals had been issued with a diamond or triangle of tin to be worn on the back of their haversacks. Although the weather had been poor, 1 July was forecast to be hot and dry, a perfect summer's day. In these conditions the triangles would work well, reflecting the sun's rays to the RFC, who would be circling overhead looking for indications of the extent of the advance.

The triangles were the lightest of the extra equipment that Frank Lindley would carry into action.

We had entrenching tools strapped low across our fronts. They should have fitted at the back but we used to strap them across the front to protect our privates from a bayonet thrust or a piece of shell or owt. We were loaded down with stuff. We had a Mills bomb in each pocket and a bandolier around us, the pouches full of ammo. I had a telephone slung on a leather strap – and they weighed a ton – and a coil of wire as well as my gun.

In the hours of darkness, the battalions were brought forward, crowding into the front line and support trenches. As they filed

up the communication trenches, they were frequently held up.
Frank recalled:

> As we stood there, one of these German shells we called 'coal
> boxes' dropped on top and covered us all. We scattered ourselves
> a bit. My knees were red-raw with the soil hitting me. The next
> bloke to me started shaking, jibbering like an idiot. He was abso-
> lutely unhinged, couldn't do a thing. We had to bypass him and
> travel on because they were shoving us forward.
>
> They were shelling us in the rear. I was cheek by jowl with one
> of our sergeants, Sergeant Jones, and this salvo of shrapnel came
> right over the top of us and rattled on our hats. Some must have
> gone down the back of the sergeant and he was done. Blood was
> coming out between his back and his haversack, and had bespat-
> tered me. I don't know if he was dead.

Just a few hundred yards from Frank Lindley, the 11th East
Lancashire Regiment was filing into its front line. Better known
to posterity as the Accrington Pals, these men were drawn primarily from the town itself or close by, from places such as Chorley,
Blackburn and Burnley. For the best part of four months, the
battalion had been out in Egypt undergoing intensive training, but in March they returned and headed for France and the
trenches near the Somme village of Serre. In April they received a
new officer, Second Lieutenant Reginald Battersby from Blackley
in Manchester – present at the front courtesy of significant string-
pulling back home. Now, as a sixteen-year-old, he was in the
trenches preparing to lead his platoon over the top in the third
wave of the attack.

Reginald was not the only sixteen-year-old officer at the front
that day. Second Lieutenant Philip Lister was serving with the
10th King's Own Yorkshire Light Infantry (KOYLIs), a battalion
due to attack in the first assault. Born on 30 July 1899, Philip had
applied for a temporary commission in January 1915, his almost

infantile handwriting evidently not impeding his application. He had trained for a year before being sent in a draft of seven officers to join the KOYLIs in June 1916 as the battalion made final preparations for the offensive. During the hours before the attack, they were holding trenches no more than a mile to the south of the German-held village of La Boiselle, and so were in a prime position to see the biggest mine explode a couple of minutes before the signal to go.

As these young lads began to move up to the line, Cecil Lewis was making for the aerodrome hangars. He wanted to make last-minute checks to his aircraft, to ensure that all would be well when he took off in a few hours' time. He turned in to get some rest but in the early hours was up again, checking once more as a final precaution.

Cecil had been detailed to be the first flight up, and would therefore have a grandstand view of the attack, which would go in at 7.30 a.m. It was fully daylight when he took off, and as he flew over the battlefield he could see the devastation resulting from the week-long bombardment.

> Square miles of country were ripped and blasted to a pock-marked desolation. Trenches had been obliterated, and still, as we watched, the gunfire continued, in a crescendo of intensity. Even in the air, at four thousand feet, above the roar of the engine, the drumming of firing and bursting shells throbbed in our ears.

All the battalions were now waiting to go. Frank Lindley recalled:

> When you stood on the fire step, your head was just over the parapet. One or two of the blokes got dinted by snipers. One in particular, he must have been dozing, because all of a sudden he came crashing down on me and his hat had a great slice in it at the side. I don't know if it'd done his skull, as there was no sign of blood, but he was out.

As Frank waited for the whistles to go, Cecil Lewis was flying up and down the line. He had been warned against flying too close to La Boiselle, where two mines were due to go up, but he would be able to watch from a safe distance.

We were over Thiepval and turned south to watch the mines. As we sailed down above it all, came the final moment. Zero!

At Boiselle the earth heaved and flashed, a tremendous and magnificent column rose up into the sky. There was an ear-splitting roar, drowning all the guns, flinging the machine sideways in the repercussing air. The earthy column rose, higher and higher to almost four thousand feet. There it hung, or seemed to hang, for a moment in the air, like a silhouette of some great cypress tree, then fell away in a widening cone of dust and debris.

In the trenches, the ground rocked violently. Frank Lindley was the best part of two miles from another mine placed under a German redoubt at Beaumont Hamel.

The birds were singing in the copses around. It was a beautiful day, beautiful. We had this morning chorus and then it all happened, just like a flash. We were stood there waiting, ready for the officer to blow his whistle, and our barrage lifted and then bang! a great big mine went up on the right-hand side. We saw it going sky high, one huge mass of soil. It shouldn't have gone up till we were on the top because it alerted the Germans and they were up and waiting for us and when we attacked they cut us to ribbons, totally ripped us to pieces.

To the right of the Barnsley and Accrington Pals were the Leeds Pals, or the 15th Battalion of the West Yorkshire Regiment as they were officially designated. Like all other units, they had their fair share of under-age boys, including several who had enlisted at fourteen or fifteen. Horace Iles was one of those boys, a lad from Woodhouse in Leeds. He was now sixteen, and had already been wounded once, hit by shrapnel when the Germans had bombarded the Pals' trenches in May 1916. He had been sent to hospital in England and had not been back long with his platoon in B Company. As they moved up the line, several men had been wounded by German shelling, but they finally reached the front line and were ready to go. All the men knew what they had to do. They must sweep over the German front, second, third and fourth lines to the south of the village of Serre, and then consolidate the gains.

As the debris settled from the mine explosions, tens of thousands of men left their trenches and went forward. The Barnsley Pals attacked up a rise towards the German trenches. Frank Lindley recalled that it was not a steep rise, but to them that morning, laden with equipment, it looked like a mountain. Even as the advance began, casualties were falling.

> One bloke was climbing out, and he'd got hold of the top of the ladder and this shell must have chopped him right across the middle. It left his feet and the bottom half in the trench and all his insides were hanging down the blinking trench wall. It was a shocking sight, looking at that lot.

Cyril José, who had been out in France for a year, was seventeen. He had gone over the top just yards away from the smaller of the two explosions on the edge of La Boiselle, following his platoon officer, Lieutenant Eric Gould. Cyril had gone over with his friend Norton Hedge, another under-age volunteer and a veteran of eighteen months' fighting. This was Norton's fourth time over the top. In two letters home, written just after the attacks, Cyril described the next few minutes in his usual upbeat style.

> We were told it would be a walk-over ... Of course we might expect to be sniped at by a stray German naturally! We would

advance, take the first line, go on to village of Ovillers then on to
3rd & 4th lines to village of Pozieres. If we met any opposition
here we would dig in and other regiments would come through
us. Quite simple!

Well, we went over . . . with the feeling in us of the song 'Over
the top, over the top & never come back again.' Some people say
you go absolutely mad. You don't! I've never felt so cool & matter-
of-fact in my life. I was surprised. But I was still more surprised
at the reception. You know what a hailstorm is. Well, that's about
the chance one stood of dodging the bullets, shrapnel etc. Of
course it must have been that stray sniper!! 'Johnny' [Cyril's name
for a German], always considerate, ordered me to have a rest when
I had got about 20 yards from his parapet.

Cyril had been shot through the left shoulder five minutes after
going over the top. He had done comparatively well, for he had
lost touch with Norton Hedge, and his officer, Lieutenant Gould,
had been killed soon after, leaving Cyril to cross almost 800 yards
of no-man's-land before he was hit.

At Serre, the German trenches were much closer, but Frank
Lindley was struggling even to reach the enemy wire.

I was in the first wave on the extreme left. We scrambled on to the
fire step and then on the top, when I glanced over. They were all
going on our right. There was nothing on our left. There was no
cheering, we just ambled across, you hadn't a thought; you were
so addled with the noise. Second Lieutenant Hirst was next to me.
He had just got wed before we came away, and was a grand chap,
but it wasn't long before he got his head knocked off.

Out of the corner of your eye you could see the boys going down
but there was no going back, they had what we called 'whippers-
in' with pistols and they could shoot you if anybody came back,
so we moved forward as best we could, it was implanted in our
heads. You could hear the bullets whistling past and our lads were

going down flop, flop, flop in their waves, just as though they'd all
gone to sleep. As I laid flat out there in No Man's Land, up on top
jumped one of our whippers-in with pistol ready, and we were all
laid out in shell holes, and he said, 'Come on, come on.' He hadn't
gone two yards before he went up in the air, riddled.

Cyril's relative success was now his potential undoing. In the
minutes before he was wounded, he had advanced far enough into
no-man's-land to make it impossible to return, and he lay close
to a number of dead and wounded men. Those who were unhurt
were now hiding in shell holes and where possible helping the
wounded. Every man carried what was known as a first field dressing, held in a little pocket lightly stitched in the front of the tunic.
As Cyril was incapable of bandaging himself, another man opened
Cyril's coat and retrieved his dressing, placing the bandage against
the wound. This quickly became saturated with blood and another
bandage was applied, but with the same result. Cyril threw away
both bandages and let the wound bleed, hoping it might clot of
its own accord. He lay back, and in doing so could well have seen
Cecil Lewis's plane as the young pilot flew up and down the same
part of the line looking for evidence of progress. There was little to
suggest the German lines had been penetrated at all. Cecil wrote:

> My logbook for July 1st contains the following entries. 'From
> our point of view an entire failure. Not a single ground sheet
> of Battalion or Brigade Headquarters was seen. Only two flares
> were lit on the whole of both Corps fronts.' . . . I was bitterly
> disappointed.

At Serre, Frank was trying to advance but the situation was
hopeless.

> We had to dodge from shell hole to shell hole to try to get through.
> All their wire was piled up in great coils, tremendous, and there

was just the odd gap. As soon as you made for that gap it was R-R-R-R-R, all you could do was dive in a shell hole, and the ground was pitted with shell holes because our guns had tried to bust all their wire up. Bullets were like a swarm of bees round you, you could almost feel them plucking at your clothes. Them that made for the gaps in their wire were all piled up where the machine guns just laid them out. Some were hanging on the wire, but it was no good. It was pure murder so we tried picking the Jerries off because they were on the trench top, some of them, cheering their mates on while our lads on the wire were hanging like rags. Some I recognized, 'that's so and so,' I thought, but one burst of one of their big machine guns and they were in bits. Arms and legs were flying all over.

I didn't know anybody in the shell holes I got in. We were all mixed up. There was no conversation, it was self-preservation, dive in and risk what you got. The final shell hole we got in was the finish, a whiz bang came over us and split, I never heard it coming. Shrapnel went right through my thigh and took my trousers in with it, I looked down and there was blood running freely and another bit of metal sticking out.

When I'd recovered a little, I thought I'd better get it seen to, so I rolled over no-man's-land and over to our trench on the edge of John Copse. There was the head of a sap there and I went in and had a smoke with another bloke, he was wounded. They dropped some shells into the copse and one hit his arm and a bit of the hot shell burnt a little hole in my leg.

I carried on. All the communication trenches were full of dead and on the way down I passed our headquarters, an old German dugout, and they were patrolling up and down, the colonel and his retinue, looking across, and they had faces like chalk.

The Accrington Pals had been annihilated, too. They had advanced from the neighbouring copse, and the same machine guns had ripped through their ranks. The first two waves had left the trench before zero hour and had lain out in no-man's-land, suffering numerous killed and injured before they even set off. The following two waves had been able to move into the front line in order to advance at precisely 7.30 a.m., but in the event none of the attacking companies had met with success. Reginald Battersby had done as well as anybody and had managed to advance up a slight depression in the ground with the survivors of his platoon. As they approached the German line, they came under attack from the right by a machine-gun post at close range. Swinging his platoon round, Reginald went to engage the German crew but was shot once in his forearm, the bullet passing straight through, and once in the right leg. The platoon faced the prospect of being wiped out when the German machine gun suddenly jammed, giving the Pals the chance to attack and destroy the position.

For the rest of the day, the dead and wounded lay out in no-man's-land. In some places the Germans allowed the wounded to be rescued, in others they sniped at the survivors, making rescue impossible. In the heat, thirst became intolerable. Cyril José realized that while the battle raged, his best option was to stay put.

I couldn't get back to our own lines until next morning. I didn't eat anything, but lived on pulling off dead men's water bottles. I was as thirsty as anything at first, but I got a few water bottles.

That night German patrols ventured out into no-man's-land looking for prisoners. Cyril had been lapsing in and out of consciousness all day, remaining calm. Now with Germans about, he was once again on his metal. 'I lay doggo clutching a Mills bomb ready to pull the pin with my teeth. Rather than be taken prisoner I would take the patrol with me. They passed me by.'

It was clear that no one was going to come for him; Cyril would have to be the architect of his own rescue.

Even well behind the lines, the gunners on Len Thomas's battery knew things had gone badly wrong. When the attack was launched in the morning the guns' elevation had been increased to shell the rear areas but by the afternoon the range had been shortened and they were back shelling the line around Thiepval. Len wrote:

> Late that evening a group of infantry were passing, and one of our chaps shouted, 'What's it like up there?' And a Sergeant replied, 'It's bloody murder, we 28 are all that's left of the Battalion.' They were Inniskillings. We kept hearing of massacres that day. All we could do to help the walking wounded was to leave buckets of water at the side of the road.

Hope of moving anywhere that day, let alone seven miles up the Bapaume Road, was dashed. Len's battery did not advance an inch for another four weeks. Cyril José was no longer interested in any advance, only a retreat to safety.

> About 6 a.m. 2 July, I began crawling back to our line – the grass was fortunately long. It seemed that I was alone in a field of dead men. The wounded had either made their way back or had been killed in their tracks Then, about halfway, I encountered Private Lamacraft – a hardened regular soldier thirty years old. He was wounded in back and legs. We struggled along together with my right arm under his body whilst he tried to walk on his hands wheelbarrow-race style.
>
> In an hour we had made very little progress. We were both too weak from loss of blood and we had made ourselves conspicuous – Jerry had started firing at us. Luckily, his shooting was very erratic – he too was beginning to feel the strain.
>
> I dragged Lammy into a large shell crater and we rested while we took stock. We decided that it was impossible to reach our lines. Lammy had to be carried. There was still a faint chance that

I could make it alone. I gathered some water bottles from nearby corpses and stacked them around Lamacraft. Then I set off again snaking my way through the grass.

The Germans continued to snipe at Cyril all the way back to the British front line.

I offered up a prayer of thanks when I dropped in our trench right by a chap on periscope who had been watching me come in. I soon got rushed back then, so now here I am in England. I heard after, that out of our battalion twenty-seven answered roll call after the battle. So you can imagine what it's like. Twenty-seven out of about 900 or 1,000 men.

Once he reached the trench, Cyril had been quickly attended to. His jacket, cardigan and shirt were caked with blood and had to be cut off before he could be properly bandaged and sent down the line. Cyril was lucky that none of the major arteries had been severed, otherwise he would have bled to death. In a letter written in a hospital bed, Cyril gave more detail of the events that day and his subsequent feelings. The letter is dated 16 July.

My dearest Mother

Thanks awfully for [the] letter yesterday & Ive's today. I was awfully pleased to get them. You want to know if the bullet is out? Yes, it went clean through. So I didn't have a chance to keep it as a souvenir, did I? Now, to answer your questions. Yes, some of the Battalion got to Ovillers. I think, at least I heard, that they got to the third line & Ovillers is only about 2nd line. In fact part of it is just behind the first. But Johnny must have had some powerful defences there, for our people had to retire to the 1st line again. However, they hung on to that. Yes, there were several dead around me but I saw some wounded a bit too far off to speak to them. They were all the result of the few minutes going across.

That's where we lost most of our men. Of course, some 'big bug'
thought it a great idea to go over in broad daylight instead of
crawling up as near to their parapet in the night under cover of
the bombardment as [possible], so that we could then dive in their
trench with hardly any losses in going across. Of course Johnny
wouldn't expect us then so much. I suppose they thought that as
he wouldn't expect us, he wouldn't see us. Certainly not! Result –
Johnny spots us coming over the parapet and we have to go about
600 yards. What brains old Douglas [Haig] must have. Made me
laugh when I read his Dispatch yesterday. '*I* attacked.' Old women
in England picturing Sir Doug in front of British waves brandish-
ing his sword & living in trenches. I'll get a job like that in the
next war. Attack Johnny from 100 miles back!! Still, we can't all
lead, can we?

God bless you all.
Best love from
Cyril

Cyril had not forgotten Private Lamacraft and he described
his friend's location while two officers of the Royal Berkshire
Regiment tried to ply him with some rum. Cyril had hoped a
stretcher party would be sent but the officers had declined to send
anyone as the task was simply too dangerous. Lamacraft remained
in no-man's-land for a further three days until he was rescued.

Philip Lister's battalion, the 10th KOYLIs, were badly cut up.
On 1 July the battalion had lost nine officers killed and sixteen
wounded, perhaps all of the officers who went over the top that
morning. The number killed included at least one officer who had
arrived with Philip's draft in June, and an unknown number of
wounded. It is not known if Philip took part in the assault that
day or was held back in reserve. On the following day, as one of
the few surviving officers, he was made acting captain and given
command of a company until 11 August, when he returned to

his substantive rank. Of those who took part, at least 157 were killed and around 300 wounded. Frank Lindley's battalion had lost 119 officers and men dead. The neighbouring battalion of the Accrington Pals had fared even worse. Some 235 of their number had died at Serre and another 360 were wounded, while the Leeds Pals had also suffered heavily, losing every single officer and at least 504 other ranks killed or wounded.

One of the battalions that did meet with success that day was Vic Cole's. On 1 July, Vic was resting in a convalescent camp when casualties from the day's fighting began to pour in by the hundred, and Vic, along with other lightly wounded, was quickly removed from his tent to make way for serious cases. Among the wounded there were few, if any, from the 7th Battalion. On the southern sector of the attack, close to Montauban, the British divisions had stormed the enemy line and held all the ground captured that day. The casualties had been relatively light: the 7th Royal West Kents had fewer than thirty killed, an achievement given the destruction elsewhere, although Vic could never quite agree with the sentiment, for among the dead was his old pal George Pulley, killed at the age of eighteen.

Such was the pressure on casualty clearing stations and the base hospitals that even lightly wounded men found themselves rapidly sent down the medical chain, on to boats and back to Britain. Reginald Battersby was back in England by 3 July and in hospital. Cyril José was not far behind – he was sent to No. 16 General Hospital, Le Tréport, and kept for a few days until his wound was cleaned, and then sent on 9 July to Southampton and eventually to Barnstaple. His friend Norton Hedge had been slightly wounded, a relief for Cyril, although he was killed later that summer.

War Office 'official' lists of the killed and wounded might take a month or more to hit the newspapers; however, with the wounded being sent home, news of the disaster reached families far earlier. Within days the press began publishing pictures of heroes, dead, wounded and missing, so that by the middle of July no one was left with any other impression than that the first day of the Battle of the Somme had been cruel in terms of lives lost.

The gunshot wound to Cyril's shoulder took a long time to heal and he remained in hospital for six months. While there, he had an unexpected visitor.

> Today a gentleman, evidently a founder or something of this Hospital, was coming round. 'What's your name, sonny?' 'José, sir.' 'Oh, so you're the Devons' chap.' 'Yes, sir.' Asked me where I had got hit. Told him, 'Ovillers'. Asked me if I knew Lieutenant Gould. 'Yes, sir, he was killed in front of me.' 'Ah, you're the man I want. He was my son!' I nearly fainted . . . I fancy it had broken him. Poor chap. I didn't half feel sorry for him. I told him he was the best officer a chap could have etc etc, he said that he had written home saying what a fine lot of men he had under him. Queer coincidence, wasn't it? He looked properly broken hearted.

The statistics from 1 July are often quoted, but remain staggering. In short, some 20,000 dead, 40,000 wounded. From the CWGC records it is possible to identify 118 boys aged seventeen or under who died that day, but this figure is misleading. They are a small proportion of those under age who were actually killed or wounded. The ages of many others who died can be identified from other sources both published and unpublished. Thomas Hartness of the 11th Borders had enlisted aged fifteen when the war broke out and was killed on 1 July, as was Thomas Norman who died at seventeen with the same battalion. In the 15th Battalion of the West Yorkshire Regiment, Horace Iles's battalion, Richard Matthews had enlisted just after his fifteenth birthday, and died aged sixteen. James Clarke of the 12th Royal Irish Rifles was killed on 1 July. Born in June 1899, he had also enlisted at fifteen and had only just celebrated his seventeenth birthday when he was killed. Another was Private John Metcalf. He was killed aged seventeen serving with his battalion, the 11th East Lancashire Regiment. They are a handful of the many other boys killed that day who remain unidentified as under age by the CWGC.

The reports of such huge casualties sent shock waves across the country and nowhere more so than among families of under-age boy soldiers. For many of the Kitchener's New Army battalions this had been their first time over the top, and the first time, too, that they had suffered heavy casualties. As after the Battle of Loos, families were galvanized into writing to the War Office to get their boys out.

Florrie Iles, sister of Horace, was appalled by the reports and decided she must write direct to her brother and persuade him to own up to his age and come home. On 9 July she composed the following:

My Dear Horace . . .

I am so glad you are alright so far but I need not tell you what an anxious time I am having on your account, you *have* dropped in for the thick of it and no mistake. I only hope you have the good luck to come back safely like your father did [a professional soldier who had served in Afghanistan] and my dear boy *I* don't care how soon. I should be more than pleased to see you, I can tell you. You have no need to feel ashamed that you joined the 'Pals' now for by all accounts they have rendered a good account of themselves, no one can call them 'Feather-bed Soldiers' now . . .

We did hear that they were fetching all back from France under 19. For goodness sake Horace tell them how old you are. I am sure they will send you back if they know you are only 16, you have seen quite enough now, just chuck it up and try to get back you won't fare no worse for it. If you don't do it now you will come back in bits and we want the whole of you. I don't suppose you can do any letter writing now but just remember that I am always thinking of you and hoping for your safe return . . .

Your loving sister
Florrie xxxxxxxxx

The letter was sent but soon returned. On the envelope was stamped 'Killed in action'. Horace Iles had not survived the attack on Serre, and his body had been lying for over a week somewhere in no-man's-land as his sister began to write her letter.

10

Dear Old Blighty

HERE LIES A MOTHER'S SON
AT HEART A MAN
WHO GAVE HIS ALL
FOR US AND MOTHERLAND

14650 Private Fred Thomson
24th Manchester Regiment

Enlisted 17, France 18, Killed aged 19, 6 February 1916

INSTRUCTION 1186 OF JUNE 1916, clarifying the issue of underage soldiers and releasing them from front-line duty, had been announced by the War Office three weeks before the launch of the Somme offensive, but there was a time-lag between the procedural decision and a public announcement reaching the press. This meant there was no time for anxious parents to make any meaningful application for a son's release before the battle. In any case, a rush would have implied foreknowledge of the events of 1 July and no one, least of all civilians, predicted any calamity. The public feeling, such as it was, had been to presume success, in which case seeking to remove boys such as Horace Iles or Cyril José would probably have left them unnecessarily devastated. Horace was after all the son of a former soldier who had also fought for his country.

Despite their own anxiety, parents were aware how much service to the country and particularly loyalty to their friends meant to boys who had rushed to join Kitchener's Army. But then what if their son were killed? Could they live with the knowledge that they could have saved him? It was a terrible conundrum, and the decision to recall a son from the trenches was invariably agonizing.

In July 1916, an unknown but undoubtedly significant number of boys began to be sent down the line. The adjutant of the 2/5th Gloucestershire Regiment chose to record their passage not by name but by number, noting down each occasion when each one left the battalion. One under-age boy was removed on 11 July and another six days later. Two more went on 20 July, followed by two more on 24 July. Yet another left on the 27th and another one eighteen days later, followed quickly by a further three before the end of August. More boys followed the well-worn route later in the year: and this was one battalion of many hundreds serving on the Somme.

When reclaiming a son the first logical step for parents was to contact their local Member of Parliament in the hope that he might give advice or point the family in the right direction. There was no guarantee that they would receive a sympathetic ear, and an approach could result in more confusion and doubt. There were, after all, MPs not averse to boys serving at the front. Sir Henry Craik, an MP and former army officer, was approached by a family in his constituency, asking if he would make an application to the War Office on their behalf. Craik refused unless they could produce a letter from their under-age son actually asking to be discharged.

I said to the parents, 'Do you realize what responsibility you are taking in the eyes of your son? It is not a responsibility I would care to take in the case of my own son. Do you think, if you summon him home, and he is sent away from his comrades in the trenches, he will ever get over it in later life, or that he will ever forgive you for what you have done?'

Within days, Craik received a letter from the family. They had been swayed by his argument and their application would not be pressed.

> I am perfectly certain that that is the feeling of many parents, and I am proud of it. I am still more sure that it represents the feeling of these young fellows . . . they do not wish to be treated as children, misled or misguided . . . They are keen to serve their country, and they are proud of the opportunity to do it.

Craik's eldest son George was serving in France, and in due course he was awarded the Military Cross of which father and son were no doubt rightfully proud. Yet Craik's opinions were as unfortunate as they were patriotic. Everybody's circumstances were different and a number of parents had sought to withdraw one under-age son from service only after the death of another, elder son. Notions of responsibility and pride were of less importance to the terror of losing further sons. In January 1916, Rachel Appleyard wrote to the authorities seven days after the death of her son Leonard. 'I have just lost my eldest son, he went down on the [HMS] *Natal* last Thursday and I don't want to lose all I have got . . .' Her other son Albert was serving aged sixteen in France. Likewise Walter Barter requested the removal of his fifteen-year-old boy from the front line after 'he had the sad news a few days ago that my elder son – twenty-two – had been killed in the Dardanelles . . .'

One tragic case concerned that of Jane Walsh. All four of her sons had joined the army, the youngest, Samuel, aged fifteen. The first son, William, had been killed in April 1915; the second, David, in March 1916, after which she wrote seeking the discharge of Samuel. While the process was under way, her third son Thomas was wounded (he was later killed in August 1917) and Jane was clearly desperate to have her son home. 'He is all that I have now left to me . . . it has been very hard on me, the loss of my sons, [and] it has left me broken-hearted and lonely.' Samuel was soon withdrawn from the front.

There was no doubt that boys were proud to serve, although after a winter in the trenches some were less keen than they once were. A few lads themselves hinted that they had had enough. Private James Walters had been overseas for a year and it had taken much heartrending consideration by his mother, Hannah, before she decided to withdraw her son from the front. There was no doubt that he had done his bit. James, a survivor of the Gallipoli campaign, was still only sixteen, and was now fighting on the Somme. Hannah Walters began the process, forwarding his birth certificate as required to the military authorities, but before her son was taken out of the line he was killed in action close to Delville Wood. James's body was found and buried in a cemetery adjacent to the wood. His gravestone records that he was seventeen, but his birth certificate, which survives, proves otherwise.

The first that an under-age soldier would know about his imminent release was an order to report to the commanding officer. Fear was frequently the boy's first reaction. Had he done something wrong? It must be serious if the CO was involved. George White had fought on the Somme and survived unscathed. Then one day the sergeant came and asked what he had been up to.

I could not think of anything that would have interested him and so replied 'Nothing, Sarge'. He then told me I must have been up to something as I had to go before the CO right away, the inference being that I had to face a charge.

The sergeant marched me in and I stood to attention facing the colonel, somewhat perplexed as I knew I had not done anything to warrant 'being on the mat'. To my surprise, the CO asked me how old I was and, automatically, as so many times before to others, I told him I was nineteen.

The officer explained that George's stepfather had provided proof that he was actually aged just sixteen. George had little option but to agree.

> The colonel's attitude then changed completely and he talked to me quite informally. He said that he admired my courage in joining up and coming to France. He congratulated me on my service with the regiment and wished I could remain with them. However, he could not keep me in France and I would have to return to England as soon as arrangements could be made. He then shook my hand and wished me good luck.

When a boy had distinguished himself by his conduct, it would have been extremely hard for the CO to berate him for having enlisted in the first place. Archibald Dall was a private with the Machine Gun Corps in the 30th Division and had served with distinction in some of the thickest fighting near Bernafay Wood on the Somme. He was keen to stay in France.

> I managed to survive and hide my age for some weeks before the fateful letter arrived informing my CO that I was only sixteen years old. I won't repeat what he said before he sent me, a very proud boy, 'down the line' to Camiers, near Étaples, where I found myself just one of several hundred such lads, of ranks ranging from private to CSM [company sergeant major] and CQMS [company quartermaster sergeant].

Not every officer had reason to be so accommodating. George Maher had run away from home to join up, and had been in France a matter of weeks. He had not had time to prove his worth to anyone; on the contrary, he was shocked by what he saw and burst into tears on several occasions although he sought to hide his shame. The winter of 1916/17 turned out to be the harshest of the war, and George was overwhelmed by the squalid conditions of the camp – and he had, as yet, not even gone into the trenches.

> I was lying on my ground sheet crying in the tent when this man said, 'What are you crying for?' Then it all came out, that I was thirteen. He went and reported what I'd said and I was taken to see a major. I can see him now, wringing wet, with rain dripping from his helmet. He swore at me. 'You bloody fool, it costs money to get you here and you bloody well cry.'

The officer would have no interest in keeping a boy so evidently unsuitable for war and, as George was a boy of 'extreme youth', the regulations enabled the major to circumvent the requirement for a birth certificate and set about sending George home; it was still a time-wasting administrative problem and one he could certainly have done without.

If a boy was removed from the firing line, it would be up to him to make his way back to safety, armed with an officer's docket confirming his status, and giving him permission to leave the forward area. Seventeen-year-old Private George Fortune of the 18th Lancashire Fusiliers had been steeling himself to go over the top when he was given instructions to leave the line. At about midnight, he heard the sergeant calling out his name but George steadfastly ignored it in the belief that he was about to be given a job. He may have been under age but he had been long enough in the army to know that it was wise to try to melt into the background. The sergeant persisted and in the end George had no option but to respond. Then, to his surprise, the sergeant said, 'Give your bombs to your section commander and go to battalion headquarters.' At the last moment George was being sent away owing to his age and so he left, finding his way by the light of bursting shells.

It was a dangerous trip and George was blown off his feet by at least one explosion. Then, as he found a road, the Germans

opened up again and started to drop shells uncomfortably close.
'I wandered about for hours. I would watch the Very lights go up
and walk the other way; I knew I was going away from the line
then.' George had been fortunate to escape so far unscathed. As
he pressed on he met an artilleryman whose friend had just been
killed. The man was visibly upset.

> He had been with him all through the war, he said. I told him
> I was going out because of my age. The man collected himself.
> 'Good luck, mate' and he gave me a good swig of rum from a
> petrol can.

Private Frederick Bird was on his way back home to Britain, just
so long as he could get out of the line safely. Fred, a butcher by
trade, from Kilburn in London, had grown considerably since the
diminutive boy, weighing marginally over seven stone, and five
feet tall, went to enlist in September 1914. He was well under
the minimum height for the army but he had been lucky to find
a 'cooperative' medical officer. A year's training had built him up
sufficiently to enable him to embark for France with the battalion
in November 1915.

The only thing he was missing was his parents' blessing, and it
was not long before Daniel and Kate Bird made an application for
their son's release; it was granted. As far as they were aware, they
could expect their sixteen-year-old son through the door at any
time. He might be peeved at his removal from France, but at least
he would be safe and sound.

The order for Fred to leave the trenches arrived at an extraordinarily inopportune moment. The front and support lines occupied
by his battalion were being subjected to a prolonged bout of shelling resulting in several casualties. It would have been safer to stay
put until the shelling stopped, as Private Horace Ham, a friend
in the platoon, advised, but 'Dickie' Bird, as he was affectionately
known, was to be on his way. Horace recalled:

We all knew he was just a lad and it did not surprise us when we heard his mother had applied successfully to have him withdrawn. He packed his kit, and although we were under fire, we all shouted our goodbyes and he made his way off down the communication trench. It was only as he reached the end of the trench that a shell landed, killing him.

In fact, Fred was not killed outright but had been seriously wounded in the back by shrapnel. He was still alive when he was taken away by men of the 19th Field Ambulance but died before reaching the advanced dressing station. The news of his death was a terrible blow to his friends in the line. Not only was he one of the first to be killed but the circumstances surrounding his death had made the loss all the more tragic.

No one could legislate for bad luck, but the new instruction would save the lives of the majority it was designed to help, and at the end of June 1916 MPs were apparently sufficiently satisfied with the safeguards to let the matter drop for the time being. It was a month before the issue returned to the House when questions were raised about the efficiency with which the instruction had been implemented on the ground. On 1 August, MPs went straight to the point.

Backbencher Henry Watt, a stalwart campaigner for the cause, spoke first. Citing the case of a Private William Dalziel of the Highland Light Infantry, he asked if the War Office's attention had been drawn to the boy:

who, although only seventeen and a quarter years of age, has been sent to France and to the trenches, and has been refused leave to return to this country, the commanding officer at the end of June writing that he has no authority to send [home] youths of that age.

The boy, according to Henry Watt, had been wounded in mid-July and was told while in hospital that he would be sent back into the line after recovery. 'Will he [the Undersecretary of State for War] see that promises made in the House with reference to boys under eighteen are fulfilled in this case?'

Standing in on behalf of Harold Tennant was a junior minister, Henry Forster. He replied that the case was being dealt with under the new instructions and that the officer in charge of records had been given fresh orders.

It was much too inefficient, argued Sir Arthur Markham, who, though he looked tired and ill, was his usual pugnacious self. He asked the minister:

Why has the War Office Order of 13th June not been observed? Only this morning I have heard from Glasgow that a boy under eighteen was shot last week whose parents had applied for his discharge over a month ago.

Henry Forster answered: 'I am very sorry; I have not heard of it. We are doing what we can to see that the instructions are observed.'

Then came the following exchange:

How long does it take an instruction to reach the proper authority?

My Hon. Friend will see that depends upon where the authorities are.

Will these boys be sent home – yes or no?

My impression is that a youth over seventeen years of age serving in France may be sent home if he is willing to come. If he is not willing, he will be sent to the Training Corps at the base, and at any rate will be kept out of the firing line.

Is not the Hon. Gentleman mistaken, and that under the Regulation a boy under the age of eighteen at the Front is sent home, and a boy between eighteen and nineteen is sent to the base?

I do not think so. I think it is my Hon. Friend who is mistaken.

Is it the superior officer who asks the boy to remain in France?

I think that is so.

Has the War Office any control over officers?

No answer was forthcoming and the House moved on to another issue. One thing was obvious. Not only was the implementation of the new instruction causing frustration, but the terms themselves were confusing. It was clear that neither Sir Arthur nor Henry Forster was entirely confident of his case. If MPs in the comfort of Parliament were using expressions like 'it is my impression', and 'I think so', was it any wonder that battle-worn officers were making mistakes?

Just over 200 miles away in the village of Westreham, sitting in his billet, Lieutenant Colonel J.H. Lloyd, commanding the 15th Lancashire Fusiliers, was catching up on correspondence. It was the end of a good day, the first in a long time, for the first day of August was Minden Day and, respecting regimental tradition, the men were given the day off.

Minden Day commemorated the battle of 1759 when a combined British and Prussian Army defeated a larger French force near the German town of Minden. The irony was not lost on some, but the Fusiliers simply welcomed the break. They had been in the thick of the fighting on 1 July and had suffered terrible casualties. Since then, the battalion had been in a state of transition, with large drafts making their way from England to be absorbed into the depleted ranks. In the meantime, it had been kept busy, returning to the front near the recently captured village of Ovillers to collect equipment and to bury the dead, eighty-six bodies having been retrieved and interred.

One of Lloyd's correspondents was a Mrs Evans, the mother of an under-age soldier in his battalion; she had taken up the Government's advice to write directly to commanding officers. News of the battalion's mauling had filtered through to Lancashire mill towns, and in particular Salford, the home of the 15th Lancashire Fusiliers – popularly known as the Salford Pals. The awful news had frightened Mrs Evans into writing. Poignantly, her letter arrived just as the survivors of the battalion had been clearing the dead from 1 July.

Lloyd wrote back to her:

Mrs Evans

In reply to your letter of 11 July I know your son quite well as he often does work as messenger etc and is quite an exceptionally intelligent man: I am astonished to hear that he is so young. He looks up to the standard of 19 or 20. I can hardly think that he ought to be discharged as under age being so physically big and strong. The rule is that if the man or boy is up to the work he stays whether he is under age or not. I should be very sorry if anything happened to him – anyhow he has come through our part of the big battle all right, though about three-quarters of the Battn were knocked out, so we have that much to be thankful for.

I am

Yours sincerely

J. H. Lloyd Lt Col, Commd 15 Lancashire Fusiliers

The boy in question was clearly aged no more than eighteen and, from the tone of the letter, was probably younger. Under the new instruction he should, at the very least, have been sent out of harm's way. However, the inference in the letter is clear. Young Evans was to stay put and serve.

Lieutenant Colonel Lloyd may not have been aware of the new rules, given the backdrop of a major offensive – or not have remembered them all. Either way, he was wrong.

Another boy who slipped through the net was Private George Collett, a big and strong former grammar school pupil, who had enlisted aged fourteen. Instruction 1186 had permitted the wishes of the young lad to override those of his parents, enabling a boy of any age to stay in France, just no longer in the firing line.

Removing George from the trenches would at least have come as some relief to his parents. They had sought to reclaim their son once, back in March 1916, when George's father had written directly to the commanding officer, but his son did not want to go home. 'I think it is my duty to stop out here,' George asserted in a letter. Before the June instruction it had remained entirely at the discretion of the army whether George stayed or not, and the verdict had come down on the side of the young boy. The divisional doctor had examined him and he had been found 'physically fit to bear the strain of active service. As he has expressed the wish to remain with his unit in the Expeditionary Force he is being retained.' The decision had then been endorsed and confirmed in writing to the parents by the War Office.

After 13 June, George if he was still 'willing' could stay in France but he should have been removed from the firing line. Nevertheless, there appeared no question of this, as George had subsequently gone over the top on 1 July. He had survived, although at least 588, or around 75 per cent, of his battalion were killed or wounded.

His escape still did not precipitate a change. Barely a fortnight later, the battalion was sent back into the line. George was killed aged sixteen when the trenches were subjected to a heavy and prolonged bombardment. His body was lost, but his name is commemorated on the Somme's Thiepval Memorial to the Missing.

It is always tempting to assume that when instructions were issued they were followed, if not to the letter then broadly adhered to. This was far from the case, and it is evident from the stream of orders emanating from the Army Council that some directives were either ignored or remained unread. While under-age soldiering was no doubt of paramount importance to worried parents back home, it was not of the same significance to commanding officers, other than how it might affect the fighting capability of the army. The lists of boys' names cited in Parliament by Sir

Arthur Markham and his colleagues are testament to a common inertia within the system.

Tragically, Markham's questions to the Government were to be his last in the Commons. They had been typically robust, but it was evident for all to see that the MP for Mansfield was far from well. During June and July he had made gestures towards protecting his strength, spending more time at home. But he had found his calling, albeit late in life, and the zeal required to pursue the issue of boy soldiering for a whole year had taken its toll on his health. Doctors' warnings that he should radically curtail his workload had been stubbornly ignored and he remained fully active, even though he was worn out physically and mentally. On 5 August 1916, Sir Arthur Markham suffered a massive stroke at home and died. He was just forty-nine years old.

Although a Liberal MP, Markham had acted like an independent, unwilling to toe the party line unless it suited him. He infuriated his colleagues in office with his statements but no one doubted his integrity or mistook his passion. His primary deficiency was one of control and, in moments of anger, his judgement could go badly astray. He had been greatly troubled by the losses on the Western Front – indeed, his hatred of inefficiency stemmed from a desire that those who had volunteered to fight were not let down by people at home. Nevertheless, in his moments of anger, he espoused ideas that were irrational and unattainable, including the exclusion of enemy goods in a post-war Britain, and even lending half an ear to the absurd notion that German music might be banned.

The following day the press reported his death. *The Times* described the MP for Mansfield as 'aggressive and independent . . . never amenable to party discipline [and] utterly fearless and honest as the day'. This was very true, but in his search for honesty and integrity in others he had also been sometimes too rash in word, to the occasional detriment of his cause.

It is difficult, with hindsight, to assess the effectiveness of one individual's campaign on the issue of under-age soldiering. As swathes of his, as well as the Government's, documentary evidence do not survive, it is impossible to prove conclusively one way or the other whether he was largely responsible for a change of direction. What can be said is that he never failed to keep the issue in front of the House. Proof, in the end, does not matter. The best memorial to his unheralded work remains the lives of boys who, without his help, would have died.

Removing a boy from the line was subject to delays, mistakes and even obstruction, all consequences of war and the pressure conflict brings. A birth certificate might be produced with all haste, but how soon that certificate might be acted upon would depend on a number of variables: how much priority a record office might give a claim; how many claims were being processed at any one time; even how sympathetic an officer was to a case.

For months prior to the Somme offensive, the fighting in the British sector had been muted as the Germans turned their attention to their own offensive in front of the French-held city of Verdun. This, coupled later with the public's optimism about the success of the offensive, ensured that before the battle there were relatively few letters to the authorities by worried parents keen to recall their children. With the offensive's calamitous first day, however, a rush of letters was received by the authorities, the processing of which would lead to inevitable delays. From the partial evidence available, the process certainly appears to have been slow at times, and Sir Arthur Markham's complaint in July that no response had been received by one family after a month may not have been untypical.

Driver George Sennett of the Royal Field Artillery had enlisted in August 1914 aged sixteen and had gone overseas the following year. In 1916, shortly before his eighteenth birthday in June, George's father, John, wrote to the Record Office at Woolwich.

The exact date of his letter is not known but a standard reply was received on 12 July.

> Sir
>
> I beg to acknowledge the receipt of your communication of the recent date relative to an application for your son No 94908 Driver George Sennett, to be placed on Home Service, and in reply I have to inform you that no action can be taken in the matter unless the Birth certificate is forwarded to this office.

If it is assumed that John Sennett replied promptly, then the response from the army was tardy indeed, for the letter confirming their son's position did not arrive at the Sennett home for another two and a half months.

> Records/British Army. No 499/190
> 30.9.16
> MEMORANDUM
> Reference your application for the discharge of No 94908 Dr Sennett G D/69th Bde RFA as being under age, this man states that he is not desirous of being posted to a training or other unit behind the firing line, but wishes to remain with the unit in which he is now serving.
>
> T. Wheatley Smith
> Lieut
> I/C Records British Army 2

George Sennett could stay overseas if he wished, but, once again, the regulations should have ensured he was removed from the line. Given the length of time between letters, it was perhaps fortunate that George was still alive to make his decision.

A similar situation arose in the case of Private Donald Price. He had enlisted in the Royal Fusiliers aged sixteen and, like George

Sennett, had been at the front since 1915. In mid-July he went over the top for the first time on the Somme and it had been terrifying.

> The battalion had lost about 400 that night and there were only about 150 of us left when we congregated. The remaining men struggled down towards the town of Albert and the band came out to meet us. It was a wonderful feeling.

His initial exhilaration and pride at coming through was immense, but the thrill soon disappeared when he realized that going over the top was not a one-off event.

> My mother saw the lists and lists of casualties in the *Daily Dispatch* and she got the wind up and wrote to the War Office and Lloyd George. Much to my amazement I was called into the company office one day and was told that I had got to be withdrawn from the line until I was nineteen. It was marvellous. They withdrew me to a school at Auxi le Chateau, about ten miles north-east of Abbeville. It was the surprise of my life to be taken out of the line without being wounded. I didn't care what anyone else thought and couldn't get out of it quick enough.

Donald's recollection, recorded seventy years after the event, gives the unintentional impression that the time between his mother's first letter and his removal from the line was short. This was not the case at all.

Mrs Price had two sons in France, and Donald was the younger. Just before the outbreak of war, she had been widowed and the strain of making ends meet, coupled with the anxiety of knowing two sons were in mortal danger, had made her ill with worry. A third brother, Harold, who was the youngest, was still living at home. To help alleviate her anxiety, he wrote on his mother's behalf, composing several letters to the War Office, enclosing his brother's birth certificate and requesting that his eighteen-year-old

brother be removed from the firing line. Some of the correspondence is now missing but it is clear what a protracted business
it was. Harold's first letter was sent on 15 July. It was almost a
month before he received an official reply, which merely stated
that the letter had been forwarded to the commander-in-chief,
and that the birth certificate was returned.

After a further delay, Harold wrote in September directly to
Lloyd George at the War Office to press his brother's case. The
Secretary of State for War was busy at the best of times, but it
did not hurt to try and, out of sheer desperation to get things
started, Harold wrote movingly, 'Please allow Donald to come
home and allow her [their mother] some joy after an agony of
suffering already coinciding with the duration of the war.'

Official confusion followed. Harold was told that his brother's
birth certificate had not been received when, as he pointed out to
Lloyd George in his next letter, it had been referred to previously
as 'returned herewith'.

Whether this correspondence in any way speeded up Donald
Price's withdrawal from the fighting line is not known. Harold's
wish that his brother might be sent home could and would not be
granted, but his persistence partially paid off. On 27 September,
the following letter was received:

Infantry Records
With reference to your letter No. RF/17164/PS dated 18.8.16
instructions have been issued for No. P.S 5473 Pte D. J. Price
20th Bn Royal Fusiliers to be withdrawn from the firing line in
accordance with Army Council Instruction No. 1186 of 1916 para
2 (b).

Capt for DAG, GHQ, 3rd Echelon

Even then, it was not until 6 October, nearly three months after
Harold's first letter, that Donald Price was withdrawn. He was

returned to his battalion the following March immediately on passing his nineteenth birthday. In September 1917 he suffered a gun shot wound to his left knee and was hospitalized.

Losing experienced men, no matter what their age, was always grievous to any command. It is certainly evident from Lieutenant Colonel Lloyd's letter to Mrs Evans that he found it hard to countenance losing a soldier, albeit under age, whom he had highly rated. The temptation must have existed for a CO to flout the rules, especially when a boy was so clearly physically capable and keen to stay. Rules and regulations regarding the use of equipment had been issued to officers in the line before and had been ignored when the CO could see that they ran counter to good sense. Would it be surprising if a CO were to resist losing a boy he trusted, particularly when so many of his experienced comrades had recently been killed or wounded?

Solid, reliable men were often at a premium and, as a rule, a number were withheld from general attacks – often those who had previously volunteered for trench raids or patrols. These men might be required to form the nucleus of a rejuvenated unit should it be needed. Invariably, some were boys, not because of their age, but simply because of their experience. By 1916 and 1917 there was a growing number of boys aged sixteen and seventeen who had been promoted to the rank of corporal or even sergeant, as well as others awarded medals for bravery.

According to Routine Orders issued later that summer by General Richard Haking, commanding First Army, boys sent down the line had to be noted in battalion returns as having been 'detached for special duty'. Accompanying the note would be a demand for replacements, yet such replacements were rarely like-for-like. No numerical compensation could replace the experience of boys each of whom might be worth five fresh-faced newcomers, lads who might be full of enthusiasm but with little or no idea of how to survive, let alone conduct themselves in the face of the enemy.

Drafts replacing those killed or wounded had to be tutored in the practicalities of trench life. Sixteen-year-old Thomas Hope, who had been so quickly disabused of his enthusiasm for war, nevertheless was one who was considered to have the requisite knowledge and was chosen to pass on his wisdom.

Each sentry has one of the new soldiers and on my turn of duty I am accompanied by a fresh-faced youth of nineteen. He is excited at being actually in the front line, not a nervous excitement but more like that of a schoolboy, all eagerness and expectancy. I explain to him the lie of the land in front, point out the supposed machine-gun emplacements in the Jerry lines, our own posts in front of our wire mostly inhabited at night, and a hundred other things a soldier should know about his particular part of the line.

To all this I add my own pet theories and devices for cheating death. How to take a slanting look through a loophole. The spare cartridge stuck in the rifle sling. It is easier and quicker to insert than a new clip when one counts life by seconds. How to distinguish the different shells by their sound, and the necessity of judging accurately the interval between the bursts. The best way to approach a Jerry trench, and the necessity of taking advantage of every bit of cover. He takes it all in and asks for more until my fund of information becomes exhausted and we lounge against the sides of the trench. 'How long have you been here?' he enquires next. 'Oh, about four months.'

Dick Trafford, the ex-coalminer, had been in France for a year and had survived the Battle of Loos. Although only seventeen years old, he was a trusted member of the company and well respected. It was fortunate for one newly arrived officer that Dick was around, for the young subaltern was a bag of nerves.

Soon after his arrival he said to me, 'You've had plenty of experience, Trafford, could I more or less keep close to you, give me an education.' I said, 'Well, sir, if that's how you want it, sir, I don't mind what-so-ever.'

In a reversal of normal roles, it was Dick who kept a close eye on the officer, until the day when the battalion was ordered to take part in an attack.

As we were getting ready to go over he came to me and said, 'Now, what I want you to do is let me follow you over, and let me do what you do.' 'Well, sir,' I said, 'you're going to be very funny doing what I do, but if I happen to get hit, in any way, ignore me and carry on, carry on the attack. Don't forget. Don't bother about me, save yourself, sir.'

Shortly after going over the top, the officer was struck by several machine-gun bullets while attempting to peer over the lip of a shell hole. Dick found his body after the fighting abated. 'And that was the end of him,' recalled Dick. 'He'd been sent out, but he'd no confidence, no confidence to do anything.'

Second Lieutenant Harold Cottrell was not lacking in confidence, only experience. He was keen to get to the front line not least so that he could set about avenging the death of his brother, George, who had been killed in a shell explosion at his gun battery in May 1915. Harold, a lad from Edgbaston in Birmingham, had applied for a temporary commission in October 1915, two months after his seventeenth birthday. In September 1916, he was given the order to proceed abroad. Taking his dead brother's revolver, he left with a draft of 110 other ranks and three other officers to join a regular battalion, the 2nd South Lancashire Regiment, currently out on rest in huts in Acheux Wood on the Somme.

Second Lieutenant Cottrell's abrupt departure for France surprised his parents, George and Agnes. They had been led to believe from statements made in the House that boys under nineteen would not be sent abroad which, in the case of their son, would mean active service in 1917. Yet from his letters Harold was only too keen to get involved. Just a couple of days after stepping foot on French soil he penned a letter to his father. It is dated 28 September.

My dear Father

You will see that I have got up into the line at last and I am glad to say I have managed to get my own battalion.

I am afraid I am not allowed to give away my position, but I am not 100 miles away from that place that we have just captured, in fact I am in the middle of the Somme Battle.

We are at present in camp in a wood just behind the line with occasional 'Hymns of hate' coming across from Fritz.

The noise is terrific, and the sky is lit up with the flashes of shells and guns, mostly our side, and I expect it is pretty awful for the Hun. How they can stand it I cannot make out. All the prisoners I have seen have been fine big men and well set up.

We are going up into our trenches in a day or two now and I expect we shall be in the next push, however, don't worry as it is quite a simple thing now . . .

With best love, ever your loving son,
Harold.

Two days later, he wrote again.

30th September
My dear Mother

Just a line to let you know that I am going into action so I shall not be able to write to you for a few days.

We are going to take a certain bit of Hun trench, but as they have had a terrible Artillery strafing for the last two days I don't suppose it will be very difficult. We have got the Canadians attacking on our right, and as they bear no love for Fritz, we shall be in good company.

We are doing this show because this Battalion failed in one of the former attacks on Thiepval and so every one is keen to wipe out this score, and I can tell you this time there will be no prisoners, certainly not on my part because I have Freddy [his nickname for George, his dead brother] to think of.

We are quite close to Thiepval at present and luckily the Hun gunners have not discovered us. We came here yesterday in the pouring rain and it was not at all pleasant, but I am glad to say it is nice and fine now, and I hope it keeps nice for the attack, to which I am looking forward.

The guns are fairly going at it now and it is very soothing to think of the state of the Hun at the other end.

Best love
Ever your loving son
Harold.

Harold had just time to scribble this letter before the battalion left its billet at noon to march up to the support trenches. Harold was mistaken in the belief that his battalion would go into action. In the event, an attack was made by the Canadians to Harold's right, in response to which German artillery fire was brought down on the trenches including those held by the 2nd South Lancashire Regiment. A number of casualties were sustained, including fourteen other ranks killed, and eighteen more wounded. One officer was also killed, and it happened to be Harold Cottrell.

Harold's death coincided with Donald Price's removal from the line for being under age, in accordance with June's Instruction 1186. Yet Donald Price was six months older than Harold Cottrell, who had been allowed to go overseas to fight. This made no sense to George and Agnes Cottrell.

In the weeks after Harold's death, his parents became involved in the usual exchange of letters with the War Office. As Harold's body had been recovered there was a burial in Pozières Cemetery and information as to where he lay passed on to the family. Personal effects were returned, although the revolver that belonged to Harold's brother was not forthcoming and enquiries were made as to its whereabouts. There was a final statement of his bank account and a settlement of outstanding monies totalling £4 16s 8d paid to his father. The formalities completed, George and Agnes Cottrell were left alone to mourn their dead sons.

Six months after Harold's death, Agnes Cottrell sent a series of seven letters to the War Office. Each was typified by yet greater anger, as she sought specific answers as to how and why her son had died. The answers could not bring her any solace, though the army reluctantly forwarded her questions to France.

April 16th 1917

To The Officer Commanding

2nd Battalion, South Lancashire Regiment

I am extremely sorry to waste your time by asking you questions about casualties, but the mother of the late Second Lieutenant H.W. Cottrell, who was killed in action at Mouquet Farm on the 30th September 1916, is so persistent in her enquiries, that I have no option but to do so.

She appears to have a grievance that certain questions addressed to Col. Craigie-Halkett [the former CO of the battalion] were not answered and so she desires to know:

(a) Approximate hour at which he was killed and hour of burial.

(b) Extent of his wounds.

(c) Manner of identification.

Mrs Cottrell has lost two sons in the war and it is evidently a case of a distraught mother who cannot control herself.

I would suggest that if you are unable to give precise answers you should record such approximate information as you may consider will satisfy her questions.

Colonel
Assistant Military Secretary

The new commanding officer replied, but there was nothing he could add to what had been said before. In a letter written by Agnes on 26 April, she refers to the fact that no further information was offered in what had been 'a most curt and callous reply' to her last enquiry. She went on to write:

> My son received his commission from Sandhurst two days before his 18th birthday – after a bombing course, he was sent to the front by Colonel Vaughan, 3rd South Lancs – before he had hardly time to breathe. He was killed nine days after leaving Waterloo . . . I wish once more to protest against the shameful sacrifice of a boy of eighteen contrary to the express announcement made in the House . . . I hold Colonel Vaughan, Colonel Halkett and the War Office who supported them, directly responsible for his death.

Mrs Cottrell was told that there had been no definite understanding that an officer under nineteen years would not be sent on active service. 'I am to add,' wrote the military correspondent, 'that he was reported to be available for overseas by his CO both from a physical and professional point of view . . .'

There was little that Mrs Cottrell could do but reiterate her position. On 1 July 1917 she wrote:

> I cannot understand your statement that no definite undertaking was given that a boy of 18 (under 19) should be sent overseas. May I say that a definite announcement made in Parliament is considered by the whole nation to be a 'definite' statement and that, had not such an announcement been made, I should never

have consented to my boy to be nominated and sent to Sandhurst so young . . .

As Donald Price was making his way down the line, yet another new War Office instruction (No. 1905) was issued, automatically superseding Instruction 1186. Much of the new instruction remained the same – indeed, 1905 was in essence a refinement of what had gone before, except for one key feature. All boys under the age of seventeen would be sent home, irrespective of whether they were 'willing' to stay in France. This stipulation was repeated down the chain of command, although the First Army's Routine Order of 20 October was even more explicit and left no room for negotiation or misinterpretation: 'All soldiers under 17 years of age . . . are to be given no option of remaining in this country.'

In another alteration to previous rules, those aged between seventeen and eighteen and a half would be allowed to go home although, as before, their removal from overseas service would be dependent on whether they were 'willing' to go or not. If they decided to remain abroad, their services would be 'utilized behind the firing line', that is, out of harm's way, most being sent to one of the Army Schools of Instruction. Those over eighteen and a half were given no option but to remain in France and were posted to a training unit in readiness for their return to the front once they passed their next birthday. Once again, none of these changes applied to officers, although this was never made explicit. At eighteen and two months, Second Lieutenant Harold Cottrell, had he enlisted as a private, could have been on his way home. Then, three weeks after his death, the anomaly was rectified when Instruction 2008 was issued on 22 October 1916: 'Officers under the age of 19 are not in future to be regarded as eligible to proceed on active service. Their names will not therefore be submitted as reinforcements.'

The instructions of June and October reflect a distinct shift in the Government's attitude to the whole issue of under-age soldiering. In the space of a few months, it had signalled its acceptance that young boys who had patriotically enlisted would not be punished for the 'crime' of fraudulent enlistment. The boys had lied, but almost everyone privately agreed that this was done with the most honourable of intentions.

An alteration in the Government's stance was to be welcomed but an important qualification should be made. Just because the civilian authorities changed the rules, just because War Office instructions were issued formalizing the change, it did not mean that the order was strictly followed by COs in France and Belgium. Acting Captain Douglas Cuddeford serving with the 12th Highland Light Infantry recorded the alteration in policy and noted that many of the 'little heroes', as he called them, did go down the line to Étaples but in the same breath he also noted that 'a few of these boys stoutly held to the lie about their age and refused point-blank to leave the battalion and the front line! They were the real stuff, and we did our best to look after them.' Of course no boy could refuse 'point-blank' any order to go back, 'little heroes' or not, but their pluck had been rewarded, against instructions.

With this change in policy, it might be argued that the authorities had little excuse for reacting so tardily to requests made by families to retrieve their sons. The problem of manpower had been comprehensively addressed by the introduction of conscription in January 1916 and, by using the National Register as a basis for this, the authorities ensured that far fewer boys had been able to enlist under age. Now, the passage of time had gone a great way to alleviating the long-term, as well as the existing, problem for the Government and the army.

Twelve months earlier the army had relied on huge numbers of under-age boys, whose service had helped to stabilize a militarily precarious situation on the Western Front. Tens of thousands had enlisted in 1914 and 1915 aged seventeen and eighteen but by October 1916 most of these lads were aged nineteen or twenty,

the age at which they could no longer be recalled, radically prun-
ing the number who might be discharged from the forces. These
boys could now legitimately be kept in the firing line. This first
tier of under-age soldiers was followed by a second: boys who had
enlisted at the age of sixteen in 1914. By October 1916 they too
were of an age at which most would be retained to serve in France,
albeit at a safe distance behind the lines; Donald Price was a good
case in point. The temporary loss of these boys, while annoying,
was affordable, for virtually all would shortly return to the fray,
ready to bolster drafts to the front on a monthly basis.

Only those in a 'third tier' – and these were the youngest of
the 1914 and 1915 volunteers – would be sent home after the
October instruction. These boys were always among the smallest
group as a proportion of those who enlisted under age. Private
George Collett would have been included among their number
had he lived a few months more.

Whether destined to stay in France or go home, all the boys
sent down from the line were directed to one of the base camps
for processing. George Maher, the thirteen-year-old runaway, was
placed on a train near Amiens, destination Étaples.

When I was taken under escort to the railway station, I found
I was one of five under-age boys from different regiments being
sent back to England, and one of them, as I discovered, was even
younger than myself.

The boys had been through a great adventure and it was natural to
chat among themselves, swapping stories and experiences.

Sixteen-year-old George White was sent on a train to Abbeville
where he had to report to the Railway Transport Officer.

I found there were lots of other lads who had just arrived from
the front. We were all put on a train which was bound for Rouen.
One had been in the trenches with an infantry battalion, his father

having been his company sergeant major. Unfortunately the father had been killed and the young chap's colleagues had given his age away to his superiors, resulting in the present journey.

The losses on the Somme, combined with the introduction of new rules, did not just facilitate a significant withdrawal of young soldiers from the front line; they also halted the progress of boys going in the other direction.

Tens of thousands of men sent out from Britain as drafts to the Western Front were held at camps along the coast awaiting their turn to join their regiments. This depended upon the normal wastage in the line, estimated at 35,000 men a week, though heavier during major offensives. As they waited, they would be given final courses of instruction, meant as a refresher and final tone-up for skills honed in Britain. Training centres, such as the Bull Ring at Étaples, were infamous for their unforgiving regimes, as men, some of whom were returning from injury, were harried and bullied into shape.

These drafts contained boys of all ages, although everyone, like Private Norman Gladden, was supposed to have passed his nineteenth birthday before leaving home. In late August 1916, Norman, along with the rest of his draft, was held in a hut at Étaples. In the distance the rumble of gunfire was distinct and each day Norman and his friends woke to the thought, 'Is this the day?' Norman, no hero in the making, was in no hurry to go anywhere. He found the camp a depressing place and watched as draft after draft was sent off, knowing it was only a matter of time before his turn would come.

As a staging-post towards the as yet unknown date of departure, a medical examination was ordered, and a few of the boys were plucked from the ranks and earmarked to stay at the base, 'a fate that most of us secretly envied', Norman conceded. Their number included a lad called Chapman who was not pleased at being held back.

A bantam in appearance and full of pluck, he was one of the few who were genuinely eager to join in battle. He was also among those who had falsified their age to the recruiting sergeant. Now, at this late stage, his parents, exercising their legal right, managed to impose a veto on his going to the front before his nineteenth birthday. The prospect of cooling his heels amid the dreary sands of Étaples gave him no pleasure. Nevertheless, his parents were right and, even if their action had saved him but a few months of the horror of the trenches, it was to good purpose. Whether it achieved more than that amount of grace I do not know, for I never met Chapman again.

Regardless of how the boys themselves felt, parents were increasingly aware of their rights and last-minute appeals to prevent a son's progress to the trenches were common. John Campbell, an apprentice butcher from Scotland, had enlisted at fifteen into the Royal Field Artillery, in April 1915. After just six weeks' training, he was placed on a draft for the Dardanelles, but his father got wind of what was happening and wired the War Office. His son, along with seven other under-age boys, was returned to Scotland to take up defence duties on the east coast.

The following May, just before Instruction 1186, John was sent before a medical board and told that as he had the physique of a boy of eighteen he was being 'requested to volunteer for foreign service'. John agreed and left almost immediately for France.

I found myself at Étaples . . . My father at this point wrote to the War Office complaining at my being abroad and still under age. One morning early, when we were expecting to move up to the Somme, the fall-in sounded and I was told to get ready for Blighty, arriving home at Kilmarnock the next morning. I was discharged on 20 June 1916 on the grounds of being under age.

It was only when these young boys got home that they were able to see for themselves the strain under which their families had lived, something to which George White admitted he had not given much thought.

> Mum and Dad explained why they had decided to have me brought from France. They had been told about the tough conditions and the appalling casualty lists on the Somme. The awful winter weather had also been stressed in reports from the front and in view of all that they felt they could not allow me to continue serving there. Of course I accepted the situation and decided to make the most of things back in dear old Blighty.

Such was the gallantry shown by many that it was frequently only injury that brought about the 'discovery' of a boy's real age. Back at a base hospital or all the way home in Britain, the boys were more ready to give up their true ages. In a hospital bed, with the crust of mud and ingrained dirt removed, it was possible once again to reveal the boy. Pride in his achievement might elicit a boy's age, keen, as he might well be, to tell a pretty young nurse of his exploits. Some too were willing to admit that they had done their bit and felt it was right to call time on their youthful adventures before their families did. Cyril José's age had been discovered in this manner while he was in hospital in Britain. His family had forwarded his birth certificate, and although he was old enough to be retained in the army, he could look forward to a prolonged stay in Britain before going back overseas.

Horace Calvert could expect similar treatment. He had enlisted just after his fifteenth birthday and had fought in one of the elite regiments in the British Army, the Grenadier Guards. In late September 1916 he had gone over the top in an attack on the village of Lesboeufs on the Somme and had been wounded and returned to England. His father, George, who had been called up under the Derby Scheme, had followed his son to France before being discharged as medically unfit. Having seen the conditions for himself, he decided his son had been through enough.

My father had written and sent my birth certificate to regimental headquarters and told them he didn't think it was the thing for me to be sent on active service again until I was the right age. The Regiment didn't say anything to me, they just put down 'not available for draft' on my record in the company office.

There were a small number of boys who under the new rules could be discharged to resume civilian life. Private Percy Marshall, a farm servant living near Hull, enlisted into the Machine Gun Corps in 1915. He served several months in France before he was wounded on the Somme, receiving gunshots to his left thigh, the back of his head and his right foot. With the publicity of his miraculous survival and his obvious youth, it was not long before Percy's real age of sixteen was revealed and he was discharged, 'Having made a mis-statement as to age on enlistment' and not, as his family preferred to point out, because he was shot in the head, thigh and foot!

To the public, these boys were heroes, shining examples of youth who had given almost their all to the nation. The affection in which they were held was in almost equal proportion to the level of animosity directed at those who attempted to dodge service in the forces. Not everyone in the army was as impressed as civilians, though. A few home-based NCOs, who talked a good war to recruits, appeared downright envious.

Frank Lindley had finally recovered from the wounds to his leg suffered on the opening day of the Somme offensive. He had been home to see his parents and he had attempted to mollify his mother who was worried that he might be sent back again. He reassured her that there was no prospect of an immediate return. Then, soon after, he went to Pontefract for a medical examination only to find out that his real age had been discovered. Instead of sympathy, he was met with threats. Two years before, Frank might have been intimidated, but not any more.

In the orderly room at the depot at Pontefract, I was called in. They'd rumbled my age. 'We find you are sixteen years old.' I said, 'Well, what does that matter?' This sergeant major said he was going to prosecute for fraudulent enlistment, so I said, 'Get yourself over there and do a bit of bloody fighting.' I tore him a sheet off in soldiers' Latin. I said, 'You can't do me now; you can't put me in clink here.' I laughed me stocking tops off.

The army might let boys like Frank Lindley go but there would be no outward appreciation of their services at home or overseas for King and Country. Boys discharged from the ranks were generally bigger and stronger than the day when they enlisted; exercise, training and, for many boys, better food, took care of that. Now back in civilian life, they feared the ritual humiliation and taunting that had once driven some into the forces in the first place: they feared being taken for shirkers.

The Silver War badge was awarded to men who had been discharged owing to wounds or because they were otherwise medically unfit. This saved them from harassment or the need to explain themselves to overzealous civilians. Under-age soldiers were not entitled to the badge irrespective of whether they served abroad or not. Private Sydney Phillips of the 16th Welsh Regiment had enlisted in 1914 and served in France for three months during the winter of 1915/16 when aged fourteen. Now he had been demobbed he was being hassled in the street. 'You will fully understand, I know,' he wrote, 'how galling it is to me [that] I am continually asked "when are you going to be called up", and after just 16 months' service . . . The regimental badge does not cover ex-soldiers as any individual wears one.'

His application was refused as was that made by Charles Barter who had served with the 6th East Kent Regiment. He had been wounded, shot in the right shoulder during the Battle of Loos. His true age was discovered after recovery at the 1st Birmingham War Hospital and he was discharged, unusually not for wounds

but because he was under age. Even on enlistment Barter, like
Phillips, was big for his age at five foot six inches tall and with
a chest measurement of thirty-seven inches. This labourer from
London had claimed to be nineteen on enlistment but was only
fifteen. Back in civilian life he would be vulnerable to the same
questions that bedevilled Phillips, yet there would be no Silver
War Badge for either lad.

The rules governing under-age service at home and abroad had
changed radically in 1916 to the boys' benefit, and Frank Lindley,
for one, would never return to the Western Front. The battles
of 1915 and 1916 had taken a terrible toll among under-age
soldiers. Now, thankfully, Government intervention had ensured,
albeit belatedly, that never again would lads be sent abroad in
such numbers.

Times had truly changed. In early July 1916, for example,
Sergeant Albert Perriman of the 11th South Wales Borderers
recorded an attack in which his platoon, perhaps numbering
between forty and forty-five men, was ordered to assault and
capture three machine-gun posts. He paid tribute to his men and
the wonderful mutual support they had given and referred to the
fact 'that on this day, there were six who had not yet reached the
age of eighteen years'. A year later, such a concentration of under-
age soldiers in a platoon was well nigh impossible. Statistics (see
chapter 16) drawn from an analysis of 251 soldiers selected from
surviving pension records at the National Archives back up this
fact. All those whose details were examined had enlisted during
wartime and served while under age in a theatre of war. Of just
seven who went abroad in 1917 five had enlisted before conscription in 1916 and the consequent tightening of the enlistment
procedure.

By 1917, it is clear how very few under-age soldiers were able
to go abroad for the first time. Those who succeeded normally
had to use considerable guile and ingenuity, as did the lad who

joined the 2nd Royal Welsh Fusiliers in June 1917. The story was touched upon by Captain James Dunn during compilation of the battalion's war hstory, *The War the Infantry Knew*. He recalled how 'the draft of one, a boy of seventeen', had turned up at the battalion having deserted from the regimental depot in Liverpool: 'Having made it overseas, he got to the 1st Battalion by jumping trains and lorries; but he wanted to serve with us, so he walked along the Hindenburg front to reach us. His declared intention is to tell the Drum Major at Litherland [the depot] that he has been "over the top". The D.M. hasn't been overseas.'

The effects of the Government's new rules were being felt. The following year, 1917, losses among soldiers under the age of eighteen were cut by 80 per cent, and those who died were drawn predominantly from among boys whose 'real' ages were ignored or remained undetected. They included lads such as Private John Banning, Private James Gray, Lance Corporal Herbert Diprose, Private Douglas Williams and Private James Stedman, all of whom had enlisted at thirteen or fourteen years old in 1914, and had served overseas for at least a year or eighteen months. All five were killed in 1917, aged sixteen or seventeen.

Amongst those who died in 1917 was one of the 'little heroes' that Acting Captain Douglas Cuddeford had so appreciated and tried to look after. On the first day of the Allied offensive at Arras in April, he came across a lad shot by a German sniper.

He was only a boy, obviously not more than about seventeen years of age, but he had always refused to be sent back to the Base Depot along with the other 'under ages'. The bullet struck him in the belly, and as usual in the case of these abdominal wounds he rolled about clawing the ground, screaming and making a terrible fuss. Certainly, to have one's guts stirred up by a red-hot bullet must be a dreadful thing, and that a bullet is really hot after its flight through the air is well known to anyone who had tried to pick up a newly spent one. However, they got the boy back into the trench, opened his clothes and put a bandage around his middle over the wound, but of course we could see from the first it was hopeless. A little later, as I was squeezing my way along the crowded trench passing the word to A Company to be ready to go over on the signal, I noticed the lad laid out on a blown-in part of the trench. By then he was lying very still, and I thought he was dead, but as I passed he half opened his eyes and said something to me. I had to stoop down to catch what he said; it was 'Good luck to you, sir!'

In 1917, fewer than twenty boys are officially identified as having died on all fronts aged sixteen (approximately the same number are listed as having died on the first day of the Somme offensive) and only one, Rifleman Edwin Elks, was as young as fifteen. These numbers underlined the effectiveness of the new safeguards and, to a lesser extent, reflected the decline in the once rampant enthusiasm among boys to serve. The major British offensives of 1917, such as Arras, Third Ypres and Cambrai, were fought by men deemed eligible to serve and drawn from right across the adult male population. The majority of boys, if they remained in France at all, were now down at the base camps. For most who were aged seventeen and eighteen, the time would still come when they would have to return to the trenches but, meanwhile, they would be safe.

II

Held to Serve

MOTHER'S BABY SON
SORELY MISSED

22243 Private Bernard Whittingham
98th Battalion, Machine Gun Corps

Killed in Action 23 July 1916, aged 17

IN THE SUMMER AND autumn of 1916, thousands of boys were shipped back to camps in Britain, many of which were located around Channel ports such as Dover and Folkestone. The boys were a mixed crowd, some relieved to be home, others resigned to their lot. Archibald Dall had considered his removal from France as almost fair game, after hiding his age – sixteen – for as long as possible. He was returned to Dover from Boulogne to join a growing number of lads who had been sent back from the fighting that summer. In Archibald's case, he should have then been transferred to the Army Reserve, but, for reasons that appear to contradict the War Office instruction, he was held to serve. The army authorities may have regretted their action. 'Within a month or two there were over four hundred of us inflicting our boyish pranks (or nuisances) upon the already overworked training and organizing staff,' he recalled.

Released from the tighter military law that prevailed on active service, the boys became prone to antics that did not endear them to their NCOs, who were used to being in control. Cyril José was

sent to a camp at Devonport in January 1917, after recovering
from his wounds. The discipline he came up against was almost
intolerable, the boys being hauled up for any misdemeanour. Cyril
and his friends speculated that it was deliberately unpleasant in the
hope that some of the older boys would be provoked into volunteering once again for foreign service. With food shortages across
Britain becoming severe – owing to German submarine attacks on
Allied shipping – the boys at Devonport found their rations cut
from half a loaf per boy at dinner, to half a loaf per sixteen boys.

> Half the camp is doing jankers. The grub here is scandalous!
> We've done nothing but make complaints about it. Not enough
> to feed a cat. We nearly had a mutiny here on Thursday night in
> the guard room. There were 33 of us on guard and an officer in
> charge and we started shouting about the grub – asked the officer
> if he was investing our ration money in the War Loan. He didn't
> half rave then. [He] picked four of us out and had us in the office
> one by one. Unfortunately for him he picked four Expeditionary
> men – we told him that we had better grub in France.

Cyril had teamed up with two other boys who had recovered from
wounds and were passing time at Devonport until they were old
enough to return to France. All three were still only seventeen
years old but, as Cyril wrote to his family, they had a status among
the other soldiers.

> We're down as the 'Dauntless three' probably because we give
> more cheek to NCOs and to anybody, in fact, than any of the
> others. We seem to be the leaders here, with one or two other
> fellows, as half the guard are recruits and we are older than the rest
> of the Expeditionary men.

Many of the NCOs, although somewhat older than the rest, had
scarcely any more service than the boys under their command.

One evening when gunshots were heard, a corporal of just four months' service dashed into Cyril's hut.

'Stand-to, my lads, stand-to!' We wouldn't get up. He danced about with a big electric torch banging the bed boards. 'There's two shots been fired, p'raps three! Catch hold of a rifle!' He went nearly daft and we started pulling his leg . . . the two corporals in charge were both windy as anything and told us we didn't know how serious it was . . . So we started singing 'Goodbye forever' and 'Farewell, farewell' and told them we had shot better chaps before breakfast. We did have some fun.

Shortly afterwards the corporal came round and posted Cyril on guard duty.

'If anyone comes, ring the bell and we'll soon be with you.'
  'If anyone comes,' I said, 'I'll shoot first and challenge after.'
  'Don't, don't. You mustn't get wind-up.'
  'Got wind-up before you were called up. Anybody would think you were going over the top or something instead of having a cushy time in Blighty.'

It was hard for boys such as Cyril not to feel superior to men who held rank but scant authority. Cyril and his friends did not have just a confidence born of overseas service, they also had insignia on the uniform that told anyone who cared to look that they had been in action: brass stripes on the left sleeve signifying a wound, blue chevrons on the right, each signifying a year's service abroad. With such swagger, it was difficult not to become the focus of other boys' attention.

We're always getting into rows with chaps who have about 12 months' service, telling us they did this and that 'before we came up'. We then show them our sleeves with stripes and service badges and tell them to 'wipe their noses on that'. Especially on sentry [duty] in the road. A lot of chaps of other regiments might pass on their way in town, and seeing the sentry try to take a rise out of him. 'Go to it, kid – we'll be doing that in France in a few weeks.' Sentry: 'Here, kid, wipe your nose on that. I was doing this in France before you were called up.' Disappearance of soldiers.

The instruction of October 1916 applied not just to British soldiers, but to soldiers of the Empire as well. Lads under seventeen from Canada and Australia would also be shipped home after a short administrative stay in England. In late 1916, Canadian William Kerr was posted to Bramshott Camp, near Liphook, on the main London–Portsmouth Road. He had been recuperating from wounds received in France while serving with the 1st Canadian Division, and was still at the camp, when he was ordered to see Captain Dunn straight away in the company commander's office.

'I have a special job for you, Corporal Kerr,' he said, while I stood to attention in front of him. 'There are thirty-eight young soldiers in this camp just turned sixteen, who have falsely given their ages as eighteen and only now been found out. They are being sent back to Canada, and I am putting you in charge of them until arrangements have been made for their departure.'

Kerr was given charge of a forty-bed hut, with a separate room at the end for himself, as the corporal. All he had to do was to take the roll call morning and night and ensure that the boys' beds were kept tidy. Then, during the day, the boys were to be taken out on route march, with the distance left up to the discretion of Kerr.

As the captain handed Kerr the hut key, he added one further point. He must ensure that every night, after lights out, the hut was firmly locked. It all seemed relatively easy, although Kerr

wondered if he discerned a wry smile on the captain's face as he
strolled away down the path, leaving him with the job in hand.

> Captain Dunn was certainly not smiling when, two mornings
> later, he paid another visit to the boys' hut and confronted me.
> 'How are your young men behaving?' he asked, but his slight
> turning away as if giving me a moment to think about the reply
> was enough to tell me there was more to his visit than that. 'All
> right, sir, no trouble at all,' I replied and went on to report how
> I had done everything he had ordered me to do. 'You did not
> know that two of them, and possibly a third, were in Liphook at
> midnight last night?'

Kerr was taken aback. It was clear that the boys had simply
resorted to clambering out of the windows before sauntering off
into town.

Boys would be boys and it was obvious that, as this group was
to return to Canada, it was better to strike a deal to maintain
discipline than to risk humiliation through confrontation. With
Dunn's permission, Kerr compromised with the boys.

> I called the roll, morning and night, marched them, rested them,
> let them break off near any sweet or lemonade shop they took a
> fancy to, made a deal with them of three or four verbal permissions
> to be out at night on condition that they were back at midnight –
> or by God I would route march them till they were ready to drop.
> It worked.

One of the lads sent home to Canada was Maurice Goulet. At
the start of the war, the fourteen-year-old was working for a local
butcher in his home city of Ottawa. Inspired by newspaper reports
of the gallantry shown by the 1st and 2nd Canadian Divisions,
he enlisted, adding two years to his age. His mother was having
none of his antics and promptly had Maurice discharged but he

tried again, enlisting without her knowledge in Hull, a town across the Ottawa River. His unit embarked overseas, Maurice reaching France the following month. At first his mother tolerated his service but in August she changed her mind and applied to have him withdrawn. She sent a letter with a copy of her son's birth certificate to the Department of Militia and Defence, but this was rejected as evidence and Mrs Goulet had to pay for a formal legal declaration to be drawn up confirming her son's age, whereupon he was withdrawn. For her, as for others, the lists of casualties in the newspapers had proved too much. Ironically, Maurice's unit had been designated non-combatant and her son had been well out of harm's way chopping down wood for the army. It took approximately ten weeks from the time Mrs Goulet first wrote until the completion of formalities, a time quicker than that seemingly taken to remove under-age boys from the British Army.

While thousands of lads eventually made their way back to Britain, thousands more remained abroad. The base camps to which they were sent were sited close to the major ports such as Calais and Le Havre. As the war developed, the size and duties of base camps expanded to meet the ever-growing demands placed upon them by the British Expeditionary Force, which had more than doubled its size by mid-1916 to 1.7 million men. These bases hospitalized the wounded, and were the point of embarkation for both the sick and those going home on leave. They acted as sorting offices for the mail, and as supply depots for vast quantities of war material destined for the front, as well as 'holding pens' for boys back from the line.

If there was a coordinated programme to deal with the flood of under-age soldiers who were removed from the front line, then history has not left the evidence. The instruction of 13 June had dictated that boys under the age of nineteen would be sent out of danger. However, when these boys arrived at a base camp there is little to suggest that specific resources had been allocated to their welfare and upkeep. It was a recipe for chaos.

In the summer of 1916, the Reverend John Hannay, a fifty-one-year-old chaplain, was working at an unspecified camp where, he estimated, there were nearly a thousand boys, all of whom had enlisted during the early days of recruitment and who had either been sent down from the trenches as being unfit to serve or picked out as unsuitable as they arrived in France. Their number had steadily increased throughout the summer, and they were becoming a problem to handle.

Their existence in camp was a standing menace to discipline. Officially they were meant to be trained, fed, lodged and if necessary punished according to the scheme designed for and, in the main, suitable to men. In reality they were boys, growing boys, some of them not sixteen years of age, and a few – it seems almost incredible – not fifteen. How the recruiting authorities at home ever managed to send a child of less than fifteen out to France as a fighting man remains a mystery. But they did.

Hannay's judgement of these lads was very much of its time. The boys, he reasoned, were of a particularly difficult kind.

It is not your 'good' boy who rushes to the recruiting office and tells a lie about his age, it is not the gentle, amiable, well-mannered boy who is so enthusiastic for adventure that he will leave his home and endure the hardships of a soldier's life for the sake of seeing fighting. These boys were for the most part young scamps, and some of them had all the qualities of the guttersnipe, but they had the makings of men in them if treated properly.

The difficulty was to know how to treat them. No humane CO wants to condemn a mischievous brat of a boy to Field Punishment No. 1. Most COs, even most sergeants, know that punishment of that kind, however necessary for a hardened evildoer of mature years, is totally unsuitable for a boy. At the same time, if any sort of discipline is to be preserved, a boy, who must officially be regarded as a man, cannot be allowed to cheek a sergeant or flatly to refuse to obey orders. That was the military difficulty.

To Hannay, the boys faced a precipice of social and moral decline. They were kicking their heels around the base camps and no one was taking charge of their welfare. This could only encourage mischief. The NCOs under whose immediate control the boys had been put found their charges nothing but a nuisance, for there was little to offer the lads in terms of education and no proper plan of physical exercise. As a result, the NCOs were aggressive and bullying – in short, according to Hannay, the boys 'were in a straight way to be ruined instead of made'.

It was an Irish surgeon working at the camp who sought to do something about the problem. Hannay referred to him simply as 'J'. J's decision to help met with total support, but that did not make the job any easier. On the contrary.

> It was not that he had to struggle against active opposition. There was no active opposition. Everyone wanted to help. The authorities realized that something ought to be done. What J was up against was the system.

The system was identified as the army machine, an intransigent monolithic structure which, once set in motion, was capable of putting two million servicemen in the field, but was ill-equipped to adapt to smaller irregular problems that required specific remedies. The wheels of the machine, as J and Hannay discovered, would only go round one way.

> Trying to get anything done in the army is like floundering in a trench full of sticky mud surrounded by dense entanglements of

barbed red-tape. You track authority from place to place, finding always that the man you want, the ultimate person who can actually give the permission you require, lies just beyond . . .

It was the YMCA, not the army, that came to the rescue. A Young Soldiers' Club was formed and was offered one of the best huts in the camp, one originally designated as an officers' club. The YMCA then procured and supplied the hut with, among other things, a magic lantern, books, games, boxing gloves, a piano, and writing paper.

Everything was set up for an inaugural meeting at which a colonel at the base camp had been invited down to give an opening address. In preparation, the boys were marched from their camps down to the hut by their NCOs, most being deposited in the hall an hour before the meeting was due to begin. The sergeants considered their responsibilities terminated once the boys had walked through the club doors, leaving hundreds of youngsters to sit around and await the colonel; it was bound to lead to trouble. Hannay wrote:

> They rioted. Every window in the place was shattered. Everything breakable was smashed into little bits. A YMCA worker, a young man lent to us for the occasion, and recommended as experienced with boys' clubs in London, fled to a small room and locked himself in. The tumult became so terrific that an officer of high standing and importance, whose office was in the neighbourhood, sent an orderly to us with threats.

It was a considerable time before peace and order were restored. No one had been hurt – although there was widespread damage, the boys were simply venting their frustration at their predicament. There had been no animosity against any staff who happened to be in the vicinity; on the contrary, when the colonel made his belated entrance to give his speech, he was met with rousing cheers, not just by the boys in the main hall itself but by boys finishing off their handiwork in other rooms, boys who had clambered up on to the balcony, and boys who stood perched in windows now missing their frames.

The colonel gave his speech, though, not surprisingly, it was not the one he intended, but one fashioned from the scene of utter carnage in front of him. Remarkably, it proved a roaring success, though he did not mince his words: 'He told the naked truth about themselves, what they were, what they had been.' Crucially, he told them what they might be, too, and they listened intently. 'I found out later on that those boys would listen to straight talk on almost any subject, even themselves,' wrote Hannay.

The boys began to settle down once a routine had been established. There were lectures in the afternoons on every subject imaginable, as talks were dependent on who was available. There were lectures on the Navy, on men who had won the Victoria Cross, a lecture on Napoleon's campaigns (given by a visiting history professor from Cambridge), and a magic lantern slide show on the wonders of Egypt. This proved a difficult talk as the slides had been sent as a present from England, and some effort had to be made to find anyone who could provide a verbal accompaniment.

Not all subjects were necessarily so gripping. A lecture on how the army was fed, given by an Army Service Corps officer, would depend very heavily on the skill of the speaker, while another on the art of saluting was always likely to struggle. Occasionally, the talk missed the mark altogether. One visiting speaker launched into a speech beginning with the observation that every boy before him must have lied to enlist. The 'talk' then turned into a tirade as he developed the idea that all lies were 'disgraceful' and that therefore the boys should be 'thoroughly ashamed of themselves'. It was an object lesson in how to lose an audience and if there was any point to the exercise it was undermined completely when, a week or two later, another speaker, starting with the same premise, roundly praised the boys for having lied, declaring that each and every one of them should be proud of their patriotic actions.

The most remarkable and interesting lecture, according to Hannay, was one given by an under-age soldier himself, when, owing to an emergency – there being no speaker – someone had to step in.

> He volunteered an account of his experiences in the trenches. He cannot have been much more than seventeen years old, and ought never to have been there. He was undersized and, I should say, of poor physique. If the proper use of the letter 'h' in conversation is any test of education, this boy must have been very little educated. His vocabulary was limited, and many of the words he did use are not to be found in dictionaries. But he stood on the platform and for half an hour told us what he had seen, endured and felt, with a straightforward simplicity which was far more effective than any art. He disappeared from our midst soon afterwards, and I have never seen him since.

The boys clearly required dedicated help. A proper routine of work was established with an emphasis on physical training under the charge and guidance of undefined 'special sergeants'. The club too was refitted, although the boys were still prone to antics, including wild boxing bouts held in pitch darkness after the club's candles had been trampled. On one occasion, Hannay found a boy lying flat on his back, using the heels of his boots to hammer the keys of the recently acquired and brand-new piano.

Further improvements were made, including the installation of electric light, and, in what was probably an astute move, the imposition of a Miss 'N'. She was placed in charge of the hut and was quickly able to modify some of the boys' worst behaviour. 'Miss N was born to deal with wild boys,' noted Hannay. 'The fiercer they are, the more she loves them, and the wickeder they are, the more she loves them.' Miss N ran the canteen at the club, boiling eggs, serving tea, cocoa, malted milk, bread-and-butter, and biscuits. Tea parties were held every day and were always full. 'She listened with sympathy which was quite unaffected, to long tales of wrongs suffered, of woes and of joys.'

In April 1917, a decision was made to collect the under-age soldiers together and place their education and training on a more professional footing, under the direct control of an officer whose sole duty would be their collective welfare.

Captain Cardinal Harford had been working as an adjutant at the 33rd Infantry Base Depot at Étaples, when he was instructed to take command of all the young soldiers who were then being held at the 26th Infantry Base Depot. His sudden promotion to the rank of major was welcome, but he now faced dealing with hundreds of boys, and the prospect left him feeling somewhat apprehensive.

> The young soldiers began to arrive in half-dozens from all parts of the line: English, Scots, Welsh, Irish, and also some South African boys . . . lance corporals, corporals, some with Military Medal ribbons, tall boys, short boys, nondescript boys, many most indignant at being taken from their units. One extraordinary boy was Sgt Conner, a pukka Sergeant, a serving soldier from, I think, the 2nd Lincolnshire Regt., aged 17½; and a most useful NCO he proved to be.

Ostensibly, Cardinal Harford had many of the credentials to train such young boys. He was a tough-looking forty-year-old officer who had served in the Imperial Yeomanry during the Boer War, and been badly wounded by a bullet in the stomach. He had an impressive group of medal ribbons on his uniform and, to go with his evident stature, he had considerable recent front-line experience, having served in the trenches with the 9th East Surreys and then with the 13th Essex Regiment.

Major Harford was given a free hand to select his training staff and, being aware of how much boys looked up to role models, he set about choosing wisely. A large number of boys under his command were from Scottish regiments, so among his staff was a fine NCO, Regimental Sergeant Major Fraser of the Highland Light Infantry. Indeed, all the NCOs who were selected were men who had seen action but, through injury, were unfit for further front-line duty. One of the more notable was Johnny Summers, a former featherweight and welterweight champion of England, who instructed the boys in boxing and was immensely popular, while another sergeant, a former music-hall artist, was taken on to keep the boys entertained. Much later, Harford was even able to procure the help of Captain Hugh Colvin of the Cheshire Regiment, who had won a Victoria Cross at Ypres. He was sent to the camp as one of the physical-training instructors.

The boys were formed into separate companies, depending where they came from. There was a Scottish Company fashioned from boys sent from every Scottish regiment; there was a Northern Company, with lads from Durham and Newcastle, as well as a Southern, Midland, and a mixed company made up of boys from Wales, Ireland and South Africa.

Within a short space of time, Major Harford had over a thousand boys under his command, including a number of lads aged over nineteen designated 'immatures' owing to the inadequacy of their physique. These boys were to be given good food and plenty of exercise, their chest measurements and weight being taken every three weeks in preparation for a move back up to the front line.

All the boys undertook a strict regime of training, with bayonet fighting and trench construction at the Bull Ring. On other days, they were taken out on route marches, to be followed by sports, including football and cricket. Harford recalled:

Sgt Summers started boxing competitions, and some really good material was soon discovered. Summers carefully arranged the weights and watched to see that no boy was out-classed. The National Boxing Association were most kind in sending me every month two medals, one silver and one bronze, to be boxed for, and these were much prized by those who won them.

With so many boys at the camp, there was plenty of raw material from which to find good boxers or talented footballers. Others had a more theatrical bent, and for them a concert party was formed, 'The B'Hoys', under the sergeant and former music-hall artist. Costumes were made in Britain and shipped out to France, and concerts were put on, not just for in-house entertainment but also for the enjoyment of other depots and hospitals.

As well as many such activities, the boys were set to work. So many casualties were arriving at the base that help was always needed. Eighteen-year-old George Fortune was waiting for his nineteenth birthday when he would be sent back up the line. He was among a group of boys who had been put to work burying men who had succumbed to their wounds. 'It was a sad business – the coffins were roughly made and sometimes blood would come through the bottom.' Shortly before Christmas 1917, a rumour came through that the authorities were to form a young soldiers' company, 'when they got enough of us', recalled George. In the meantime he was kept on burial fatigue.

That year, the war had not been going particularly well for anyone, but it was at least going more badly for the enemy. Economically, Germany was in deep trouble. An Allied naval blockade of German ports had cut off essential imports, yet the country's own economic mismanagement was as much to blame for growing war-weariness and unrest. Domestic problems were compounded by the knowledge that the Americans had joined the war and were on their way to France and, once the men of the American Expeditionary Force (AEF) took to the field in numbers, these fresh, if inexperienced, troops would seal the fate of the central powers. Germany would be beaten and with it the Kaiser's principal allies, the Austro-Hungarian Empire, Bulgaria and Turkey.

The Americans took the decision to join the Allies in April 1917 and began to gear up for the conflict. A small regular force under its commander, General John Joseph Pershing, was dispatched to Europe, while at home conscription would potentially draw on an available pool of 24.5 million American men. Daunting though this figure was, it would be a while before the AEF could take to the field and make any meaningful impression on the war. In the meantime, the Germans would have the chance to strike first.

In preparing for their offensive, the Germans had to fully utilize their one huge, if short-term, advantage. After the October Revolution of 1917, the new Russian Government had immediately signalled its desire to cease hostilities and end the war. Negotiations began in December 1917 and, well before the peace treaty was signed in early March 1918, the Germans had begun to transfer artillery and infantry divisions from East to West. In all, well over a million men, mostly battle-hardened, would be ready to attack when given the order.

After the offensives at Ypres in the summer and Cambrai in the autumn, British troops were in need of rest and training. As always, the C.-in-C., Douglas Haig, was concerned about the number of troops at his disposal on the Western Front that winter. The British line in France was 123 miles, if all the twists and turns were included, the longest held by the BEF in the war to date, and a third longer than in 1916. Furthermore, five divisions, effectively Haig's reserve, had been siphoned off to fight in Italy. Little wonder he felt that the number of men available to him ensured that there could be no Allied spring offensive, and that the initiative would inevitably pass to the Germans. They, he believed, would undertake offensive operations of their own against the weakened British divisions in France and Belgium.

Haig's problems were exacerbated by the deep mistrust between himself and Lloyd George, who had replaced Asquith as Prime

Minister the previous year. After the perceived failure of recent offensives, Lloyd George had taken it upon himself to rein in the commander-in-chief, starving him of reinforcements; he was fearful that he would not be able to overrule any proposal made by Haig to launch a new offensive. Only by deliberately holding reserves in Britain could he ensure the predominance of his will over Haig's.

By the middle of December, it was quite clear that the Germans were beginning to shift the first of their infantry divisions from East to West. Haig expected thirty or thirty-two to be moved, over the course of three or four months. At first he doubted that the Germans would risk an all-out attack but, if they did, it would signify, as he wrote in his diary, 'a gambler's throw'. The outcome of the struggle for power in Germany between military and civil authorities would, in Haig's eyes, decide the next move. 'If the military party won, they would certainly attack and try and deliver a knock-out blow against the Western Front. We must be prepared for this.'

Meanwhile at Étaples, the rumours of a change proved true and with the new year the young soldiers were moved down the coast to the No. 5 Convalescent Camp at Cayeux; the camp's war diary notes: 'Jan 1st 1918. Boys under 19 and immatures requiring further training are in future to be sent to this Depot. The first batch arrived on this date.' Two days later they were joined once again by Major Cardinal Harford who, almost straightaway, took the boys down to the beach for a swim. For many of the lads who had been born into industrial poverty, this turned out to be their first dip in the sea and, for a few, the first time that they had been swimming at all. Harford recalled:

In due course, the numbers reached between 1,000 and 1,200, and a nice packet of trouble seemed collected together – but not a bit of it. We were a really happy lot and there was never any trouble.

A monthly parade was held, a necessary but uncomfortable duty, to say farewell to the boys who had reached the age for front-line service, and immatures whose physical stature was such as to warrant a return to the trenches. These boys were on their way to their respective depots in France, the first stop en route to their battalions at the front.

In March, the Germans launched a massive offensive that put pressure on Allied medical officers to send back as many boys as possible, and, while many were willing to go, not all who had seen action were prepared or happy to go back. Private Alexander McConnell of the 16th Highland Light Infantry cut his own throat with a razor in the early hours of one Monday morning. He had been to the front and had been one of those designated 'immature' when he had been sent down to the base for building up. An investigation was launched but the results are unknown; a return to the line and all its attendant terrors would undoubtedly have been difficult, too difficult for some to stomach.

Major Cardinal Harford, who had grown to know these boys, found it hard to see them leave.

It was a parade which I hated, they were such lads, and one found oneself much drawn to them; and one hated to think, after the happy days we had spent together, that they were once more on the way to the Front Line with all its horrors. It was indeed strange, and almost unbelievable, looking at their youthful faces, to realize that all had served in the trenches and that Fate had decreed that they should again be due to return to them.

It was perhaps as well that the major could not have foreseen the heavy bombardments that, in the last year of the war, were to take the lives of many of 'his' boys.

12

1918: The Year of Decision

BRAVELY HE ANSWERED
HIS COUNTRY'S CALL
HIS BRIGHT YOUNG LIFE
HE GAVE FOR ALL

13095 Private Albert Povey
6th Royal Berkshire Regiment

Killed in Action 23 September 1915, aged 17

THE NATURE OF WARFARE had changed radically by the last year of the war. In particular, there were more efficient and accurate techniques for hitting targets, including photo-reconnaissance and improved methods of judging location and distance by the use of flash-spotting and sound-ranging. Fuses were made more reliable to cut the number of dud shells, while the shrapnel shell was complemented, and to an extent superseded, by all manner of high-explosive shells, which could devastate trenches, penetrate strong-points and cut barbed wire. With the advent of smoke shells to hide advancing infantry, and the use of gas shells to subdue the enemy in their trenches, artillery by 1918 was no longer a rather blunt tool of predictable destruction but an incisive battlefield weapon.

Artillery was the big killer during the Great War, responsible for well over half of all battlefield casualties. Commanders were well aware of this and had spent much time asking for more and heavier guns and greater quantities of shells. Although the number of British field guns and light howitzers had not risen substantially on the Western Front between July 1916 and March 1918, up by around 12 per cent, the number of heavy-calibre guns and howitzers had grown exponentially. In July 1916, 576 were in use on the Western Front; by March 1918 this had risen to 2,093.

A war based increasingly on mechanization and heavy industry had never looked so splendid or so utterly fearsome. In March, April and May 1918, the overwhelming power of these guns would be unleashed and into the resulting maelstrom would be hurled tens of thousands of eighteen-year-old boys, many with barely four months' training and some with as little as fourteen weeks. The Government, under military advice, had considered the question of sending eighteen-year-olds to the front on many occasions in 1917, but had declined to do so. Now, in March 1918, owing to the pressures of the German offensive, ministers felt compelled to reduce the limit to eighteen years and seven months and subsequently to eighteen years and six months.

Eighteen-year-old Private Percy Williams of the Northumberland Fusiliers was one of those boys sent to France in March 1918. He never forgot the impact of the bombardment and recalled it in detail many years later.

I was in a dugout in the third-line trenches when an officer came round and said that there might be action tonight. I'd not been under bad shellfire before and I was shaking and was almost sick with fright.

When the shelling started we were told to leave the dugout and we scrambled up into a trench that had been practically destroyed. Gas shells had been falling all night and saturated everything, covering our masks with a sulphur film. You couldn't see. I had stomach ache. I felt faint and sick and had to spew up, forcing me to take the gas mask off and vomit as best I could, trying not to breathe in.

Casualties were being suffered and between the din we could hear them shouting for stretcher-bearers, stretcher-bearers. I thought, 'Oh my God, I'm going to die, I'm going to die!' We did not know what was happening, not fifty yards on either side of us.

It had been true for much of the war that those holding a trench tended to have an advantage over those seeking to take it. In 1918 this balance altered radically. Artillery, when integrated with new infantry assault tactics, would break the deadlock of the Western Front. If the modern battlefield tactic of 'shock and awe' ever had an origin, then it was surely in the fighting of 1918. And if these bombardments could rattle window frames in London, as they did, what effect might they have on the boys drafted out to France in the last spring of the war?

The fighting would test the boys' resolve to the limit and, in time, their gallantry would humble the highest in the land. When the Prime Minister, Lloyd George, addressed the House of Commons as the tide of war finally began to turn against Germany, his words bordered on a eulogy.

I remember coming at nine o'clock one dark night to Boulogne, after I had been to see the generals, and I met these boys coming up by torch-light from the boat, and they went straight to the front. No sooner were these boys in France than they had to face veteran and victorious troops. No veterans ever fought with greater courage and with greater steadfastness than those lads. They hurled back these legions who had vowed to destroy the British Army. We must all be proud of the boys who have so upheld the honour of their native land, and helped so valiantly to save the cause of the Allies from disaster.

These boys had indeed helped save the Allies but their victory was based upon a lengthy period of preparation. Haig might not have had the troops he wanted in France but with the knowledge that the German offensive was coming he had set about accumulating and hoarding huge quantities of ammunition, including 16.5 million shells sent to France in the 'quiet' months of January and February 1918. Medical supplies were also stockpiled, and with the supplies came young VADs, nurses of the Voluntary Aid Detachments created to augment the medical services. At the outbreak of war, there were over 47,000 VADs, belonging to either the Red Cross or St John Ambulance. This number nearly doubled during the war. Initially, the lower age limit for going to France was twenty-three, but in time this was largely ignored. Even so, only around 5 per cent actually served overseas, forty-two VADs died, thirteen through enemy action.

One of those who left for France in February that year was an eighteen-year-old Red Cross nurse, Marjorie Grigsby. In 1916 she had become sick and tired of hearing her father talk about her brother Herbert and his service in Mesopotamia, so when she returned from boarding school in July she had gone to Devonshire House, the home of the Red Cross in London, and sought out an interview with anyone who could help.

> I saw the Head of the Red Cross. He interviewed me over a double desk and I was always very good at reading on the other side when I was sitting there and he said, 'How old are you?' So I said, 'Twenty, sir.' I saw him write down, 'Age twenty. Apparent age sixteen.' I said, 'Now you've written it down, sir, in black and white, you can't alter it, but it isn't sixteen, it's seventeen.' He grinned and left it as it was, and passed me. I think he thought if I'd got the cheek to tell him that, I could do anything.

After working in a London hospital for eighteen months, Marjorie, with parental permission, was sent to France. As she left, she was given command of a group of General Service VADs. Coming from an upper-middle-class family, Marjorie was charged with delivering these primarily working-class women to France.

I felt a perfect fool. All the General Service VADs had to be in the charge of a VAD because we were voluntary and the service ones were paid. To use the old-fashioned word, they were really char-women and they had to be taken and lined up on the quay. We were going to the Hotel Christol in Boulogne, so I marched them down the quay, round the other side and down the road and into the hotel, stood them to attention and then handed them over to the office. That was the end of them as far as I was concerned. Lots of them were old enough to be my mother at any rate, if not my grandmother, and there was I. I suppose you look more mature in uniform, but I couldn't have looked very old.

Marjorie was unaware of the increasingly bleak outlook in France. The morning after she arrived, Field Marshal Haig had held a conference with all his army commanders to discuss the arrange-ments for defending the front, which included agreeing the dispo-sition and use of the reserves and the crucial role of the artillery during the German offensive. Then, after returning to London, Haig continued to press for fresh drafts, stressing the urgent nature of his demands, but, while supplies continued to pour across the Channel, reinforcements did not.

By the end of February, Nurse Marjorie Grigsby had been sent to work at No. 2 Red Cross Hospital, Rouen. When she arrived, she had opened her suitcase to find a letter from her mother offer-ing a few friendly words of advice: she must always remember how she had been brought up and not mix with the wrong people.

Marjorie was acutely aware of her youth and was less concerned with getting in with the wrong people than with how she was going to be accepted by the other nurses. The early signs had been mixed.

When I went into the staff room the nurses were having their break and they were all smoking. They would make fun saying, 'Oh, yes, here comes the baby, she won't want a cigarette, she won't want a gasper.' I got sick of it, so I went and bought a packet and one night I walked in and pulled out a little packet of Woodbine Willies, five in a little green packet, and lit up – God, I nearly choked. But smoking made me feel that I was the same age as the others, so that I could be on a par with them.

The nurses could afford to relax. Casualties at the front in February were the lowest since November 1915 and the third lowest monthly total of the whole war. It was the silence before the storm.

As the dark clouds gathered, a fourteen-year-old boy, Henry Stevens, made his way to France for the first time. By 1918, boys of his youth serving overseas were extremely rare although not as rare as the circumstances of his case; these were probably unique.

His story began in December 1917 when his brother George returned home on leave. George had been serving on the Western Front since July 1916; he had been wounded by shrapnel in June 1917, returning to front-line service after a spell in hospital. George was fed up. While in hospital, he had voluntarily given one and half pints of blood in order to save the life of a wounded officer, an act for which a doctor promised a month's leave. The doctor had given George a strongly worded letter of recommendation to take back to his unit, the 7th Northamptonshire Regiment, but no leave was forthcoming. Eventually, as a matter of course, two weeks' leave was granted in November, at the end of which George disappeared. Over the next few weeks the Metropolitan police made several visits to the family home in Barking, Essex, but were told that nothing had been seen of him since he left to rejoin his unit.

Then suddenly, on the evening of 25 February 1918, George surrendered himself to Police Sergeant Samuel Pyle at Ilford Police Station, confessing to being a deserter. His identity was established by Sergeant Pyle and next day he was conducted under military escort to a Rest Camp at Southampton before being sent back three days later to France. The problem was that the soldier was not George but his brother Henry, seven years his junior.

Henry was sent via Le Havre and Boulogne to Hancourt to join his brother's regiment where it was acting as Corps Reserve. Henry's duplicity was quickly, if not immediately, unmasked, leaving him no option but to own up to his antics. It was just two weeks since Henry had arrived in France and on the day of his fifteenth birthday he found himself sitting in a guardroom being interviewed by the Assistant Provost Marshal. It appears that Henry was released back to the battalion awaiting further instruction. The order was sent from the 73rd Infantry Brigade headquarters and directed that Henry should be sent to the Base at once. However, this order arrived only on 20 March, on the eve of the German offensive, and no one was going anywhere.

The offensive was launched against two British armies, the Third Army in the north and the Fifth Army at the extreme right-hand end of the line where it met with the French. The enemy attack at this point was intended to drive a wedge between the British and French armies, and ultimately to drive the British back against the Channel ports. In launching their offensive, the Germans used new tactics of rapid infiltration. A devastating but brief bombardment of the British lines was followed by an infantry attack by the pick of the forces available. The British defences were quickly breached in most sectors, the enemy bypassing strong points in the line; these were mopped up later. This initial success was aided by the weather, a thick mist that hid the attacking troops, so that the first many of the British soldiers saw of the enemy was large numbers sweeping to their rear. In this way entire battalions could be encircled and captured. Such was the rapidity of the enemy's advance that in just two days the British troops were flung back over the old Somme battlefield, the Fifth Army retiring twenty-five miles.

In Britain, news of the German offensive brought about the immediate release of the reserves. But by keeping them in Britain, Lloyd George had endangered the BEF's capability to withstand the onslaught. The vast majority of the drafts rushed out to France had not experienced any form of the battle-hardening experience acquired only by serving in a war zone.

At Newmarket, seventeen-year-old Eric Hiscock was not expecting to cross the Channel so soon. He had enlisted in the army in 1915 aged fifteen, and the officers who had overseen his progress had pledged 'faithfully' to his parents that he would not see active service until he was at least eighteen. As he wrote:

So much for well-intentioned promises. The Kaiser decreed otherwise and when all hell broke loose on the Somme in March 1918, Private E. Hiscock, 59333, was dispatched with all haste to help stem the advance to the French ports.

Eric was not the only boy to go out under age. 'The widely cast net for men caught up other under-aged soldiers,' he noted, including one lad called Brook, and another seventeen-year-old friend, 'a cheerful, lazy-minded, fresh-complexioned Cockney called Ernest Jackson'. All three were given the dubious compliment of being made lance corporals (unpaid) before setting sail.

On 23 March, seventeen-year-old Reginald Kiernan was also in the process of getting ready to go, but everything was in a state of commotion.

It appears that there is a very big stunt on in France. The physical training staff have the wind up. The whole camp is being cleared, and they are afraid they will be put on draft. There is a PT sergeant who has been the terror of recruits since 1915. Men he trained in that year have been back, wounded, in 1916 and 1917, and each time he was the same. He is utterly changed now and is very quiet. We feel triumphant over these NCOs – we know we will soon be the real soldiers, and we do not care a damn about France. We feel twice as strong as they are.

On Sunday 24 March, Fred Hodges heard that his draft was off to war. He and his friends were billeted in Norwich, and talk spread quickly among the boys who thronged the city streets that they would be sent to France without completing their training.

On Monday, 25 March, the rumours proved to be true; at the early morning roll-call, as we paraded outside the billets, we were officially told. The situation on the Western Front was so grave that all those who had reached the age of eighteen years and eight months were to be drafted to the Front immediately. My age was eighteen and eight months on 18 March, and so I was eligible.

War-readiness included the rigmarole of queuing for extra kit, gas mask, identity tags, first field dressing, steel helmet, iron rations, and, most exciting of all, ammunition. Queuing, which had always been a chore, was tinged with excitement and expectation. Back in their huts, the boys repeatedly tried on the full equipment, before laying the kit on the floor to make minor adjustments to straps and buckles. Then it was off to get bayonets dulled and boots re-soled where needed, and rifles given a final check by the armourer. Last, but not least, there was a trip to get a haircut to ensure that gas masks would fit properly. They were ready to go, or almost. Reginald Kiernan, an Irish Catholic, went to confession. Skipping tea, he managed to leave the barracks for the short walk to the church and a priest.

He did not seem too pleased to be brought out into the church at six o'clock in the evening to hear a confession, though he tried to hide it . . . The priest never said a word to me, except the words of absolution. Perhaps he was tired.

Charles Carrington, who had himself enlisted at seventeen, was by 1918 in England overseeing the training of young conscripts, primarily Yorkshiremen. Every six months, the reserve battalion received seven or eight hundred boys, mostly eighteen years old, into the fold to be fashioned into soldiers. Untrained but nominally fit, they were given the classification A4, and it was Carrington's job to see that they were trained and A1 by the time they were embarked for the Western Front.

The transition he saw in these boys during six months' training was remarkable.

> The skinny, sallow, shambling, frightened victims of our industrial system, suffering from the effect of wartime shortages, who were given into our hands, were unrecognizable after six months of good food, fresh air, and physical training. They looked twice the size and, as we weighed and measured them, I am able to say that they put on an average of one inch in height and one stone in weight during their time with us . . . Beyond statistical measurement was their change in character, to ruddy, handsome, clear-eyed young men with square shoulders who stood up straight and were afraid of no one, not even the sergeant major.

In 'the dark days', as Carrington called them, of 1918, these boys would not receive even six months' training. In time, questions would be asked in the Commons about this. The new Undersecretary of State for War, James Macpherson, replied:

> The minimum period of training for such lads is four months, I can assure my Hon. Friend that no lads have been sent to France unless they are sufficiently trained to take their place in the firing line.

There were allegations that some boys had received just fourteen weeks' training, denied at the time but later conceded by the Government. Fourteen weeks or four months, either way the time granted for training had been shortened dangerously and it was a moot point whether it was possible to teach a boy to be a competent soldier while simultaneously developing him physically.

The boys' departure for the Western Front was 'painful' to witness, according to Carrington.

> I knew well that under their forced cheerfulness there were mixed sentiments and I did not much like the headmaster's – I mean the colonel's – set speech of valediction. The boys suddenly looked much younger, loaded down with their marching order, their new steel helmets and gas masks, their pouches stocked with live ammunition, and with their iron rations tied to their packs at the last moment in white linen bags – the unmistakable sign by which you recognized a new draft in France.

There was anything but cheerfulness as far as Private Percy Williams was concerned. Percy, a lad from the heart of Wales, was feeling miserable and not in the slightest patriotic. He had prayed long and hard that this day would never come.

> You may call me a bit of a coward, but I didn't want to join the army. I could see by the casualty lists that so many had died during the Battle of the Somme, I could read between the lines and I was hoping and hoping that the war would be finished before I was called up.

Soon after his eighteenth birthday in September 1917 Percy received a telegram directing him to Whitchurch Barracks in Cardiff. He left home feeling very apprehensive, clinging to the belief that he would not be sent abroad until he was nineteen; that was what he had been told.

Not a bit of it. I was sent abroad at the end of March 1918. In the short time I was out in France, I hoped, along with others, that I'd get a blighty, a slight wound that would get me back to England.

Fred Hodges was the antithesis of Percy Williams. Fred, a grammar school boy of the most patriotic type, had enlisted aged seventeen in March 1917 with two friends from school. The prospect of a commission had been suggested but rejected, as it appeared to forestall their chances of getting abroad. They could not wait. They were fit, strapping lads, and made a nice contrast to the blighted youth that all too frequently shuffled into the recruitment office. When Fred and his friends had walked in on that March day, he had been proud to overhear the medical officer say, 'Ah, these three look more likely. I'm pleased to see three young chaps raring to go.'

In the last days before leaving for France, Fred's draft was moved to Norwich. All embarkation leave was stopped but Fred managed to contact his parents and they came to the city to stay for a few days. On the day before embarkation, the boys were taken to a local park to be inspected by a senior officer.

We marched past the general, column after column. It was a cold frosty morning; our breath was ascending from our mouths as we marched, and then the general got up on his dais and spoke to us. 'You men,' he began, and then paused as he surveyed our eager young faces, 'of course I know you're not men, you're only boys, but the Germans have broken through our fortifications and you're needed at the front at once. You've now got to play the part of men.'

The general then descended and walked along the lines of boys inspecting each one, stopping, Fred recalled, to talk to a few who appeared particularly young or small or both. It was a young draft. Fred estimated that it was three-quarters boys, and only one-quarter men.

The next day the draft left the camp and marched to the railway station. The crowds grew ever deeper as they approached the train, but Fred spotted his parents and for a moment they were able to say goodbye.

> The pavements were full, mostly of women; we were their boys. Some waved and said, 'Good luck', some were crying. We could hear comments: 'Poor little buggers,' I heard one woman say. 'Fancy sending them out to France to die for us.'
>
> My parents were there on the station platform and I remember my mother putting her arms round me and saying something about 'If you don't come back . . .' I don't know what she was going to say but I interrupted her and said, 'Don't worry, Mum. I shall come back.'

Reginald Kiernan had left his camp and was already on a train to Dover. As the train went down to the coast, a crackle of rifle fire was heard as some of the lads, excited at owning new weapons, took pot shots at grazing sheep and cows. By evening the joviality had calmed and men slept against each other, or sprawled out in the passageways of the carriage.

> It was night when we passed through London and children and women came on to the verandas of the slum tenements and cheered us. Their cheers sounded shrill and faint over the noise of the train. Many were in nightclothes, and we could see them dimly, and their little rooms, by the light of their tiny gas jets.

After arriving at Dover, the men were temporarily discharged to several houses overlooking the port, and awaited the order to move. When it came, they traipsed down the hill to the ship and joined the queue to board. As they waited, Kiernan became aware of a lady dressed all in black approaching the line. The words she spoke were unforgettable – born, as they clearly were, out of her own personal grief.

'Finish it off this time, boys,' was all she said.

13

All or Nothing

A MOTHER'S HOPE, A FATHER'S JOY
GOD HAS CALLED OUR ONLY BOY

79210 Private Harold Carter
9th London Regiment (Royal Fusiliers)

Killed in Action (Epéhy) 18 September 1918, aged 18

THE MEN AND BOYS who poured into France at the end of March were given one undertaking: to halt, by whatever means, the unremitting enemy advance. It was a huge obligation to place upon the shoulders of those who had never seen combat before; nevertheless, lads such as Fred Hodges were not about to shirk the responsibility. The draft sent out with Fred would join the 10th Lancashire Fusiliers, but first they needed ammunition. As the boys queued at the base camp for their extra rounds, Fred heard the voice of a Private Ablethorpe, a usually mild-mannered and refined lad, but no longer. 'Well, now they've given us all 120 rounds of ammo, I intend to use it, and shoot as many of the buggers as possible before I'm killed.' Fred was more thrilled than taken aback. 'I realized that we boys were going to face death or wounds for our country. I said to Ablethorpe, "We've GOT to STOP THEM whatever OUR fate."'

The situation at the front dictated a short stay at the base, often less than a day, before the drafts were entrained on cattle trucks and sent to join their new battalions. The trains were slow, cumbersome and jolting, and it was perfectly possible to jump out of a carriage and run down the track to catch up. On Fred Hodges's train, a few boys fired their rifles at barns, while others climbed out on to the roof of the train, returning, after it had passed through a tunnel, with blackened faces. There was an atmosphere akin to going on a picnic, but the tranquillity of the countryside belied the danger ahead and one old campaigner knew it. In the truck was a man named Brandon, an old soldier who wore the medal ribbon of the 1914 Mons Star.

> He was watching our boyish tricks with some interest when, grinning, he said, 'When Jerry sees your lovely pink faces he'll say "Mein Gott!" rat, tat, tat, new troops, rat, tat, tat, tat.'

Often drafts were roughly hewn apart, 200 being sent to one battalion, 300 to another, frequently separating friends in the process. Fred was fortunate in being sent to the battalion he joined in 1917. Now he had the chance to listen to 'old' soldiers and pick up tips about life in the line, but there were not many left to tell the tale.

> These survivors of the Old Tenth had only just come from the forward area of the line, their numbers reduced to less than a hundred very tired, dirty, unshaven men, whose faces showed the strain of the past fortnight.

The boys looked on in awe at these men, whose clothing was muddy and torn and yet their rifles were spotless, and in return they were greeted by these battle-worn soldiers with a mixture of pity and amusement.

Not all new boys were made welcome. Harold Lawton, an eighteen-year-old lad from Rhyl in Wales, was one of those who were numbered off and directed to join a battalion with which he had no prior association, the 1/4th East Yorkshire Regiment. This unit had been practically annihilated in March, being reduced from a nominally thousand-strong battalion to three officers and thirty-six other ranks. On 5 April, Harold was one of 500 reinforcements sent to make up the numbers. Harold remembered:

> The regiment was resting after a very nasty time. We were the new boys and the old soldiers took no notice of us whatsoever; they were utterly exhausted and had to look after themselves, but it meant they told us absolutely nothing.

The following day the battalion was sent forward.

> We were to hold a line of trenches which were little more than a scrape in the ground and we had to get digging straight away. We hadn't been there long when one chap, a lad who'd come out with us, John Peacock, looked over our new parapet and he was immediately shot through the head and killed. I was shocked. No one knew what was going on! We were cold, wet and hungry.

Fred Hodges, in contrast, had moved up to the Somme in stages, and had more time to acclimatize. These boys were naive, and, as Fred remembered, prone 'to behave like a crowd of tourists'. A group had stood near a battery trying to spot the flight of the shells and had already been told to clear off by a gunnery officer.

Fred's march to the front line had been full of interest and incident. The battalion had been broken up into platoons to minimize the risk of casualties from shelling. As it happened, the threat materialized from the air, a plane swooping low to drop a couple of bombs, scattering the boys, most running for an empty trench. The corporal was annoyed and turned on the platoon. 'I thought I'd brought some men up the line, not a lot of bloody scared kids.'

These kids may have felt like soldiers but, to the experienced eye, kids were all they were and moving up to the front with the weight of fear, expectation and a full pack was utterly exhausting. An unknown Australian who saw these lads wrote home:

> For two days companies of infantry have been passing us on the roads — companies of children, English children; pink-faced, round-cheeked children, flushed under the weight of their unaccustomed packs, with their steel helmets on the back of their heads and the straps hanging loosely on their rounded baby chins.

It was a sight that could not but evoke pity.

Reginald Kiernan, one of a 400-strong draft sent to join a battalion in the line, wrote:

> We were in full marching kit, and we marched on with no band, just slog, slog, slog on, not even keeping step after about five kilometres. I have never had such an agonizing bodily strain as the last kilometre. We had not one halt. Some of the men were screaming at the end, though I don't know about what, unless it was the fear that one's head would burst. It seemed as though we would march for ever. A great many men fell out and lay by the roadside . . . I tried to keep upright when we were marching, instead of leaning forward, slipping the fingers through the shoulder straps of the equipment to relieve the weight.

Eric Hiscock wrote of his experience:

> It is difficult, at this distance from the dread reality of those frontline nights, to communicate what it was like for a youngster still well under the age of enlistment to be included in such hazardous fatigues. Most journeys were made in single file, on treacherous duckboard tracks perched precariously across the sinister, stinking, death-filled mud flats . . . I don't know what happened mentally, but physically I occasionally broke down under the sheer weight of equipment that had to be carried, lack of sleep, and the

intolerable discipline that was necessary to keep tired and bored
soldiers up to something like scratch, and away from mutiny . . .
I wanted home with all my being.

Later that summer, Eric was tempted to get out of the line by
means of a self-inflicted wound. It was while his company was
resting for ten minutes by the side of the road that an opportunity
presented itself. Heavy howitzer guns on caterpillar wheels were
passing.

Suddenly I saw one such vehicle approaching that I might use as a
means of getting myself shipped home and out, finally, from this
world I had never made.

No one, I decided, could accuse a flaked-out schoolboy, seemingly asleep during a ten-minute rest, of a self-inflicted wound
if one of his feet was run over and crushed by a heavy vehicle in
the dark. All I had to do was stretch out a short distance in my
pretended sleep just as the caterpillars approached and I would be
incapacitated for ever from that painful moment.

The instrument of release rolled nearer and nearer. I stirred in
my simulated sleep and my right leg stretched out. In a matter
of moments the foot of it would be crushed and mangled into an
inoperable mess and I would be headed for home, minus a foot
but for ever free from nightmare marches, fatigues, machine-gun
bullets . . .

At the last moment he withdrew his dominant right leg and
substituted his left, but the caterpillar had passed. 'A sense of
relief flooded my stupid mind and my tired body,' he recorded.

Why would any soldier, let alone a seventeen-year-old boy,
willingly mutilate himself to get out of France? The reality of war
is one of intense extremes and the same moment of madness that
could propel a man to win a medal was, in the climate of war, a
primary reaction that might also cause him to run headlong in the

opposite direction or to put a foot under the track of an oncoming heavy vehicle.

The number of self-inflicted wounds (SIWs) had officially grown from just thirty-four cases in the year to the end of September 1915 to 2,239 cases in the last year of the war. Better medical detection of such 'crimes' was no doubt partly responsible for the remarkable increase, but then, as such recognition improved, so did the ability of soldiers to disguise their efforts at self-mutilation. Many cared little for the risk of detection: like Eric Hiscock in his moment of temptation, they had reached the end of their tether and were going to get out one way or another.

It would have been easy, believed Reginald Kiernan, to shoot oneself to get away from the line. If a man was careful and shot through a water bottle into the leg, there would be no tell-tale 'burn', the giveaway mark of a rifle discharged from just a few inches. 'But I could not do it. The thought of it had always filled me with disgust. Someone has to do the fighting.'

A particularly fierce bombardment, indeed, faced Fred Hodges's platoon soon after it arrived in the front line.

Captain Drummond came along and said, 'Now do what I'm doing,' and he sat on the fire step and pulled his feet up so his heels were touching his backside and he put his arms around his head and shoulders and said, 'Now you've covered your vital parts, so there's nothing more you can do. If you do stop some shrapnel, what better place to die than in the front line in defence of your king and country?'

Such lessons had been learnt in the past when there was time to acclimatize, and generally not while shells peppered the parapet; new battalions were sent to 'quieter' sectors to learn the ropes. In April 1918, many were so utterly depleted, so completely replenished by drafts, that there were few men left with any experience to impart. The younger soldiers would have to turn, where possible, to those in the draft itself who had served at the front before.

One boy fortunate to be going the other way was the imposter Henry Stevens. Quite what part Henry played in the retirement is not clear. The fighting in the previous three weeks had been brutal: eleven officers and 275 other ranks of the 7th Northants were killed, wounded, or missing. Henry had managed to remain with his unit, probably with the transport. He was a civilian in an army uniform and was, as likely as not, kept out of harm's way as far as that was possible in a fighting retreat. By 8 April the exhausted battalion was relieved and out on rest, at which time Henry could be disposed of, being sent under escort to custody at the Military Police barracks in Boulogne where he was interviewed once again. He repeated the story as told to him by George of how his brother had given blood and why he had decided to stay on in Britain and desert after his official leave had ended.

> In February 1918, the police were making enquiries about my brother, who had left home with the intention of crossing to Ireland – he told me that he hoped to secure a passage for the 2nd of March [to Cork]. To stop the police enquiries I dressed in my brother's uniform, [he also had his kit and pay book] and impersonated him and gave myself up as a deserter to the Ilford police.

The statement taken down by an Intelligence Officer ended with an assessment of the case and the verdict that 'the Prisoner has committed an offence in England Viz:- "Falsely describing himself as an army deserter", for which he is liable for three months imprisonment.' Henry Stevens was brought before Folkestone Magistrates and charged with 'Being an unauthorised person wearing Military uniform "without authority".' Sense prevailed, the case was dismissed and Henry returned to his parents.

In Britain's darkest hour of the war, this was a good news story and details of Henry's pluck appeared the following week in *The*

Times under the title 'The Family Honour: Boy Who Killed Many Germans', the journalist unquestioningly repeating the boy's own embellishment and the guff that he had attached to his recollection of events. 'When the German offensive began, the youth, although he had no military training and did not know how to use a rifle, went up with his unit. He said that he killed many Germans, and that he "could not help it when they came so thickly".' Henry's local paper also ran with the story, repeating Henry's claims and adding: 'I think it will be universally agreed that young Stevens is made of the right stuff.'

Twenty-two-year-old George Stevens was in all likelihood never in Ireland. Wherever he went, he surrendered to police on 8 April. In June he was subjected to a Field General Court Martial for desertion. He pleaded 'not guilty' but was found guilty and given seven years' penal servitude for his crime, the sentence being suspended for the duration of the war. George returned to his unit and was reported missing during a daylight trench raid on 22 July 1918. His body was never found.

George Stevens was an experienced soldier and despite his crime he was needed at the front not languishing in a prison cell. Cyril José's crime had been to lie about his age but this was now irrelevant and he too, as an old soldier, was required back in France.

Sent home after being wounded on the Somme, Cyril was swept up in the rush to get men abroad, embarking for the port of Le Havre on the night of 31 March and arriving back in France on his nineteenth birthday. Cyril had assumed that he would be sent to join his old battalion, the 2nd Devons, but on landing he and his friends were sent as a draft to the 2/4th Oxfordshire and Buckinghamshire Light Infantry, which had been very badly knocked about on the first day of the German offensive. Cyril was an experienced hand and, as he sported a wound stripe from his actions on 1 July 1916, he was afforded instant respect by the 'kiddies', as he called them, sent across from England.

Vic Cole was back, too, although not as part of a draft. The 1st Royal West Kents, to which he had been transferred in late 1916, had been part of Haig's reserve hived off to Italy at the end of 1917. For a few months Vic and his friends had been having fun in this relative backwater. Unfortunately the fun had gone too far and Vic had been demoted, losing his only stripe after a drunken night in Padua. Then came the March offensive and his division had been rushed back to the Western Front, the Royal West Kents arriving at Doullens on 6 April before being marched to the town of Armentières.

The March offensive against the Fifth Army in particular had been ferocious but the Germans had failed to separate the British from the French. A fresh onslaught was now ordered, and unfortunately for Vic Cole and Cyril José the direction was switched so that this time it was against the thinly held line just east of Armentières. The front line around this town had been generally quiet – indeed, new battalions sent out to France in 1915 and 1916 had often been directed to this sector to get used to trench life. For the first time since 1914, the town would be in the direct line of fire.

The intensity of this second phase of the campaign would hardly slacken as the German High Command threw in division after division in their desperate bid to make a decisive breakthrough. Geographically, this attack looked extremely dangerous for the survival of the BEF in France. The front under pressure was further to the north than the fighting hitherto in March, as it was the Germans' intention to capture the three significant heights to the rear of Armentières. This would enable them potentially to surround the town of Ypres to the north, making the whole British line untenable, and ultimately threatening the Channel ports. Vic and Cyril would be right in the way of the proposed advance, as indeed would the thousands of teenage boys shipped to France, one of whom was eighteen-year-old Corporal Ernest Stevens.

Ernest had been in France only a matter of days. His father had been a professional soldier and had fought and died for Britain during the Boer War. His son had grown up with a picture of a proud father holding him on his knee, and ever since he was a small boy all Ernest had wanted to do was follow in his father's footsteps and serve overseas. The army granted his wish by drafting him to France at the end of March, and with ninety-six other lads he joined the 20th Middlesex on 7 April.

The first day with the battalion was peaceful enough, and that evening Ernest's company moved into a farmyard.

We slept on the hay that night, and next day we were put on trucks which took us up as near to the second line as they dared go. We then marched along both sides of the road with at least four feet between each man in single file, to reduce the risk of heavy casualties if we happened to be shelled.

We were to be in support but when we arrived we found there wasn't really a trench at all; all we had was a built-up earthwork.

The company dug in, improving the position and deepening some shallow trenches, but the weather was bad and these soon filled with water.

That night was hectic and we were shelled for at least two hours, not with high explosive but with poison gas. I was tired and managed to sleep but the bombardment woke me up many times. Everybody was alive to the fact that the Germans were strafing behind our lines where the reserves would be congregated, to try and knock them out and isolate the men in the first and second lines.

At daybreak, a ration party came up with bread and cheese and this was dished out. I had just got my share when the platoon sergeant shouted out, 'Stand to!' It was a very misty morning and we were in low-lying ground, but it was also quiet at this time and I don't recall any shelling. Two figures were seen coming through the mist and the platoon sergeant ordered us to fire five shots, rapid fire, thinking they were Germans. As soon as we started firing, up went their hands, and as they approached we could see they had no helmets and that they had discarded their arms and equipment. They were our lads and one of them had a bullet wound in the back of his neck. The Germans had obviously reached our front line and had probably been reorganizing for the next attack, and these two managed to get away.

The position of the 1/4th East Yorks was just as precarious. On the morning of 9 April, Harold Lawton and his company had been told to pull back from their hastily constructed positions, but in doing so the men had become split up into groups.

The Germans had infiltrated our lines and had already swept around the flanks. We could hear plenty of firing but we hadn't a clue what was going on, not an officer was to be seen, it was shocking. We were stuck, and began to eat our iron rations hoping all the time that we would be found or someone would tell us what to do. Eventually the Germans returned and mopped us up; there were only half a dozen of us so there was nothing to do but put up our hands.

Ernest Stevens remembered:

We stood behind the earthen wall we had built up, when suddenly we heard this chatter of a machine gun behind us. We knew we were in for some trouble but we thought we were going to be attacked from the front, never imagining that we would be machine-gunned from our rear. That was extraordinary. I heard the bullets whizzing past me as I made a run for a small slit trench and I jumped in to find myself up to my waist in water, next to my platoon commander. He was new out to France and looked very worried. He turned to me and said, 'Corporal, I'm afraid we're absolutely hemmed in, it's impossible to make a fight of it. The only thing I can suggest is if you have a handkerchief bring it out, tie it to the end of your bayonet and indicate to the Germans that we are prepared to surrender.' I didn't want to do it but as an NCO I had to obey commands, but being taken prisoner, oh, what a disgrace!

A large proportion of the 20th Middlesex, Ernest's regiment, managed to escape, but the battalion lost a total of eight killed, fifty-nine wounded and 281 missing, almost all of whom became prisoners of war.

Ernest Stevens and Harold Lawton were each marched away to captivity. Unfortunately for Harold, he was taken to a fortress known in the British press for its dire reputation as the Black Hole of Lille. As he and the other prisoners went there, the towns-people came out and tried to offer them bread, even though they were hungry themselves.

Once in the fortress, we were taken down underground to a room, a truly awful place. Hundreds of men were crowded into cells, men lying on wooden shelves for day after day. The conditions were terrible. Men were dying in there from wounds and dysen-tery but there were so many prisoners you couldn't move in the filthy conditions. I was kept for twelve days, hardly able to move, and it came as a relief to be taken to Germany.

The German battle tactics, although costly in terms of men and equipment, were pushing the British troops back at an alarm-ing rate. Huge numbers were taken prisoner, and battalions, once more, almost ceased to exist.

The casualties on both sides were huge but there was a criti-cal difference between those inflicted on the Somme two years before and those of 1918. In July 1916, British and Empire troops had suffered 187,300 casualties, of whom just 8.8 per cent were prisoners, and over 41,300 were dead. In 1918 the figures were reversed. In March, nearly 40 per cent of all 165,000 casualties had been taken prisoner, and fewer than 19,000 were killed. In the six weeks to the end of April, over 93,000 British and Empire prisoners were taken, testament to the successful infiltration tactics of the Germans, helped, in part, by the lack of battlefield experience of thousands of eighteen- and nineteen-year-old boys.

Despite the numbers being taken prisoner, there were still plenty of wounded filling the casualty clearing stations (CCSs). VAD Marjorie Grigsby had been asked to volunteer to go forward to a CCS just a few miles behind the lines. Some nurses had been taken ill, she was told, and the rest could no longer cope with the wounded.

It was hell, absolute hell. We were doing things we knew nothing about, giving injections to people with legs hanging out of trousers, heads half blown off, and using the same needle, just dipped in carbolic twenty, one after another. All we were anxious to do was to put them out of their pain. A lot of them were not even conscious. Some were moaning, some groaning, calling for their mums or girlfriends; one particular lad I remember singing 'I'm Forever Blowing Bubbles', he kept on all the while and I got sick to death of it, I wished he'd stop.

The CCS itself was an old barn which was full, there was no room for anybody else inside, so the wounded were just put down on stretchers, perhaps a mackintosh sheet, or pieces of fencing, just put down and left. Remember, they were not coming in in ones or twos but in twenties and thirties. First thing they wanted was a cigarette. I had cigarettes in my pocket which I used to give them. You lit it yourself and put it in their mouth and hoped they'd be able to hang on to it; they used to say 'cig'. Often they'd have a puff or two and it would drop out of their mouths.

It was a slaughterhouse more than a clearing station, and if they died you had to clear them away as quick as you could. You took off one of their identity discs and took everything out of their pockets and handed it all in at the office where belongings were put in a bag with their name on it. The bodies were just put into bags and driven off.

We worked around the clock and got very little food. They would bring some milk round, they seemed to have plenty of milk – the cows didn't seem to get shot as much as the men. Then, when you couldn't carry on any longer and just had to stop, you just plonked down wherever you were, perhaps leant against a tree, then you'd pull yourself together, enough to go to your bed for a while. I mean, you reached a stage where you were too exhausted to do anything.

You don't cry easily, not when you've got things to face up to. People think you would cry but you don't, not when you're really up against it with your back to the wall. You don't cry then. It's afterwards, when you think about it, perhaps years afterwards.

Helen Gordon-Dean, also working at a CCS, was even younger than Marjorie Grigsby, and it was debatable whether she should have been in France at all. At her interview – an intimidating experience with a panel of no fewer than eight people – she had lied about her age.

I told them I was nineteen but I was a year younger. I got away with it; telling fibs is a gift, but you've got to be convinced yourself. I wanted to go to France very badly. One lady was very sceptical about my answers. 'What age are you? What year were you born?' I resented the questioning, because of all the things I could have chosen to do it was nursing that inspired me.

Dad had to pay for everything when I joined up, but then I could always get round him. I could make the job sound frightfully important. I don't think I thought much about patriotism. There was a war on and we had to win it, I knew that. At home we were on the fringe of things, in France I would see things other people would never know.

Interestingly, in the medal rolls held at The National Archives, she is listed as 'VAD/Unofficial Overseas'. Whether she was official or not made not a scrap of difference to Helen herself, treating the wounded and holding the hands of those who were about to die.

It's funny how quite strong men that you looked up to would want to hold your hand during these moments. It was a very real expression of what I believed in very, very firmly, the physical contact with other life. It generally came from them, they wanted to hold your hand and you wanted to hold theirs. It was a horrible feeling to know that somebody is going right into eternity that moment, and you have to hold their hand, maybe patting it to give them courage. So often, so often these young men would look at you and say, 'You remind me of my mother', who would be three times my age. It was something that happened and always the same words, 'You remind me of my mother.'

Marjorie Grigsby tried to remain detached.

Some of them were quite youngsters. Remember, lots of them were only boys of seventeen and eighteen, they'd joined up – they thought it was a joke I think, you know what children are. They entered into the spirit of the thing and found it wasn't fun when they got there but they had to carry on – there were lots, lots. We knew how old they were and of course we felt sorry for them but they were just patients. You didn't know them. It wasn't a friend or a relative. You had no particular sentiments. But if you were the same age as they were you couldn't help thinking, 'Oh Lord, I wonder if he's got any brothers,' or wondering if he was an only child. It's an absolute mêlée really of blood and thunder.

Helen never forgot the bloody reality of the whole experience.

> You heard the shelling and sometimes it seemed very close and noisy, but I never remember fear, naked fear. I was conscious of the shells, but I thought, well, a shell could kill anyone and if it is me, then so be it. But there was so much to do, there wasn't time to stand back and think. Ambulances were always arriving, generally in convoys, and you would go out and help those who could walk or limp along, and the rest would be carried in for treatment.
>
> The wounds were smelly. I think very often the smell was the worst. Every wound was treated with a swab doused in Lysol, a red solution. The Lysol was in a dish and you held the swab with forceps, dipped it in and applied it to the wound quite brutally to clean this nasty place up. These wounds were so dirty, sometimes full of maggots, and on one occasion I saw lice in the wound, too.
>
> Bad wounds were quite horrific, shocking beyond belief. You didn't want to believe what you were seeing, the horror of what people, responsible people, were doing to each other. I remember the first amputation I saw. They said, 'Go on, Nurse, you can help, this is quite a simple one,' and they shoved me into the room with the others and it suddenly struck me how simple and ordinary it was to deliberately cut off a hand.

Throughout the spring months of 1918, tens of thousands of wounded men were evacuated, from advanced dressing stations to casualty clearing stations, and as quickly as possible down to the base hospitals. There was always a brief time-lag between casualties at the front and the sudden rush at the base camp, as trains pulled into the sidings and released their cargo of maimed men for treatment. The under-age soldiers living in huts nearby could not help but be aware of the seriousness of the situation, and it would have come as no surprise to them that moves were under way to sift out from among their number anyone who might go up the line. On 25 March, an entry in the war diary of No. 5

Convalescent Camp at Cayeux noted that all 'strenuous efforts are being made to evacuate all men for general duty', followed four days later by a note confirming that an order had been issued that 'all boys aged 18½ who were "Fit" and immatures of category "A" were to be discharged to their Bases'. That day, 151 boys left Cayeux, ready to go back to the line. When the Germans renewed their attacks on the Lys in early April, an effort was made to reduce the numbers in the depot still further.

The decision to cut the age at which a boy could be sent abroad had not been taken easily, but the dire military position necessitated the change. On the very day that the Germans launched the second phase of their offensive, the Prime Minister addressed the Commons and spelt out to MPs the extent of the crisis.

> There was an understanding as to boys under nineteen years of age, that they would only be used in case of emergency. We felt that the emergency had arisen. In so far as those who were over eighteen and a half were concerned – those who had already received four months' training – we felt it necessary that they should be sent across to France.

Two days later, on 11 April, the commander-in-chief felt compelled to release a 'Special Order' addressed 'To All Ranks of the British Army in France and Flanders'. Underlining his admiration for the men under his command, Haig told them:

> There is no course open to us but to fight it out. Every position must be held to the last man; there must be no retirement. With our backs to the wall and believing in the justice of our cause, we must fight on to the end. The safety of our homes and the Freedom of mankind alike depend upon the conduct of each one of us at this critical moment.

Nowhere was the fighting more intense than around Armentières, and the fifth division was sent forward to try to stabilize the front.

It was the morning of 11 April, and Vic Cole was reluctantly on his way back into action.

> As we advanced, line after line, in extended order across the green fields and into the sprawling forest of Nieppe, there was no sign of war, the sun shone, birds sang in the trees and startled deer ran leaping off into the brush. We eventually came out on the other side of the forest, still no sign of the enemy.

For a brief moment the fighting appeared to have subsided. A halt was ordered and the men dug in. It was then that Vic saw a farmhouse and absented himself from the shallow trenches to investigate. He found a cellar full of wine and, liberating six bottles in a sandbag, he returned to the trench to find his friend Ralph Newman. They were already quite merry when the rum ration came round; they would have been in serious trouble if anyone had suspected how drunk they were.

> With the sun shining, the birds singing, and the mellowing effect of the wine and rum, we were feeling at peace with all mankind – even with Fritz himself! Then, all of a sudden, with a shattering crash, the fun commenced – with a mighty roar the German barrage opened up and in a moment the air was full of bursting shells, flying shrapnel and the smoke and noise of battle.
>
> Pulling myself together, I noticed that most of the stuff was going over our heads and dropping in C Company lines. All the world seemed full of the whine and crash of shell splinters. To our front across a ploughed field, the ground rose a little so that we had hardly any real field of fire, then suddenly, quite close, I saw the Germans – at least I saw the tops of their helmets bobbing up and down as they ducked and dodged in our fire. Aiming at these moving blobs, I fired again and again until there was no longer anything to shoot at and the 'cease fire' whistle brought respite.

> With much gusto, a battery of our field guns now joined in the game. Concealed in the forest behind us, they fired over our heads at the again advancing enemy. As poor Fritz came on, our guns shortened their range until their shells were falling just in front of our own position. One fell right among our men, then another, and several men were wounded.

It was demoralizing enough to be shelled by the enemy, but to be fired upon by one's own side was heart-breaking. In any successful attack, a small proportion of such losses could be expected: shells sometimes fell short, or infantry advanced too quickly into their supporting barrage. Firing on your own entrenched infantry was pure loss. Vic, being a signaller, tried to telephone back but the line was cut, so he was ordered by an officer almost incandescent with anger to go and get a message through ordering the guns to lift. Vic shook hands with Ralph and set off, but by good fortune he found another signaller who could relay the message, and within minutes the gunfire relented.

> As I turned to leave, something hit the tree behind which we were crouching, there was a blinding flash, a whirling sound of splinters, parts of the tree flew all about and there I was lying flat on my back looking up at the startled signaller. I had been hit in the back and was already feeling numb from the waist down. In a few minutes, stretcher-bearers arrived on the scene. A couple of them dragged me over to a hole for temporary cover and turned me on my face. One of them let rip a stream of swear words as he cut away my leather jacket and saw the wound.

Vic was taken first to a dressing station, labelled, and then evacuated to a farmhouse with a Red Cross flag above the door.

> My stretcher was laid on the floor and the bearers went away. The place was crowded with wounded men swathed in bandages. At

one end of the big room, a couple of RAMC doctors were bending over a stretcher raised on boxes and it looked to me as though they were trying to amputate a leg. It was dusk, and the room was lit by an oil lamp. A soldier sitting opposite, his head in bandages, suddenly fell forward and crashed to the floor.

Despite the pain, I managed to doze and awoke to find myself crying like a baby. Nerves, I suppose. The doctors made their rounds, put fresh dressings on us and marked most of us up for a CCS. Then came the ambulance driver – a woman! This was the closest I had ever seen a woman to the firing line, and although big shells were still whistling overhead the girl took no notice of them – she just carried on with her job. 'I can take four,' she said. So four of us were carried out and lifted into the little Ford ambulance. The girl gave us cigarettes and to me she said, 'Don't worry, chum, I'll take it easy over the shell holes.'

It was the end of Vic's war. The metal could not be taken out of his back, and remained there until he died in November 1995, a few weeks short of his ninety-ninth birthday.

The girl who gave him a lift was exceptional, although not unique, in being so far forward within the battle zone. Normally, the CCS was the farthest a nurse would be permitted to go, but these were exceptional times, to the point that even CCSs were under direct threat of being overrun. Marjorie Grigsby was still serving at the CCS when the order came to evacuate. The German forces were getting perilously close, and the decision was taken to remove all the casualties and head towards the coast.

So we all put together what we could in the way of anything we could carry, and went to the ambulances. We worked until about midnight. It was a pouring wet night and ours was the last ambulance to leave. On board we had six stretcher cases, a girl driver by the name of Griffin who, for some reason, was practically stone deaf, and myself. We set off and I suppose we'd gone about four or five miles – bang – 'Oh, my

God' a tyre had gone. The Germans were quite close and no one to help us. Now, I knew about nursing but I didn't know a thing about changing a tyre, so I just tried to do what Griffin told me. She said do so and so and 'Put that spanner on'. 'What's a spanner?' I felt so hopeless, the water was dripping off me, and I was cold and frightened. I don't know how we did it but we got that tyre off and put another one on and set off again with German artillery firing quite near.

The Germans attempted to press their advantage and drove the British further back, but the line was beginning to stabilize and, by the night of 14 April, the great advances of the previous few days came to a grinding halt.

Cyril José had been rushed forward to join his new battalion, the 2/4th Ox and Bucks, which was resting just behind the line in a village that Cyril recognized as the one in which he had spent Christmas 1915. Within hours of his arrival, the battalion was ordered forward, extending in an open field to await the Germans. As they dug in, they came under attack both from shellfire and from snipers lodged in some farmhouses, and several men were killed or wounded. Promptly, Cyril and five others were sent off to dislodge the Germans but, by the time they arrived, the snipers had pulled back fifty yards. Both parties traded shots for half an hour before the Germans pulled out on horseback.

The next day, the Ox and Bucks were ordered forward. Cyril later wrote:

We went over the top on Sunday afternoon [15 April] and again on Monday evening when we took our objectives but were wiped out. In the end there were about fifteen of us left, no officers or NCOs . . . I took charge, as they were mostly young kiddies from the training reserve battalions.

In what Cyril was humorously to call a 'thin red line of khaki', the survivors waited for reinforcements, but with no support on either flank the position was hopeless. It was only a matter of time before the enemy regrouped and came again.

> Jerry surrounded us on three sides and advanced in front, in three waves, so we showed him how fast we could run. We fired a few rounds into them now and again when we got out of breath, then on again. We didn't stand a chance of holding him. I suppose Jerry got those who were wounded and couldn't run. Didn't stay to argue the point myself.

As he fell back, Cyril turned to run again and was shot in the left arm. By pure chance, the bullet passed through the wound stripe on his sleeve. Now injured, he could legitimately drop his rifle and equipment and escape. He was fortunate. By Sunday 21 April, he was back home, in hospital once more. He had lasted less than three weeks in France and no more than three days back in the firing line.

The German offensive continued until 29 April, when it was finally called off. Once again the Germans failed to capture their objectives, and although they had taken the town of Armentières and seized one of the three strategic heights, Kemmel Hill, they had not succeeded in taking the critically important railhead of Hazebrouck. The success of the first few days of fighting could not be sustained and, although a deep salient appeared in enemy territory, salients were, as the British had found at Ypres, costly to hold.

After a pause of a month, the third German offensive was launched in a final attempt to win the war before significant American forces took to the field. On 27 May, 4,000 guns fired a short bombardment at Allied defences on a ridge known as the Chemin des Dames. The British divisions included the 50th Northumbrian, which had suffered particularly badly during the German offensives of March and April.

Private Percy Williams, aged eighteen, of the Northumberland Fusiliers, and Private Frank Deane, nineteen, of the Durham Light Infantry, were both there. As before, the Germans had overwhelmed the British forward line, forcing the opposing units to fall back, frequently in total disorder. This time there had been no helpful mist to support the attackers, but a saturating cloud of gas had been almost as effective.

Percy recalled:

> By this time the gas had lifted and I could see the Germans running across, scores of them, I was so confused, you see, and the noise had left me all of a muddle. I didn't know where I was.

He was captured at bayonet point minutes later. Frank Deane managed to fall back further.

> I recall seeing my platoon officer and he was just sat on the fire step with two men doing absolutely nothing, he just watched us go by and didn't say a word. He seemed to me to be just waiting there until the Germans caught up with him.
>
> We left the trenches and passed through a wood, crossing a road then up a hill on the other side. A couple of officers on horseback were on that hill, where they'd come from I don't know, possibly headquarters, and it was they who lined us up facing these woods, waiting for the enemy.

The Germans came on as expected, and Frank was captured.

> A machine-gun bullet crashed through the first joint of my thumb before going up my hand. My corporal friend next to me said, 'Your hand is bleeding.' I didn't even know I'd been hit.

Both Percy and Frank were stripped of their webbing and marched to the rear.

The offensive continued to be pressed against both British and French forces, the Germans penetrating ten miles into Allied territory; once again a large salient appeared in the Allied lines. The Germans had crossed the Aisne, east of Paris, and reached the river Marne. They inflicted 130,000 casualties on the Allies, including taking 50,000 prisoners, but the German losses were commensurate, and Germany could no longer afford to suffer on such a scale. This offensive, like the others, fizzled out.

Prisoners such as Percy and Frank were marched into captivity but, as they were taken behind German lines, they were able to see for the first time clear evidence that their separation from home would only be temporary. Frank was encouraged.

> I became quite cheerful because they seemed to have such a ramshackle lot of transport, an old harvest cart being pulled by a donkey, a mule and a horse. I didn't see any motor transport, so I thought, 'Well, if that's the sort of equipment they've got, they won't last long.'

He was right. A final offensive was undertaken against the French and American forces in July, but within two days the Allies were on the counter-attack. To all intents and purposes, the Germans as an attacking force were spent. A brief respite, particularly on the British front, enabled the Allies to concentrate their forces for an offensive, a long, costly but eventually victorious campaign, which the Germans fought hard to delay but which they could never stop.

Even before the end of July, the improving situation on the Western Front was being reflected in Parliament, as MPs questioned the Government on the continued need to send boys aged eighteen and a half to the front. On 30 July, Percy Harris, MP for Leicester South, asked the Undersecretary of State for War: 'Am I to understand that . . . now that the emergency has passed, the Army Council and the Government are reconsidering their decision?'

James Macpherson replied: 'I cannot, of course, admit that the emergency is passed, but I may assure the House and my Hon. Friend that this matter receives the gravest consideration.'

Richard Lambert, a backbencher, asked: 'Is the Army Council considering the opportunity, if it arises, of withdrawing these young lads of eighteen and a half years from the fighting line?'

James Macpherson confirmed: 'Certainly.'

A week later, on 7 August, the issue came up again when Percy Harris rose and addressed the House:

> To take lads from homes as absolutely raw recruits, only give them three months' training, and send them overseas is not doing justice to them or to our army . . . Military experts will agree that there is no better soldier than the fully trained youth or young man of nineteen and a half, the young man who has had six or nine months' training in this country, who has been through camp life, and who has had the advantage of good food and proper care, but to take them before they are trained, and before they are fully grown and send them overseas is a profligate policy . . . Modern war is Hell indeed . . . I ask [the Government], now that the emergency is over, to toe the line with our Allies, and not to send overseas boys until they are nineteen. I say that in no spirit of criticism – I am not complaining about the past – but I think the House and the nation have a right to ask.

In reply, James Macpherson clarified the Government's position:

> The War Cabinet had decided that an emergency had arisen so great that it was absolutely necessary to send from this country every officer and man who was available. Unfortunately, within that category came boys between eighteen and nineteen years of age . . . [However] we have now decided at the end of this month that we shall return to the old regime.

Not only was the emergency over but the Government's decision came just hours before events at the front improved spectacularly. A counter-offensive by the Allies east of Amiens against depleted German forces proved an outstanding success, the Australian and Canadian Corps advancing twelve kilometres by early afternoon. Thousands of enemy prisoners were taken and Allied casualties were relatively light. The day was a disaster for the German High Command and was later dubbed the 'Black Day of the German Army in the History of the War' by Erich Ludendorff, the General commanding the German forces.

At the end of the month, the decision to halt the front-line service of boys aged eighteen and a half was implemented as promised, and new drafts due to embark for France were suddenly shorn of boys under nineteen, lads literally being plucked from the ranks as they were about to set foot on the boat. Those already in France were kept at base camps, but those serving at the front remained in the line, for, despite representations made by the Government in September, the C.-in-C. felt unable to agree to their withdrawal. Haig was determined to press the enemy as hard as he could to win the war outright; it was not the time to release soldiers from the firing line. 'It seems to me to be the beginning of the end,' he wrote in his diary on 10 September.

A final flurry of questions was asked by MPs in late October about the issue of keeping boys in the front line, but Haig remained steadfast in his resolve and, in essence, the whole subject of under-age soldiering had, at last, been drawn to a close.

During the summer and autumn of 1918, the Allies fought a series of rolling battles that pushed and harassed the retiring Germans, slowly sapping at the will of the enemy to continue the fight. In the first three and a half years of the war, 127,000 German prisoners were taken by British forces on the Western Front; in 1918, over 387,000 were captured, 186,000 in the last three months of fighting.

By early September, some soldiers too began to believe that the war might reach a conclusion, not in 1918 but perhaps the following year. Ernest Steele, the seventeen-year-old recruit of 1914, who had warned his brother not to serve under age, was now twenty-one. He remained on the Western Front for three years, gaining a commission on the way. His letters home became cautiously optimistic as time passed.

September 5th

I expect we shall be getting a little excitement shortly. Everything is going well, even better than the papers say, and I hope to be home for good in less than a year.

September 11th

We advanced umpteen kilometres carrying all our kit and got absolutely no sleep. I hope to have a couple of days' real rest now, before going up again.

Jerry is beginning to make a greater show of resistance now, and it is harder work pushing him.

Lieutenant Steele was approaching the Hindenburg Line, the massive German line of defence, which for a long time had appeared impregnable. Before an all-out assault was possible, the forward outposts had to be taken, and an attack was ordered for the early morning of 18 September. British infantry would attack near the village of Epéhy, supported by a creeping barrage of 1,500 guns. Ernest Steele, serving with the 21st Battalion MGC, would take forward a section of machine guns in order to support the attack. The night before, he wrote a letter home.

September 17th

Dear Mater and Pater

As I don't suppose I shall have a chance of writing to you again for a few days, I thought I'd take this chance of letting you know, so that you shouldn't worry.

We had a bit of a storm last night, but today the sun is out again and it is quite fine. There is a strong wind too, to dry up the ground.

I think we are winning the war hand over fist now, and it won't last much longer.

When I come home on leave I shall be able to tell you quite a lot of facts, which of course can't be mentioned at present.

While I am out here, Mater and Pater, I realize more than ever all that you have done for me, and wish I could have a chance to repay you at least a part – I shall never be able to do it in full. However, the time will come after I get home, when I shall have that chance and then you will see, as I know you realize now, that I understand exactly what a lot I owe to you.

I spoke to our Padre the other day about my confirmation, and he told me that it would be difficult to have it done out here, but he thought I could consider myself a communicant until it could be done. So I feel easy in my mind about that.

Well, au revoir, Mater and Pater, God bless you and keep you safe till I come back.

The best of love from
Your eldest affectionate Son,
Ernest

P.S. – Please kiss Marie and Leslie for me, and give my love to Harry, and also to Grandma and everybody else.

Seventeen-year-old Reginald Kiernan would also take part in the fighting at Epéhy. After six months in France, his attitude to the war had profoundly changed. Just a few days before the attack, he had been deep in thought.

What I've thought of most today, and it has been running in my mind all the time for we had to learn it by heart, is Rupert Brooke's

'The Soldier' ['If I should die . . .'] I cannot feel like that. I do not want my body to rot away under this field, with its yellow earth and thin, pale grass. Perhaps Brooke could feel like that because he'd *had* something in this world. He'd been to Berlin, and he'd had lovely warm afternoons in Cambridgeshire, beside decent, quiet rivers; and he's had time to *think* and enjoy things. *I* have never had time to think. I have had *nothing*, *nothing*. I want to get back from all this, back out of it – and sit and think, and look at clean things, and hear my people's voices again . . . Rupert Brooke had longer than I've had to see things and enjoy them. He was ten years older than I am now.

Reginald was endlessly reminded of his short life by the dead. These bodies, he knew, received no attention. Even the living, the other men in his company, did not know one another's names, so often were they replaced by new drafts, while the officers barely knew their own men by sight.

It's the lying like those fellows we've passed – on your side with a fixed grin on your face, or on your back with your eyes turned up – and no one caring! And it's the thought that you don't die a hero. That would help. There are no heroes here. No one cares.

It was in this frame of mind that he prepared to go over the top. At 4 a.m., just eighty minutes before zero hour, he scribbled some notes, and wondered what the next few hours would have in store.

September 18th 1918, 4 a.m.

We have come up and are 'lying out' to 'go over'. The air is alive and shaking with fire. It is hardly dawn yet, just grey and black. Along the railway line our barrage is down, a great wall of grey smoke covered with yellow flashes. It is the first time I have seen a barrage from behind. It is raining and very cold.

Everything is banging and roaring, and there is the steely shriek of hundreds of shells, and that great wind overhead. There's the big whistle and 'shee-ing' and hammering of the machine guns, firing over us from the railway embankment.

I do not feel at all afraid. A boy is lying near me on his back in the rain. He was tall and lanky and K-legged, and had a very small, grey face. He looked like a stalk a minute or two since, when he was standing up with his ground sheet round his shoulders. I noticed him suddenly then, and remembered I had seen him before, somewhere. He is on his back now, and his legs are wide apart. He has been killed by a stray bullet. No one knows who he is, or what his name is, or where the bullet has hit him, and no one has bothered to notice him. He looks quite natural, gazing up at the sky. But he is dead.

I think, myself, that he was always tired; tired beyond anything anyone can know, and that he is resting now.

I have come to write this in a little dugout, cut in the railway embankment. I have made an Act of Contrition, and I think that this time it was perfect. Before, there has always been fear in it.

The roar is greater outside, and the machine guns are madder and madder. The grey light is getting stronger and is creeping along the floor, whitening it. We shall go forward soon.

They are shouting outside. I must go.

Reginald Kiernan was lucky; he was wounded sufficiently to see out his war back in Britain.

Lieutenant Ernest Steele died that morning. He had been reconnoitring a position for his guns near a railway track when he came into close contact with the enemy who began to bomb and shoot at the machine gunners. It was at that moment that the young officer was killed, shot by a sniper. Ernest's body was recovered and his private possessions handed in to the orderly room by the section sergeant, who remained with his officer despite being wounded himself. The next evening, at seven o'clock, Ernest was buried in the village churchyard under the shadow of the crucifix that still stood, though the church itself had been destroyed. The

Battalion Pioneers made a wooden cross and letters of sympathy were sent to the family, not just by the CO of the 21st Battalion MGC, but also by the CO of the company, the battalion padre, and Ernest's wounded sergeant. Their loss was felt very deeply by everyone, not least the company CO, Major J. B. Hardinge.

I can say perfectly truthfully that, without exception, he was the best Officer I had. He was so exceptionally straight and conscientious. His men thought the world of him, and he gave his life for England as one could have imagined he would, in a gallant way, leading and protecting his men. He was not more than 20 yards from the enemy when he was shot straight through the heart and killed instantly. I saw him afterwards and although I have been out nearly four years, I have never seen so peaceful and wonderful a look on anyone's face as was on his. I am glad to say he was buried, not on the battlefield, but by our own Padre in the Churchyard at Heudicourt. I feel sure he is at peace with his God.

'Geordie' Steele, as we called him, was also one of my dearest friends. I feel his loss so much that I can understand a little what it will mean to you. We had so much in common. We used to keep up our knowledge of German together.

He and I used to be very keen on chess and I think I knew a good deal of his private affairs. For instance, it was only three days before he was buried that he had gone to see the Padre about his confirmation. I knew he was engaged and I should very much like to have written to the lady concerned only I have no address.

He also often talked of his young brother, to whom he seemed so devoted, that I should like to have written to them all . . . Will you therefore express my most deep sympathy to all, but more especially to your wife and yourself.

Believe me,
Yours sincerely
J. B. Hardinge

A little to the north-east of Epéhy, Lieutenant Jack Pouchot was flying with 56 Squadron RAF. The fifteen-year-old DCM winner was now nineteen and flying SE5s against the Germans above the Hindenburg Line, close to Cambrai. He was enjoying a lucky month, having been reported missing in action once, only to turn up miraculously, plane-less but uninjured. In the build-up to the breaking of the Hindenburg Line he was flying daily to suppress enemy surveillance. On 27 September he took part in an early-morning sortie with nine other aircraft when they met and engaged the enemy. The attack proved highly successful and on his return Jack filled out a combat report claiming yet another victory for the squadron.

> While on patrol at 15,000 ft over Cambrai we attacked a formation of E.A.[Enemy Aircraft]. I got in a short burst at close range at one [a Fokker biplane]. He went down in a spin and crashed a few miles N.E. of Cambrai. I was then attacked by 4 E.A. and driven down to the ground east of Cambrai and crossed the lines at 1,000 ft.

Two days later the most heavily fortified part of the Hindenburg Line was stormed. The line, which had been under construction since September 1916, was irreparably breached in a matter of hours, a remarkable feat of arms. The Germans, with no proper defensive position to fall back on, were forced to begin a retreat with no expectation that they could hold the Allied forces anywhere on foreign soil. Defeat was inevitable.

Sadly, Jack Pouchot, like Ernest Steele, would not enjoy the fruits of his four-year service. On 5 October he was shot down and killed; he is buried in the Marcoing British Cemetery near Cambrai. The two boys, who had independently chosen to join the Queen's Westminster Rifles in 1914, were both dead.

The pursuit of the enemy continued and for six weeks, until the Armistice, it was relentless, stretching the lines of resupply to the

British and Dominion forces to the absolute limit. Dick Trafford, the fifteen-year-old miner who had also enlisted in the heady days of 1914, was still at the front. He had been wounded – he had lost a finger – and he had also been gassed. He had fought at Loos, on the Somme, at Passchendaele and throughout the campaigns of 1918, and he was still only nineteen years old. Like the rest of his platoon, Dick was both exhausted and hungry.

We seemed to be getting the Germans into a tight corner, and the officers were telling us 'keep on, lads, keep on.' They urged us to give everything we'd got because there were a couple of times when our fellows nearly gave up. They were that tired, with marching and they'd nothing to eat or drink for a couple of days, and there was no sign of rations because the Germans had blown up the crossroads and that had made it difficult to get supplies up. The men had all eaten their iron rations, which they weren't supposed to, except in emergencies, well, the men put down that it had been an emergency and they'd eaten the biscuits and cheese a while back. Anyway, we were all of one mind, unless we had something to eat, we wouldn't go on.

It was the officers who solved the problem. By pure luck, a bakery was found that had just made some bread. It was of dubious quality, 'blackish stuff' according to Dick, but it would do, and the officers bought a number of loaves out of the cash in their pockets and issued them to their men, so averting a potentially nasty situation.

Dick recalled:

We were capturing the enemy all the time. I wouldn't say young boys, I'd say young men, I mean to say a young boy could be anything from about eight years old to about twelve, whereas a young man, he'd be about sixteen to eighteen, that's the way I look at it. They were glad it was ending because from their point of view they would be right for meals, that's what they tried to explain to us, they'd not seen a decent meal in a long time. The only thing they could do had been to kill their horses and use the meat for food. You saw dead horses on the side of the road and you could see where lumps had been cut out, from the stomach or off its side, and that was a sure sign they were short of food.

'We'd got them on the run,' agreed Smiler Marshall. Like Dick Trafford, this one-time under-age volunteer had gone right through the war and was enjoying these final scraps.

I thought this was smashing, we'd got them beat. I can't tell you any dates, but we noticed the last lot that held us up were young boys and they hadn't got the fight in them that the old ones had. If they saw the cavalry coming with their swords drawn, they'd scamper. They kept putting their hands up, 'Kaput, kaput!' The Germans would stand their ground if they'd got to, but if there was a chance to get away they would.

When the end finally came on 11 November, it met with a muted response by the men on the battlefield, who frequently felt at a complete loss. The army had dominated their lives for so long; now, all of a sudden, the yoke of war had been lifted, and many looked at each other as if to say, 'What do we do now?'

Smiler was then a twenty-one-year-old man serving with the Machine Gun Corps (Cavalry). He wanted to go all the way into Germany.

We were in a factory in the town of Lille when the news was broken to the men and they were not happy. The officer came along and he said, 'I've got some great news for you, the war's over, there's an Armistice.' Oh, you never heard such language in all your life, you see, they were angry, we were all angry because we'd been going on two or three kilometres a day for the past fortnight.

Right at the end the Germans were throwing their rifles away. They weren't going to fight any more, they told us that. One or two spoke English, one had been a pork butcher from York before the war, another had been a hairdresser in London, and they'd had enough. They were ambling along, without their rifles, walking towards Germany, accepting defeat. We believed we could go all the way to Berlin.

The casualties in 1918 were by far the heaviest of the war. Month after month a continuous offensive had been conducted by one side or the other as decisive victory was sought. It had been the war's worst year for British casualties but few were under-age soldiers. The number of these who had managed to gain entry into the army was now very small indeed, and the losses numerically insignificant. Only 109 boys from Britain aged seventeen or under are recorded as having been killed, with a further forty-seven deaths at home, an unknown number of whom had succumbed to wounds. Very broadly, these figures represent less than a tenth of those *known* to be killed under age in 1915. Given that the size of the British Army in 1918 was between three and four times the size it had been in 1915, so the number of under-age deaths per head of the BEF in the last year of the war, compared to 1915, is equal to a ratio of roughly 1:40.

Nevertheless, the death in action of exceptionally young boys had not been eradicated entirely. Two boys in particular stand out. Private Frederick Steward of the 1/18th London Regiment, a lad from Surrey, was killed aged fourteen on the first day of the German March offensive; while David Ross, at fourteen and three months, was killed just four days later on the 25th while serving with the 2nd South African Regiment. Frederick is buried in Heudicourt Communal Cemetery, next to the small extension in which Ernest Steele lies buried.

The real tragedy of 1918 concerned the boys who had once been designated under age but who, in the March crisis, became legally old enough to serve abroad. Their losses in the final year of war grew remorselessly until the Government, in response to the ending of the German offensive, withheld such drafts from going to the front. In the end, slightly more than 10,000 boys aged eighteen died at home or overseas in the army between March and November 1918.

The majority of these boys, over 60 per cent, died in three months: April, August and September 1918. Contained within these figures is the interesting statistic that three times as many eighteen-year-olds died as a daily average in April compared to the daily average in March, underlining the desperate need to send out boys to France to shore up the front. The losses later that summer, in August and September, reflect the heavy casualties that were suffered as a rolling battle was joined with a determined, if retreating, enemy.

In one of the final actions of the war, in mid-October 1918, a soldier from Newfoundland called Thomas Ricketts volunteered to go out with his section commander and a Lewis gun in an attempt to outflank an enemy battery causing casualties at point-blank range. They were still 300 yards from the battery when their ammunition was exhausted. Private Ricketts, under heavy machine-gun fire, doubled back a hundred yards to replenish their supplies and, amazingly, got back to the Lewis gun alive. Together, the two then drove the enemy and their gun teams into a farm, and the platoon was able to advance, capturing four field guns, four machine guns and eight prisoners.

For this action, Thomas, who had already been presented with the Croix de Guerre, was awarded the Victoria Cross. At his investiture after the war, King George V presented him as 'the youngest VC in the army'. He was just seventeen.

If the standard for winning the Victoria Cross was maintained throughout the war, and there is no reason to doubt that it was, then the number of men awarded the honour for conspicuous bravery is testimony to the terrible nature of the conflict in 1918.

Between August 1914 and December 1916, 172 Victoria Crosses were awarded, or 6.14 decorations per month. Between January 1917 and the end of the war, 287 VCs were won, on average 13.04 per month, but, if 1918 is taken alone, then the average stands at 16.5 VCs per month, more than one every other day. Many were won in the final hundred days of the war, when, after the German forces suffered their catastrophic reversal on 8 August, the enemy were remorselessly pushed back across the old battlefields of the Somme and Ypres, and then, for the first time in four years, over open countryside largely untouched by war.

A predominance of Allied firepower, the superiority in the quality of equipment and its regular supply, superb training combined with the ascendancy in troop numbers, were fundamental ingredients which, once in place, could only ensure victory for the Allies. Nevertheless, owning the tools of victory was not in itself victory: the war still had to be won and that was achieved by the willingness and determination of the men on the ground to see it through. It was won at great cost, although few expected, until the very last days of the war, that the Germans would capitulate so soon.

14

Aftermath

HE GAVE HIS YOUNG LIFE
FOR ENGLAND

28407 Private John Harris
1st Cheshire Regiment

Killed in Action 25 July 1916, aged 17

AT 11 A.M. THE GUNS stopped firing, and an almost uncanny silence lay across the battlefield.

Fred Hodges always remembered the effect the ceasefire had on him.

> I was silent too, feeling no desire for any conversation with the gunners, who began to clean their guns and tidy up the gun sites. The occasion was too big, too poignant, for words and I walked slowly back to the village, mind and spirit strangely numbed.
>
> I looked again at the German graves as I passed, and I thought of the relations of those men in Germany. I thought too of the many who also would never return home to their families.
>
> I was trying to realize that it was all over, that I was alive and that I had a life to live. It was almost unbelievable. For seven months I had lived a day at a time, but now I could look forward as well as back.

More than a year earlier, in mid-1917, Private Thomas Hope was undergoing battle training with his battalion, well behind the lines. It was beautiful summer weather and, after a hard day's training, Thomas and his friends meandered back to the billet for rest, a peaceful evening and a chance to chat. They were housed in an old barn and, as there was a full moon that night, a soft light was diffused throughout the building. 'The hooting of an owl outside, the rustling of leaves and the sound of restless cattle,' as Thomas recalled, were things to be appreciated while the men puffed contentedly on their pipes and cigarettes and talked well into the night.

> When will the war end? What will happen to us? Questions we can never agree on.
>
> The first we can find no definite answer to; it is something only to be dreamed about, something that, deep down in our hearts, we doubt if we'll ever live to see. Nevertheless, that does not prevent us from speculating and surmising on just what will happen to us when the miracle takes place.

The older sages of the group had firm ideas that post-war life would be no bed of roses. Hope's friend Webster was frighteningly cynical.

> I'll tell you what will happen to you duration soldiers. You'll have the time of your lives, you'll be hugged and kissed, treated and petted, they'll have banners strung across the streets: 'Welcome Home, Our Heroic Tommies', you'll be received with open arms, they'll let you mess on their doorstep and thank you for doing it, you'll be the heaven and earth and all that therein is for just one month, then some morning they'll wake up and realize the war is over, and that's when you fellows will have to start using your own toilet paper. You'll get the cold shoulder, as they'll have no more use for a penniless, out-of-work, fighting man who stinks of trench manners and speech . . . Ah, you can laugh, boys; you're little tin gods just now, but when it's all over you'll find you've

not only had to fight the war but you'll have to fight the peace as well, and a damned sight harder too, if you're going to win through, so get it out of your thick heads that you're in for a cushy time.

Webster's opinions caused consternation in the barn, not just among Hope and his close-knit friends, but also among those who could not help but listen to this doom-laden prognosis. 'Smother him, somebody, he's too cheerful,' came one response, amid calls to ram a sock in his mouth, or kick him.

At sixteen years old, Thomas was inclined to listen intently to the older men, who had taught him not only how to survive but how to live. Taffy, another old stalwart who was keen to continue the conversation, decided to put forward his views.

All I know is that there will be a couple of million men suddenly thrust back into civil life ... men accustomed to look on life cheaply, all of them coarsened in different degrees by the exacting life they have been forced to live. As in war, so it will be in peace, and anything might happen.

Taffy pointed out that although the post-war struggle would affect hundreds of thousands, not every struggle was applicable to every man. For younger soldiers there would be specific difficulties. Thomas listened carefully, aware that his friend had given the subject on which he was talking some detailed thought. He watched Taffy, 'with his head to one side and his pointing index finger wagging away in tune with his ideas'.

'Some of you, of course, have jobs to return to. For you, the war will merely have been an episode, but there are others like Mac, Duggan, Barham and a few more, who had just started an apprenticeship. To them the war will have been more than an interruption; the most valuable years of their lives have been wasted here;

they'll have to start all over again, handicapped by age. Then there are the babes like Jock [Thomas] there.'

'Hold on, Taffy,' I interrupted.

'It's quite true, Jock, there are dozens like you out here, straight from school into this, men before you were youths, the only trade you know – that of killing. Yes, unless the old country can dig up a Solomon, peace is going to bring one glorious mess, an unequal fight against a public who will soon forget our sacrifices, and new generations who will know nothing of the war and what it meant to those who served.'

The convivial party broke up shortly after but, while the majority of men were soon fast asleep, snuggled under blankets and great-coats, Thomas's mind was active.

I toss restlessly, thinking of the different opinions . . . Webster's, well, like all old soldiers he dearly loves a grouse. Taffy now, he has evidently given the subject serious thought and his words keep returning to my mind.

Their speculation proved with hindsight to have been remarkably accurate. Books abound detailing the post-war world, the prime minister's 'Homes fit for heroes' promises that in the end left thousands of former soldiers out in the cold. There are harrowing stories of post-war hardship, of beggar-soldiers hawking matches on London's Embankment, of former officers offering in newspaper advertisements their manual and mental labour to anyone who might see their way to employ a former lieutenant or captain, now living through hard times. Then there were perhaps the saddest cases of all: soldiers driven to suicide, whose death was not believed to have been in any way attributable to war service, leaving a widow and children to fight their own battles to survive.

And there are stories, too, of the medical boards that sought excuses to cut a man's war pension to a pittance, despite his continued suffering from wounds.

George Parker, holder of a medal for gallantry, won when aged seventeen, was still recuperating in hospital in February 1919. He was just one of many who were misled after the war, persuaded to sign away his rights.

> We wounded were waiting in the usual way for the disability pension people to sort us out with our grades of disablement. I was graded C. It might take months but, and here lay the cunning, if we signed a paper called Form Z22 in which we would agree to accept whatever pension they awarded, we could be discharged at once. I was still young, not twenty-one for another seven months, so like others I signed it. A great number of us have been sorry since.

Many wounded boy soldiers had spent so much time in hospital that the war was over by the time they left. Cyril José was still recovering from wounds he received in April 1918; George Coppard, who had been wounded in the leg, was demobilized as medically unfit. He always regretted that he had not been in France at the end of the fighting. 'To have celebrated survival with those left of my old company would have been a privilege indeed,' he acknowledged.

George was left, early in February 1919, to face the world with a £28 gratuity and a 25s-a-week pension for war injuries, which dropped after six months, then ceased altogether after a further year. He, like many others, found that his old clothes would no longer fit and spent almost all his gratuity in clothing himself so he could resemble a civilian.

> The youth had become a man but with only the capabilities of a youth to meet adult realities in civvy street. Although an expert machine-gunner, I was a numbskull so far as any trade or craft was concerned . . . No practical steps were taken to rehabilitate the broad mass of demobbed men, and I joined the queues for jobs as messengers, window cleaners and scullions.

For the boys who had thrown up their apprenticeships, there was indeed a price to pay. Even if their old jobs had been saved, they were frequently expected to begin again, to work their way back up a ladder they had already climbed partway. Norman Collins, who as a teenager had walked away from his apprenticeship in the drawing office of shipbuilders William Gray and Company in Hartlepool, found that he could not bear to go back at the age of twenty-one and start afresh, even though, as he admitted, he had forgotten most of what he had once been taught. Many were now men with a man's pride; they wanted to earn money, enough to marry and support a family, yet while that was possible for those who had learnt a trade and could apply for, or return to, work fully qualified, for those in their early twenties it was not an option.

George Head, who had joined the Royal Engineers, was in this position, having resigned his employment as a junior draughtsman to enlist under age. At seventeen, he had been earning 12s 6d per week in the drawing office and when he left he had been patted on the back and given extra pay, a reward for his patriotism.

> I was now twenty-two; what would I earn, taking into consideration that I had lost five years' professional training and was no further advanced mentally as far as being an engineering draughtsman was concerned?

In the end, George warily returned to his job in the drawing office and was paid £3 10s a week. It sounded like an improvement, but owing to inflation his pay was not enough to marry and live on in 1919. He also discovered that other draughtsmen of his age who had not served or who had completed their apprenticeship before enlisting were being paid £5 a week. He was, in effect, being penalized for his patriotism.

Cecil Lewis, the Royal Flying Corps pilot who had flown on the Western Front since the age of seventeen, was aware of what he, and others like him, had lost in the intervening years. Comparing himself to men who had pursued careers uninterrupted, he began his autobiography, *Sagittarius Rising*, with an acknowledgement of what war had cost.

> To me, and thousands like me, the easy developing pattern [of his life] was completely thrown out of symmetry by the First World War. It took me from school at sixteen, it destroyed all hope of university training or apprenticeship to a trade, it deprived me of the only carefree years, and washed me up, ill-equipped for any serious career, with a Military Cross, a Royal handshake, a six-hundred-pound gratuity, and – I almost forgot to say – my life.
>
> There were men older than I whose education was complete. To them, the War was a setback, disastrous but not irredeemable. There were others, older still, who had positions to which they could return. But we very young men had no place, actual or prospective, in a peaceful world. We walked off the playing-fields into the lines.

Near the village of Flesquières, close to the town of Cambrai, there is a small Commonwealth War Graves cemetery with about 300 gravestones. One in particular cannot fail to move the visitor. At the foot of the grave is the inscription, paid for by the family: 'School, War, Death'. The soldier who lies there, Private Arnold Statham, was not under age, at least not when he was killed, but the words tell the reader something of the truncated nature of his short life and the few life-experiences he sampled. Yet this was also true of those who survived but who had enlisted so young as to know little else. They had come through the war but were ill-equipped for any peacetime occupation; so intense was the experience that the rest of life paled into insignificance.

Former Seaforth Highlander Norman Collins acknowledged the feeling.

> The years of war seemed to last longer than all of the rest of my life put together . . . I really felt much older than my parents, and I think that feeling continued for the rest of my life.

For Norman, as for so many of that generation, their epitaph might read 'School, War, Life', but what were they going to do with their lives? How were they going to live with the memories, or justify their existence when their friends had died so young?

In response, Norman and other men used the maturity the war had given them as a springboard to accomplish things faster than might otherwise have been the case, and discovered that those lost years, in terms of career development, could be recovered. Norman became a director of Perkins Engines; Cecil Lewis one of the four founder members of the BBC in 1922; Ben Clouting the owner of a successful industrial window-cleaning company.

For others, what was taken from the war is, to outside eyes, more oblique. A veteran who had served under age, one of four centenarians who attended a service at the Cenotaph to commemorate the ninetieth anniversary of the outbreak of war, was one of the thousands who remained entirely silent upon the subject of his service for the whole of his life. He died in October 2004 aged 104, taking whatever he saw, whatever he did, to the grave.

Former soldiers like George Coppard, George Parker and Cyril José were still the lucky ones. For all the empty promises the Government had made, for all the disappointment that peace might bring these men, they were alive, they could still have families, children who, in their turn, would produce the next generation.

Dick Trafford also survived the war, despite being wounded and gassed. In 1919, he returned home.

> We got on a train to Liverpool and then from Liverpool to Ormskirk, and the first person I saw going to work was my dad on his way to the shipyards. Of course he downed tools and told his

mates, 'Tell them I'm not coming in today, tell them why.' And I went home. Of course my mother was there; she couldn't believe her own eyes when she saw me, I think she thought she'd lost me for good. Oh, she broke her heart, threw her arms around me, her long lost son. They never thought about my feelings about being home 'cos they'd got feelings of their own, they'd got me home and that was all they bothered about.

At home we did away with our uniforms that were full of lice. I'll always remember my mother's face. 'Well,' she said, 'you lousy devil, all your clothes, dump 'em,' she says, 'dump 'em and get one of your old suits.' Of course my old suits didn't fit. I'd put weight on, you see, and I'd grown; I had been a boy when I went to war. I had nothing to put on so my father had to lend me a suit while he went to Liverpool to buy me one ready-made.

For Dick Trafford's mother, the constant fear had ended and the separation was over. For those whose sons had died, there was only continuing grief; the pain and despair they felt could prove unbearable

Harriet Diprose's son Claude Damant had died in the most unfortunate of circumstances. His was one of the few cases where had he remained at the front he might have survived. As it was he came back, contracted meningitis, and died shortly after walking through the family's front door in July 1916. Six years later in June 1922, Claude's stepfather had cause to write one last time to the military authorities. A letter, a 'Verification of Address Form', had arrived at the family home concerning Claude's entitlement to the British War and Victory Medals. Unfortunately the letter was addressed to the dead son.

Dear Sir, I have again to point out that this lad died within a few hours of his discharge from the army of which fact the military authorities were duly notified and it is to say the least hurtful to his mother to have communications addressed here in his name . . .

The army duly apologized and amended the file. Harriet Diprose, whose husband had died when her son was barely a year old, had also lost her only son.

Agnes Cottrell's plight was not dissimilar. She too had lost her husband but only after the death of both her boys at the front. Agnes' younger son Harold, killed on the Somme in 1916, had been the subject of a long correspondence in 1917 with the military authorities, as she repeatedly sought for information about why he had been sent abroad so young. Now, having lost both sons and then her husband, she was alone. Before the army's file was finally closed in 1922, she suddenly corresponded again, but this time she was irrational and rambling, referring to 'conspiracies that would have to be exposed'. Mrs Cottrell was now 'distinctly eccentric and unbalanced,' a memo in the file concluded.

Her final, painful letter stands as a testament to the depth of her loss and there was little point in the army pursuing the matter. The last file note ends: 'No reply was asked for really. It was a diatribe.'

The parents of Ernest Steele were also devastated by the loss of their son, killed so close to the end of the war, but their suffering manifested itself in a beautiful velvet-lined wooden box. It contains a book with 'In Glorious Memory' imprinted in gold letters on the front and sets out to commemorate their son's life with pictures of Ernest as a baby and as a boy, the house from which he left to enlist and his letters from the front. Among the book's pages are lines of remembrance written by his father over the next twenty-five years.

Memory keeps us close to him
But time brings us nearer. 18th Sept. 1921

The years will by – and time speeds on
We still don't realize he's gone

His memory's with us all the while
And time brings scarce relief.
Pater

Nine long years that seem at times but a day. 18th Sept. 1927

At the end of the war, the boys who came home were men. Exactly what they took from the war, good or bad – and invariably it was a mixture of both – was up to the individual concerned. Hal Kerridge, who had enlisted aged sixteen, firmly believed that the war, for all its obscenity, for all its horror, was something that he would not have missed. 'It's an experience that can make or mar you for life but I have no regrets.' Right up to his death in 1999, aged 100, Dick Trafford felt the same.

I've never regretted anything at all from joining up to today because I knew what I was doing. I must have done, else I wouldn't have done it, that's the way I look at it.

15

Counting the Cost

DO GOOD & BE GOOD

11117 Private George Edwards
11th Essex Regiment

Killed in Action 24 September 1916, aged 15

THERE HAS ALWAYS BEEN a sense of comradeship between under-age soldiers, a mutual recognition of the conditions in which they served, regardless of where, when and with whom. Thomas Hope understood this and dedicated his book, *The Winding Road Unfolds*, accordingly: 'To the volunteers under military age of all the belligerent countries who served 1914–1918'. Perhaps he already suspected, when his book was published in 1937, that the next generation was about to go to war.

The vast majority of under-age soldiers in the First World War, like Ernest Steele, became men during the war. Only those who died remained forever boys, alongside a few extraordinary cases of lads who enlisted so young that they were still under age on Armistice Day. George Maher was one. He had enlisted aged thirteen in 1916, but his sojourn at the front had been brief, before his tearful confession. At the end of the war, he was still only fifteen. Another boy who was also under age when the war ended, but who had seen lengthy front-line service, was Charles Thurlby. He was born on 29 November 1900, and had served in the Gallipoli campaign with the 1/4th Northamptonshire Regiment.

According to military records, he landed on the peninsula in late October 1915 and there, the following month, he celebrated his fifteenth birthday.

Charles's brief story came to light in 1935, when, after an item on a radio programme, *In Town Tonight*, he responded with a letter to the *Radio Times* under the heading 'Youngest soldier in the War'. The programme had examined the whole issue of under-age soldiering, and the question of who was the youngest became of increasing interest to veterans. Many would stake a claim to the title, Charles included.

After Gallipoli, he had continued to serve with the same regiment until discharged in 1919. Later, he wrote:

> At the time of my enlistment I was barely fourteen years and five months old, and on 11th November, 1918, I was still eighteen days off my eighteenth birthday. In view of this, I think I can claim to have been the youngest soldier on active service during the war.

The question of the youngest veteran has commanded many inches of newspaper column. As the years have passed and the boy soldiers themselves began to die, newspapers ran obituaries and inevitably picked up on their extreme youth, and at times, largely because the veteran himself had believed it possible, speculated as to whether he was the youngest soldier. Any claim could only be conjecture. Stuart Cloete wrote in the 1970s that when he received his temporary commission in 1914, he was not only a proud officer in the British Army but 'Probably the youngest officer in it. I was seventeen and two months old.' He might have been surprised had he known the truth.

Charles Thurlby may have a good claim to the title of youngest British soldier with the longest record of service at the front, but he was not the youngest veteran. That distinction perhaps belongs to a so far unidentified soldier. Known only as Private S. Lewis, his story appeared in the *Daily Mail* in 1916: he had reputedly served several weeks on the Somme. He was twelve years old when he enlisted.

The truth about the identity of the youngest soldier will never be conclusively known; the same is true of the total number of boys who served under age. Both can at best be only the subject of informed speculation.

The figures given in this book are estimates, extrapolations from information sourced from the Commonwealth War Graves Commission. Over the period of a year, I examined the details of every man listed by the CWGC, noting relevant information whenever the age of a boy was given as seventeen or under. For those aged eighteen, a simple head count was taken.

I took the age of eighteen as the cut-off point. The minimum age for overseas service was nineteen until the last year of the war, when it was lowered to eighteen and a half. It would be impossible to untangle those who were killed aged eighteen and two months from those killed six months older. Purists will argue that this technically skews the figures; they are of course correct. However, I feel that other influences cited below tend to offset any discrepancy.

So much depends on what constitutes an under-age soldier. Many boys who enlisted were kept back and served for years in Britain before being sent abroad. One veteran I knew, Alfred Wood, enlisted at fifteen into the 6th Leicester Regiment, but was kept back because of his obvious youth and eventually became a training sergeant. He was sent overseas only in 1918, when he was nineteen.

Perhaps 'under age' should be determined not by service at home or overseas at all, but service in a theatre of war. Many boys, such as Christopher Paget-Clark, who enlisted at fourteen, were sent on garrison duty to India to release regular units from those countries to serve at the front. Although Christopher lied about his age and enlisted during the war, he was actually no younger than some other boy soldiers sent out to India in peacetime.

It has been claimed that a disproportionate number of younger as opposed to older men will have had their ages registered with the CWGC. This is because older men, perhaps those aged thirty and above, were less likely to have had a living parent to register their ages. However, spouses and siblings could also supply personal information and a great many did. And besides, how many boys' ages were not given by families too distraught or too disgusted at the loss of their son at fifteen or sixteen to bring themselves to contact the authorities again? How many boys could never be traced because they fought and died under an assumed name? It will never be known, but I cannot help but think that the number of unknown ages among boys at least equals those among adults.

One of the most interesting discrepancies that has come to light from my research has been the apparent rounding up of ages on the Commonwealth War Graves registers and website. The ages that appear on the website were given by the families themselves in response to a form sent out to every family who had lost a loved one in action. Around 50 per cent were completed. I have found a significant number of cases where the age of the casualty is given as a year higher than was actually the case.

What has become clear is that a family itself may have 'rounded up' the age, perhaps if their son was about to have a birthday when he died. William Brayshay of the 16th West Yorks Regiment is listed as dying at seventeen, yet he died in 1915 during training before his seventeenth birthday. James Walters's grave in Delville Wood Cemetery gives his age as seventeen when he was killed on 9 August 1916. He was actually born on 15 September 1899, making him a month short of his seventeenth birthday. Could it have been that James was in his seventeenth year, and this was the reason for the error?

George Pulley, who enlisted with his friend Vic Cole, was aged eighteen when he was killed on 1 July 1916, not nineteen, as listed by the CWGC. Similarly, his brother Edward, who was killed in April 1918, was aged twenty-two, not twenty-three. In Edward's case, his surviving records at The National Archives show that when he enlisted in March 1916 he gave his age as twenty years and fourteen days. Unlike his younger brother George, Edward had no reason to lie about his age, and census records show that he was indeed born in 1896. The same source also shows that George Pulley was born in 1898.

This apparent rounding up is not restricted to other ranks. Lieutenant Jack Pouchot, the boy who won the DCM at fifteen, is listed as having died at twenty in October 1918, yet his date of birth was 2 April 1899, making him nineteen when he died.

This naturally leaves the question: how many boys who were killed aged eighteen, and so should have been included in my figures, were omitted because they are listed as being nineteen?

The figures I have given do not include any from the Royal Naval Voluntary Reserve, or Royal Marines who served with the Royal Naval Division at Gallipoli and the Western Front. Nor do they include casualties from among the men of the Royal Naval Air Service. Some of these men served and were killed fighting on land alongside the army's own infantry. John Roxburgh and Albert Davie of the RNVR were seventeen when they were killed storming Beaumont Hamel on the Somme in November 1916, the same age as Lieutenant Edgar Platts of the Royal Marine Light Infantry when he was killed at Arras in April 1917 – he had already been wounded at Beaumont Hamel. They were technically naval men but they were being used as infantry, and hundreds of them died aged eighteen or less.

Lastly, the dead of the Dominions are omitted. In total, around 140,000 men from Australia, New Zealand, Canada and South Africa died in the war, an enormous sacrifice by nations willing to commit their menfolk to a conflict thousands of miles from home. Many of these soldiers had in fact been born in Britain and emigrated some time before the war. Lads like Percy Layzell and Thomas Tombs still believed that the land of their birth held a legitimate call over them, despite their obvious debt to the countries that had offered them new lives. Their deaths at sixteen are not included in the statistics. Yet what distinguishes them from the likes of John Mears, who had emigrated with his parents to Walkerville, Ontario, but who chose to return to Britain to enlist in the 2nd Cameron Highlanders? Or John McLachlan, who had emigrated with his parents to New Zealand but chose to enlist in Britain with the 1/6th Black Watch? Both were killed in action during 1915 and because they were serving in British regiments, they are included in the figures given. In reality there was no difference at all between any of them.

In short, 14,108 boys were counted as having died abroad aged eighteen or under during the war and are listed by the CWGC. If approximately 50 per cent of all the names listed have no known age, then, very crudely, the figure of 14,108 is doubled, giving a total dead of 28,216. As the ratio of dead to wounded averaged around 1:2.4, a total of killed and wounded is reached of 95,934. This figure excludes 2,516 boys who died at home from injuries, accidents or illness, with perhaps another 6,000–8,000 who recovered and were discharged. So perhaps a figure of between 100,000 and 110,000 would be a fairer estimate. As around 55 per cent of all those who served on the Western Front were killed or wounded, so in theory the number of under-age soldiers who can be said to have served may, very broadly, be double this.

Interestingly, the proportion of under-age soldiers in a battalion can sometimes be calculated by taking a snapshot of a unit involved in one catastrophic event before drafts began to dilute the original composition of the battalion. The disaster that overtook the 1/7th Royal Scots is just such an example when, on 22 May 1915, 216 men were killed in the train crash on the first part of their journey to the front. Looking closely at this incident, it is possible to calculate that of the 116 soldiers with known ages, a quarter were under age. A similar calculation can be made for the Accrington Pals who suffered so appallingly during the attack at Serre on 1 July 1916. Thanks to the author William Turner, whose long-standing interest in the unit enabled him to put ages to 95 per cent of those killed that day, it is clear that around 10–12 per cent of those who lost their lives had originally enlisted under age. Likewise the detailed work undertaken by Jack Alexander in his book *McCrae's Battalion: The Story of the 16th Royal Scots*, elicits further useful information. He identified the birth dates of 1,009 other ranks serving with the battalion in December 1914 of whom 145 were aged between sixteen and eighteen or 14.77 percent. This figure excluded a further thirty boys who were found to be under the age of sixteen and were consequently ejected from the battalion on mobilization. Not all boys of such extreme youth were identified at the time. Private Charles Hyslop, for example, went undetected and served in France aged sixteen. He was killed in September 1918 aged nineteen and therefore would not figure in any calculations in this book.

On a smaller scale numerically were the losses incurred by a battalion of the Birmingham Pals in June 1916, when, shortly before it was relieved from the front-line trenches, it was subjected to a very heavy bombardment, followed by the explosion of three mines, one of which caused considerable damage and loss of life.

Sixty-seven other ranks were killed. An examination of those who died reveals that all but a handful were original members of the battalion. Of their known ages, one was sixteen (Willoughby Greaves), two were aged seventeen (Stanley Hold and John Ludlow), four were eighteen (Percy Antrobus, Arthur Franklin, George Gilbert and Lawson Williams) and four were nineteen (Clarence Bradley, Leslie Bromwich, Oswald Baker and Matthew Barlow). In other words, at least eleven of those killed had enlisted under age (16.4 per cent) and a further ten were killed aged twenty, making it possible that they too joined up, albeit narrowly, under the specified age of enlistment.

It would be dangerous to extrapolate too much from such snapshots, but all of the four examples given appear to clearly indicate an under-age enlistment in 1914 of at least 10–15 per cent.

Furthermore, from figures given in the following chapter, there is no reason to believe that that proportion dropped in 1915.

Anecdotal evidence of the prevalence of under-age service, collected from different sources, constantly surprises me, and while it does not in itself prove very much, collectively it has also led me to believe that there were more under-age soldiers than I, for one, would have believed. At the back of George Coppard's book, *With a Machine Gun to Cambrai*, the author reproduces letters he received in the late 1960s and early 1970s from appreciative readers, all but one of whom were veterans of the war. Of the fourteen letters he quotes, four came from men who served under age, a fifth enlisted at eighteen and a sixth can be deduced from census records as serving under age. Of the remaining eight, four make no mention of their age. Recent research through soldiers' surviving enlistment papers at The National Archives in Kew threw up many interesting details. One such search, for a known under-age soldier called William Roberts, elicited a number of men all with the same name who had served under age. The records were revealing. William Roberts from St Helens, 'of fair physical development', enlisted aged nineteen, but was in fact under seventeen years of age and later discharged. William Roberts, aged nineteen, a gardener from Llandudno, was under age when he enlisted in April 1915 and was discharged in September. William David Roberts, fifteen years old and a steel worker from Swansea, enlisted into the 6th Battalion Welsh Guards, claiming to be nineteen years and three months. He was wounded on the Somme in July 1916, his post-war discharge papers proving that he was born in 1899. And William Frank Roberts from Walsall enlisted aged nineteen years and two months into the Warwickshire Yeomanry, but was aged sixteen years and six months when he was discharged in February 1916.

Looking up one under-age individual frequently drew my attention to another. The case of Norman Gunn, highlighted during the war by the National Service League, was typical. He was sixteen years old when he was killed serving with the 1st Cameron Highlanders in 1915. He had just two namesakes in the British Army, one a sergeant, considerably older than Norman, the other a private in the Yorkshire Regiment. The records for the latter survive, and in the first instance gave no indication that he too was an under-age soldier, except for a letter attached to his file, written after the war from his home in Middlesbrough:

> Dear Sir
>
> If possible I would like a copy of my Discharge from the Army as I have lost the original one . . . I will try and give you a few particulars which may help you. I enlisted in the P.W.O. [Prince of Wales's Own] Yorkshire Regiment on the fifth of January 1915 as 19 yrs and 11 months, at the same time I was not 17 years old. I was drafted to the 8th Battalion . . . Went to France in August 1915. Wounded and returned to England . . .

In July 1916, this Norman Gunn suffered a gunshot wound to his right leg. He was discharged at the end of the war.

As noted, the exact number of boy soldiers can never be known. Many years trawling through wartime issues of every newspaper would no doubt elicit thousands more under-age boys whose ages are not listed by the CWGC, especially in local papers which invariably paid tribute to men in the area who were killed or wounded, and frequently noted their ages. Where such a trawl has been undertaken by particular researchers or authors, concerned about the men from their own town or city, interesting results have been found. Books published in recent years on the Pals Battalions, for example, have highlighted many of those who originally enlisted and served abroad under age until they were killed.

David Bilton's history of the four Hull Pals Battalions identifies the ages of 653 other ranks, out of 1,062 original Pals who died in the war.

These four Pals Battalions reached the Western Front in March 1916 where they remained. Only nine lads have been identified as having been killed under age, eight aged eighteen, one aged sixteen. Yet scores more died before the war ended aged between nineteen and twenty-two, men who were originally under-age recruits in 1914. In addition to the nine already identified, a further 103 of the 653 were aged eighteen or under when they enlisted, while another twenty-five were possibly under age, that is, they were aged either eighteen or just turned nineteen when they made their way to the recruitment office. These figures are not necessarily typical of all battalions, but they are highly significant. They show that by counting young soldiers purely on the basis of the date of their death, many tens of thousands who were under age when they actually enlisted but nineteen or over when they died are entirely left out of the calculation.

As I started writing, my estimate of the total number of boys who enlisted under age was a conservative figure of 250,000. From the research I have undertaken and from all the anecdotal and hard evidence seen since, I believe this figure is an underestimate. Tens of thousands of boys who enlisted under age were discharged, some after a matter of days, or trained but held back in Britain ready to serve abroad once they were the right age. If these boys are all factored into the equation, a total number far in excess of 250,000 is reached, a remarkable testament to a generation born to serve the country in time of war.

And these boys did not just serve their country but it is arguable that they saved it too. The British Army was relatively small in 1915 compared to 1916–18, and under-age soldiers formed a substantial proportion of the forces committed abroad. Had they been instantaneously withdrawn at a time when Germany was militarily predominant, the outcome of the war might have been very different.

Cecil Withers was one of the final half-dozen surviving under-age soldiers. I saw Cecil after he had taken to his bed after a fall.

It was summer time 2004, and although the weather was hot, he was tucked up in bed. I felt privileged to be allowed upstairs to talk to him, for Raymond, Cecil's well-brought-up octogenarian son, was at first unsure whether it was the right thing to do. I sat on Cecil's bed, tape recorder in hand, and listened to the old soldier, who, as he lay at right angles to me, could only look at me slightly askew. He addressed the issue of under-age soldiers and the ones who hid their true names from the army and so from history as well.

When you think back on it, thousands and thousands of decent boys left their homes and were blown to pieces: scattered all over the place. At night the rats would be feeding on the dead bodies too, it's shocking and an almost unbelievable blasphemy, that's the way I thought about it, a blasphemy. And when these boys were killed in action, their identity disc would be taken from them with their name and number on, and that number would be looked up in the records and would be found to be untrue, and so they became, in a sense, unknown warriors.

16

The Final Reckoning

OUR ONLY REGRET
'TOO YOUNG'

8720 Private John Reid
2nd Gordon Highlanders

Killed in Action 17 May 1915, aged 16

IN DRAWING CONCLUSIONS about under-age service in the Great War from the service records of 2,046 under-age soldiers, some clarification is needed. The first 1,000 records I examined were found by randomly searching through the microfiche pension records (WO364) at the National Archives (the microfiche rolls are no longer publicly available) while the remaining 1,046 records were gathered by close examination of the same records available online through Ancestry.co.uk. Through Ancestry's search fields I was able to narrow the hunt, for example by checking enlistment amongst supposed nineteen-year-olds in 1915, making it easier to find records of under-age soldiers as opposed to looking remorselessly through *all* records in the hope of finding relevant evidence.

It is important, then, that in a subsequent examination of all these records I use the first 1,000 for any extrapolation of figures, purely because they were a random sample. In the main, the remaining 1,046 were gathered during my ongoing search for the records of 250 (in the end I had 251) under-age soldiers who served abroad so that I could discover, with additional qualifications, such things as the ratio of those who served in Britain only to those who subsequently served overseas. Any lads who legally enlisted for Boy Service were automatically exempted from my research.

In the case of WO364, there were more than 5,300 microfiche boxes at the National Archives, of which I studied every record in 157 boxes, or one in thirty-four of the whole. Each box was picked at random from across the full range available. From these, I extracted 1,000 under-age soldiers who were discharged from the army. Of these 119 or almost 12 per cent had served overseas. On the basis that WO364 holds approximately one million records, I would expect to find around 34,000 under-age soldiers were I able to look through every box. As there were between five and five and a half million servicemen in the army alone, it could be said that between 170,000–190,000 boys served in khaki. However, there is a problem with this crude calculation.

In all but a small number of cases, it is possible to identify an under-age soldier only if he is discharged as having made a 'mis-statement as to age'. Yet there were several other reasons why a boy might be discharged, any one of which automatically super-seded a declaration of true age as the cause for discharge. A boy might be discharged as 'unlikely to make an efficient soldier' or for 'being no longer fit'; he might be claimed as an apprentice, or his file might merely state that he had been 'irregularly enlisted'. All of these hint that he could be just a boy, especially where, on enlistment, he declared his age as precisely that required by law. Equally, if a soldier was discharged as 'medically unfit', then that too would hide his true age. This category would disguise the records of those under-age soldiers who were sent home not first and foremost because of their age but because of their wounds and were discharged solely on this account.

It is impossible to quantify just how many boys I would 'miss' owing to these alternative reasons for discharge, but it would certainly run into many thousands, probably tens of thousands over the whole of WO364. Furthermore, the records hide another large and relevant group: those soldiers unidentified by their youth who survived at home or overseas until they reached the age of nineteen; the same lads who made post-war claims for physical ailments. All this evidence, circumstantial though it is, is indicative nevertheless of a truly astonishing number of boys who chose to enlist into the British Army in 1914 and 1915 from amongst the 2.47 million men who volunteered for the Regular and Territorial Army.

In 1914 the authorities had been besieged by boys driven by patriotic fervour to enlist. Thousands went overseas, often with territorial units that struggled to raise the necessary numbers to reach establishment. These battalions were already flush with lads aged seventeen or eighteen who had lawfully enlisted before the war, but then lost members who were free to transfer to regular units, including those raised by Lord Kitchener's appeal. Kitchener's battalions also harboured many youngsters swept up in the general excitement and clamour to raise so-called Pals Battalions.

In looking at the enlistment years of the first 1,000 under-age soldiers I examined, some interesting details emerge.

Year of enlistment	Number of under-age enlistments
1914 (five months)	157
1915	736
1916	78
1917	26
1918	3

These figures reveal three significant details:

1. That the rush of boys to enlist was not necessarily greater in 1915 than it was in 1914, but that the examination of recruits was tighter in 1914, that is, many boys clearly under age were turned away when so many willing men stood in the queue to enlist.

2. That as a result of falling numbers volunteering to enlist in 1915, recruitment became more urgent and therefore far less

discerning as recruiters came out from behind their desks to chivvy boys into the army.

3. That civilian registration and subsequent conscription quickly cut the numbers of under-age lads able to enlist. It is noticeable that around 30 per cent of all volunteers post January 1916 came from Ireland where the day of National Registration (15 August 1915) had not applied. Interestingly not a single volunteer, in my sample, came from Ireland to England to enlist in the two months after the Easter Uprising of April 1916.

Under-age recruits by month:

1914

August	29
September*	46
October	21
November	36
December	25
Total	157

1915

January†	55
February	30
March	56
April‡	97
May	99
June	72

* The known 'uplift' in volunteers in the second and greatest rush to the colours in early September 1914, after news of the imperilled BEF's retreat from Mons.
† The result of boys such as Smiler Marshall, who were keen to enlist but decided to wait until after Christmas before volunteering.
‡ Also includes the next month, May: the effect of Spring warming and the news of the Germans' launch of their offensive at Ypres (22nd April) and their dastardly use of poison gas in May (7th). Other significant influences were news of the German sinking of the American Liner *Lusitania* off Ireland, and press reports of the ongoing Zeppelin attacks.

July	67
August	86
September	38
October*	65
November	43
December	28
Total	736

Although the sample of 1,000 under-age volunteers is small, their recruitment month by month resembles closely the ebb and flow in the national recruitment of all volunteers. The one anomaly is July and August 1915 when the total number of volunteers was almost identical at 95,413 and 95,980 respectively and yet the number of under-age volunteers increased by almost 30 per cent, owing to the start of school holidays and the increasing pressure on recruiters to find volunteers.

As the number of civilians stepping forward to volunteer fell dramatically from early 1915 (156,000 enlisted in January, 88,000 in February), so boys helped fill the breach. These lads were supported not only by overzealous recruiters but by medical officers who either turned a blind eye or assumed that a poor physical specimen was likely to develop under the tutelage and feeding of the army. It appears that there was very little effort made to discipline the most lax and venal of these men, who were still receiving a bounty for every recruit, and only where an enlistment was subsequently deemed preposterous was there any attempt to ask why the lad in question had been signed up. A fifth of boys were discharged after less than a month's service, and almost half of these during the first fortnight. In my sample of 1,000 boys, thirty-three did not even last a hundred hours in uniform, having been rejected almost as soon as they reached the depot for training.

---

* Response to the introduction of the Derby Scheme and the national anxiety over the lack of volunteers. Further news of enemy atrocities included the execution of nurse Edith Cavell.

Boys who enlisted under age came from every corner of the United Kingdom and from a myriad of largely menial jobs. Of those I identified as later serving abroad, 216 stated their occupation prior to enlistment: fifty were labourers or farm servants, twenty-two were clerks, twelve were miners, twelve assistants (often in a shop). There were apprentices, footmen, bookbinders, carters, porters; lads who worked in cotton mills and bakeries, post offices and butchers. There was one lad who described his profession as a dental student and one who claimed to be a scavenger.

On enlistment, boys either chose to lie about their age or were cajoled into doing so. Recruiting sergeants must have been aware of the number claiming to be nineteen exactly, or perhaps nineteen and one month to add a sliver of authenticity to their declaration. Of all those claiming their age to be nineteen or over, 37 per cent plumped for nineteen exactly, 15 per cent chose nineteen and one month, 8 per cent decided on nineteen and two months, leaving 40 per cent to pick any other, greater age. Very few ever attempted to use outrageous bluster, such as claiming to be aged twenty or over. One exception was James Rowan, who claimed to be twenty and two months when aged sixteen and two months. Yet his was not the greatest differential between stated and true age. This accolade goes to Edward Barnett, who was nearly five years and nine months younger than his stated age on enlistment. It is worth noting at this point that in my sample not one boy who served overseas reached his stated age before embarkation, giving the strong impression that the army either discharged those under age and certified as such, or sent them overseas: relatively few were held to serve at home if they were not eligible to go abroad in the foreseeable future.

When it came to physical measurements, the under-age soldiers' statistics were remarkably close to the minimum required to enlist. Of those who would serve abroad, the averages were as follows:

Chest 33.3 inches
Height 63 inches (five foot three)
Weight 120.2lbs (eight stone eight pounds)

However, the differential between some of the best built and the weakest framed lads who joined was considerable. There were a number of boys who were giants for their age, like fourteen-year-old Private Harry Aspinall, who stood five foot eleven inches tall and had an impressive thirty-eight-inch chest measurement, and lads who were weaklings, such as Private William Bain who stood at five foot two on enlistment and weighed not a pound over seven stone.

Overall it is clear that the majority of under-age soldiers, perhaps in the order of 65–75 per cent, did not succeed in going abroad at all because their true age was either revealed or suspected. There is no doubt that some boys were sent overseas even if their youth was known, either because they themselves wanted to go and were adjudged physically capable, or because a colonel, in his annoyance or frustration, decided that the declared age was what mattered regardless of the empirical evidence before his eyes. Those in my sample who enlisted after 4th August 1914 and who served overseas, embarked in one of the following years:

1914	3
1915	141
1916	98
1917	7
1918	2

The length of training received by these boys varied considerably. Of the 251 boys who served overseas, only seventeen received more than a year's training, with the average receiving a few days short of seven months. It is interesting to note that 132 had between one and six months' training, a figure that includes fourteen who received fewer than eight weeks' training and a further fifty-four who were given between three and four months' instruction before departure.

These boys were not, in the main, original recruits to Kitchener's Army. Lord Kitchener wished to keep his new force as an army, not used piece-meal in action. His army would arrive on the front as a complete new force, although circumstances dictated that some divisions would begin arriving on the Western Front from mid-1915. Nevertheless, the desire to keep this force together ensured that the majority of Kitchener's Army received at least a year's training.

A few of the boys in the sample did join those Kitchener battalions raised later in the war, such as the 15th Hampshire Regiment raised in April 1915, or the 11th Royal West Kent Regiment raised in May 1915, by the Mayors of Portsmouth and Lewisham respectively. Rather more lads headed off to the territorials, which traditionally recruited at seventeen and which, as noted, often struggled to raise the numbers required for overseas service. However, most boys were simply sent out as reinforcements, usually to the regular and territorial battalions that took heavy losses at the front in 1914 and 1915, and before the arrival of most divisions of Kitchener's Army.

The majority of the lads received sufficient training to go overseas although, once there, whether they were able to cope with the circumstances was quite a different matter. In particular, as winter drew near, many succumbed to the intense cold. Of the records examined, it is noticeable that 47 per cent did not last longer than three months from the moment they touched foreign soil to the moment of their departure. A small number of these would have returned owing to injury but most were pulled out either because a parent reclaimed them, or the evidence on the ground proved they could not manage. Out of 240 whose length of stay could be ascertained, only five lasted longer than a year: overall the average sojourn was just over four months. In so many cases these young lads, who had dreamed of serving their country in time of war, were quickly disabused of their adventurous, romantic thoughts, by the extraordinary and gruelling conditions of the Western Front.

Acknowledgements

A SPECIAL THANK YOU TO the staff at Bloomsbury, particularly Bill Swainson, the senior commissioning editor, who purchased the rights to *Boy Soldiers of the Great War* and re-published it after the book went out of print in 2010. As always I am very grateful to Emily Sweet for her editorial support and advice, as well as to Nick Humphrey, Anya Rosenberg, Ruth Logan, David Mann, Paul Nash, Andrew Tennant and Justine Taylor for their excellent work and kindness. I would also like to thank, once again, my agent, Jane Turnbull, for her encouragement and support.

I am also grateful to all at Testimony Films who helped in so many ways, including Steve Humphries, Mary Parsons, Nick Maddocks, Melissa Blackburn, Clare Titley, and in particular Lizzie Cosslett for all her devotion to the cause. I would also like to thank Mike Humphries, Madge Reed, Mike Pharey and Daniel de Waal.

As with any book that is oral-history based, the final product is only as good as the information used and, during the course of my writing this book, hundreds of people responded to adverts placed in the press for stories and images. There are far too many people to name but I would like to thank everyone for their kindness and help. In particular I thank Ron Alpe for the letters of his relative, Cyril José; Betty White and Ian Packham for the memoirs of George White; Alex McGahey for the letters of Ernest Fitchett; Lesley Molyneux for the letters and pictures of her grandfather Christopher Paget-Clark; Jim Grundy for the story of Howard Peck; Anthony Battersby for the story of Reginald Battersby;

Carl Jackson for the documents of his grandfather Percy Marshall; Peter and Joan Fearns for the cover image; Jeff Bugg for the story of James Walters; George Flint for the picture of John Flint; and the family of Horace Iles. A big thank you, too, goes out to David Empson for the story of Ernest Steele, and Peter Doyle for the story of Archie Gardiner. I would also like to offer my gratitude to John Cooksey for his interview with Frank Lindley, and Anne Pedley for her wonderful generosity, forwarding stories and information about under-age soldiers that I would never have otherwise found, and Mary and Jackie Greenwood for the image of Lance Corporal William Plant.

Thanks are also due to Jeremy and Liz Skipper, Barry Bliss, Vic and Diane Piuk, Raymond Withers, Michael Stedman, David Bilton, Jeremy and Clair Banning, Peter Barton, George Heron, Mike Tyldesley, Sanjeev Ahuja, Martin Booth, Sam Eedle, Julian Johnson, Bill Walton, Peter Francis of the Commonwealth War Graves Commission, William Spencer at the National Archives, Nigel Steel at the Imperial War Museum, Nick Fear for the interview with Bill Pain, Brenda Field, David Lock, Clive Hughes, Peter Simkins, George Heron, Jack Clegg, Jimmy and Dave James, and Lynda Welch, Michael Richards, M. Birkin, Mr Jennett, Brian Spear, John Rogers, Michael Green, Charles Bateman, Les Rideout, Harry Taylor, Barbara Jones, William Denyer, Elizabeth Lumb, John Tennant and to all those others who remain nameless but who have so kindly offered their help and precious stories. I hope this book does justice to the memory of all their relatives who served, and, in many cases, died so young.

I would like to pick out my friend Taff Gillingham for especial thanks. His remarkable knowledge of military history has proved incredibly reassuring and helpful, and the points he has made have been very gratefully received.

I would also like to offer huge heartfelt thanks to those who inevitably 'suffer' when I write, in particular my wife, Anna, who has to put up with the hassle and dislocation that being married to a writer presents, and my mother, Joan van Emden, whose assiduous attention to detail and remarkable knowledge of the English language has given me support I can never repay.

Lastly, I would like to thank the veterans themselves, who have not just given me their remarkable stories, but who also offered their encouragement and friendship over so many years.

Sources

Select Bibliography

Alexander, Jack, *McCrae's Battalion: The Story of the 16th Royal Scots*, Mainstream Publishing, 2004

Bilton, David, *Hull Pals*, Pen & Sword Books, 1999

Birkin, Andrew, *J. M. Barrie & The Lost Boys*, Constable, 1979

Birmingham, George, pseud. John Hannay, *A Padre in France*, Hodder & Stoughton, 1918

Blake, Robert (ed.), *The Private Papers of Douglas Haig 1914–1919*, Eyre & Spottiswoode, 1952

Cardinal Harford, H., 'They Had Lied About Their Age', in *I Was There*, ed. Sir John Hammerton, Volume 3, The Amalgamated Press, 1939

Carrington, Charles, *Soldier From The Wars Returning*, Hutchinson, 1965

Carter, Terry, *Birmingham Pals*, Pen & Sword Books, 1997

Clark, Reverend Andrew, *Echoes of the Great War*, ed. James Munson, Oxford University Press, 1985

Cloete, Stuart, *A Victorian Son*, Collins, 1972

Cockerill, A. W., *Sons Of The Brave*, Leo Cooper, 1984

Cooksey, John, *Pals*, Pen & Sword Books, 1986

Coppard, George, *With a Machine Gun to Cambrai*, Papermac, 1980

Douie, Charles, *The Weary Road*, The Strong Oak Press, 1988

Edmonds, Charles, *A Subaltern's War*, Peter Davies, 1929

Gladden, Norman, *The Somme 1916*, William Kimber, 1974

Graves, Robert, *Goodbye to All That*, Penguin Books, 1984

Haldane, Maldwyn, *A History of the Fourth Battalion, the Seaforth Highlanders*, H. F. & G. Witherby, 1928

Hiscock, Eric, *The Bells Of Hell Go Ting-A-Ling-A Ling*, Arlington Books, 1976

Hodges, Frederick James, *Men of 18 in 1918*, Arthur H. Stockwell Ltd, 1988

Holmes, Richard, *The Little Field Marshal*, Weidenfeld & Nicolson, 2004

Hope, Thomas Suthren, *The Winding Road Unfolds*, Putnam, 1937

Kiernan, Reginald H., *Little Brother Goes Soldiering*, Constable & Co. Ltd, 1930

Lewis, Cecil, *Sagittarius Rising*, Peter Davies, 1936

Macdonald, Lyn, *1915: The Death Of Innocence*, Headline, 1993

Markham, Violet, *Friendship's Harvest*, Max Reinhardt, 1956

Milner, Laurie, *Leeds Pals*, Pen & Sword Books, 1998

Parker, Ernest W., *Into Battle*, Leo Cooper, 1994

Parker, George, *The Tale of a Boy Soldier*, QueenSpark Books, 2001

The War Office, *Statistics of the Military Effort of the British Empire*, The War Office, 1922

Turner, William, *Accrington Pals*, Pen & Sword Books, 1998

van Emden, Richard, *Tickled to Death to Go*, Spellmount, 1996

van Emden, Richard, *Last Man Standing*, Pen & Sword Books, 2002

Walkinton, M. L., *Twice In A Lifetime*, Samson Books, 1980

Winter, Denis, *Death's Men*, Allen Lane, 1978

Newspapers

The Times: 10 August 1914, 14 May 1915, 10 March 1916, 6 August 1916

Daily Mail: 12 July 1915, 14 July 1915, 22 June 1916

Daily Sketch: 27 July 1915

Magazines

Boots: *Comrades in Khaki*

Issues 1–12, April 1915–April 1916

Stand-To! The Journal of the Western Front Association

Number 13 Spring 1985, *Communication Lines*, letter, Len Thomas, p. 48

Number 14 Summer 1985, *My Experiences In The Great War*, Alec Stringer, pp. 5–6

Number 23 Summer 1988, *One Man's War: 4*, Herbert Gutteridge, pp. 13–15

Hansard

Official Reports, Fifth Series,

Parliamentary Debates 1914–1918,

Volumes 59–110

Unpublished Sources

Unpublished war memoirs of Victor Cole

War letters of Ernest Fitchett

War letters of Cyril José

Memories of an Old Contemptible by Charles Parke

Unpublished war memoirs of George White

Imperial War Museum

Department of Documents:

Diary of Len Thomas, 74/148/1

Unpublished memoirs of George Fortune, 04/5/1

MS letter of Lieutenant Colonel J. H. Lloyd, Misc 208 (3013)

Papers of Sir Herbert Creedy, Con. Volume 1, Folios 86–90

Unpublished memoirs of Lieutenant Colonel William Kerr MBE MM, 86/53/1

Sound Archives:

Horace Calvert, 9955/19

Donald Price, 10168/14

British Library of Political and Economic Science, London School of Economics

Markham, Violet Rosa: *MP's Correspondence Files 22/9-37*

Liddle Archive, University of Leeds

Documents relating to George Adams, GS 0006

Documents relating to Albert Harvey, RNMN (REC) 042

Documents relating to John Campbell, CO 017

The National Archives, Kew

Borstal Association Records: HO 247

Field General Courts Martial Records June/July 1916: WO 213/9

Officers' Services, First World War, Long Number Papers: WO 339

Soldiers' Documents, First World War: WO 363 & 374

Records of the National Service League: WO 105/41/48

Recruitment: WO 32, 106, 159 CAB 1, 37, 41, 42, and Registration: WO 159

Unit War Diaries: Army WO 95 & RFC/RAF AIR 1
War Office Instructions: WO 293/1/2/3

Interviews conducted by the author with the following Great War veterans

Alfred Anderson

Horace Calvert

Ben Clouting

Vic Cole

Norman Collins

Frank Deane

William Easton

Edward Francis

Helen Gordon-Dean (née McNeil)

Marjorie Grigsby

Horace Ham

Albert Harvey

Frederick Hodges

Hal Kerridge

John Laister

Harold Lawton

Frank Lindley

George Louth

George Maher

Albert 'Smiler' Marshall

Royce McKenzie

Donald Price

William Sims

Norman Skelton

Ernest Stevens

Tommy Thomson

Dick Trafford

Percy Williams

Cecil Withers

Alfred Wood.

Index